MATTHEW REILLY

Mr EINSTEIN'S SECRETARY

MATTHEW REILLY
Mr EINSTEIN'S SECRETARY

ORION

First published in Great Britain in 2024 by Orion Fiction,
an imprint of The Orion Publishing Group Ltd.,
Carmelite House, 50 Victoria Embankment
London EC4Y 0DZ

An Hachette UK company

1 3 5 7 9 10 8 6 4 2

A CIP catalogue record for this book
is available from the British Library.

ISBN (Hardback) 9781 3987 2127 2
ISBN (Export Trade Paperback) 9781 3987 2128 9
ISBN (eBook) 9781 3987 2130 2

Printed and bound in Great Britain by Clays Ltd, Elcograf S.p.A.

MIX
Paper from
responsible sources
FSC® C104740

www.orionbooks.co.uk

For Kate Freeman, CFA

The physicists of the 1920s and 30s were the witch-doctors of their age, the brilliant keepers of a new kind of sorcery, that of the atom. And their high priest was Einstein.

– From: *The Nuclear Age* by Scott Sollers
(W.M. Lawry & Co., London, 2010)

The model secretary should put as much care into her appearance as into her typing. For ultimately her job is to make her boss look good: to perform all the dull chores so that her boss is free to apply his mind to those matters of business that all know are more suited to the masculine brain.

– From: *Modern Secretary*
(pamphlet, published circa 1939)

Life is like riding a bicycle. To keep your balance, you must keep moving.

– Albert Einstein

1948

PRINCETON PUBLIC CEMETERY

THE GREAT EINSTEIN IS the first person to arrive at my funeral, despite his age, ill health and the biting cold of the New Jersey day.

It is truly an odd thing to watch your own burial.

To see who comes. To see how many come. To see what they say about you.

Mine is a dismal affair.

Only four people turn up.

New Jersey in the winter is a hard place, but on the day of my funeral it is doubly so: the sky is grey, snow falls, the frozen soil crunches underfoot.

I tell myself that perhaps the weather is responsible for the low turnout.

Or maybe this is just how it is for spies. The whole point of my secret life was *not* having anybody know what I did, even when it was dangerous, horrifying and, a few times, historic.

More than anything, seeing your own funeral makes you think.

Makes you remember.

3

Seeing Einstein totter through the gates, leaning heavily on his cane, brings back memories of him as a younger man: so vibrant, so animated, so energetic of mind and body. No-one—*no-one*—had more enthusiasm than Einstein: for physics, for discovery, for life, for the sheer pursuit of joy.

He was 68 on the day of my burial.

He would be dead in a few years.

At his side, as ever, gripping his elbow, helping him along, was his loyal primary secretary, Helen Dukas.

Since 1928—just after I had worked for Einstein the second time—she had been his diary-keeper, housekeeper and gatekeeper.

It was in this final capacity—gatekeeper—that she truly excelled.

Unlike me, Helen was as firm as iron. She was as stern as Einstein was affable, as organised as he was shambolic. She could decline an invitation from a king without even blinking and she did that on numerous occasions.

Protecting Einstein wasn't her mission. Protecting his *time* was. This made her, without doubt, one of the finest secretaries in history.

Mrs Katherine Graham-Coulson would have approved. (Rule Number 1: 'Your job is to help your boss to do *his* job!')

As I stare at this scene, I find myself remembering my life.

It appears in my mind's eye in splinters, flashing stretches of time from over four decades.

Stretches that found me in the presence of the truest of geniuses like Einstein, Curie and Bohr, false geniuses like Speer and Heisenberg, and the greatest of monsters like Heydrich, Bormann and even Hitler himself.

Or the times I raced teams of Nazis to secure documents regarding the new science of the atom. Or when I faced off against the Soviet Union's deadliest assassin–spy.

Curiously, it is the smells I recall the most, the scents of my life.

My mother's prized perfume, the only thing of value she ever owned.

Human shit in a Russian torture room.

Einstein's aftershave, mainly because he used it so rarely. ('It is only for special occasions!' he'd bark happily. 'Like meeting heads of state and my mother-in-law.')

The scents of New York in the 1920s: the burnt electric cables of the subway; cigar smoke in the speakeasies; Brylcreem in the hair of gangsters like Baby Face Mancino; dead bodies in a fish warehouse; and the smell of the cement shoes worn by one fellow who couldn't pay his debts to Baby Face.

The fresh ink of a Model No. 5 Underwood typewriter.

Cherry blossoms announcing spring in Berlin.

The smell of exploding bombs in Berlin.

The reek of panic in Berlin as the Russian Army swept into the city searching for Germans to rape or kill or eat.

The dread stink of the ovens at Auschwitz.

You cannot forget the odour of burnt human flesh.

Fanny arrives with her loyal husband Raymond by her side, right on time. (Rule Number 3: 'Always be on time!')

She joins Einstein at the graveside and they shake hands familiarly.

How Fanny has changed. She's so confident now, so self-possessed. I'm very pleased to see this.

With only those four in attendance—Einstein, Helen Dukas, Fanny and Raymond—it really is a desultory affair.

What a poor showing, I think.

Einstein looks around, shrugs, and there in the falling snow, begins the eulogy.

'I first met Hanna Fischer in Berlin when she was a little girl,' he says. 'She was a sweet thing and she showed signs of her brilliance at a very early age. We were next-door neighbours and I was friends with her father . . .'

Not a bad start, Albert.

Having known me since I was a child and intermittently through my adulthood, he knew much about me.

But not everything.

He can't tell the whole story.

For instance, he can't recount what I went through in Germany both before and during the war. Nor can he tell of the three interrogations I endured, one in America, one in Nazi Germany and one while in the custody of the Russians.

And as I watch Einstein—the incredible scientist, my one-time boss, and the kindest soul I have ever known—speaking at my pathetically small funeral, I find myself remembering those interrogations, as somehow, they give form to the splinters of memory in my mind.

FIRST INTERROGATION
NEW JERSEY, U.S.A.
1933

Few are aware that the Nazis put a price on
Einstein's head.

On three occasions, Nazi agents tried
to assassinate him. The first occurred near
Princeton in 1933 during one of Einstein's
visits to the United States . . .

– From: *Einstein* by Thomas McMahon

EWING TOWNSHIP COUNTY JAIL
TRENTON, NEW JERSEY
FEBRUARY 12, 1933, 3:05 A.M.

THE TWO AMERICAN COPS guarding me looked at me in total
confusion.

It was hard to know what they made of me: a skinny 31-year-old
German woman in a sundress, with blood on her forehead and her
hands tightly cuffed.

'Please,' I said. 'If you'll just call Mr Einstein, Mr Albert Einstein,
he'll explain everything.'

'You think we're stupid, lady?' the fatter of the two policemen
said. 'If you know Albert Einstein, then I'm having dinner tonight
with Franklin Roosevelt.'

I didn't know what to do.

In all the commotion at Princeton, Einstein had been whisked
away by Agent Kessler's people from the Treasury Department and
I didn't have the first clue where they had taken him.

I had been brought here, to a cold grey holding cell in the local
county jail . . . *with* the two assassins.

At that very moment, the two would-be killers of Einstein were in the cell next to mine, separated from me by a dozen iron bars.

If officials from the German embassy—Nazi appointees—got here before the Treasury people did, the two National Socialist killers would vanish into the night, jump a ship to Europe, and never be seen again.

'All right,' I said. 'Call Special Agent Daniel Kessler—Dan Kessler—of the Department of the Treasury. He will tell you everything.'

The two cops stared blankly at me.

'Don't you worry, honey,' one of them said. 'We've called someone all right. You'll meet some nice federal agents before this is all over, you damned Kraut assassin.'

I sighed and turned away.

I could see how it looked.

Even though I'd lived in America for years, I still had a German inflection to my speech and here I was with two *real* German spies who had tried to kill Albert Einstein during a visit to Princeton University.

And I had no way to prove my innocence.

Thirty minutes later, a man in a U.S. Army uniform and claiming to be from Army Intelligence came to my cell and proceeded to interrogate me on and off in a windowless back room for the next day-and-a-half.

As he did, two armed Army troopers guarded the door.

He said his name was Major Gil Willis and he asked me about everything.

My recent life in America. My youth in Germany before that.

When I implored him to call Einstein—which I did many times—he just said he'd get to that when the time was right.

And then, after thirty-six hours of answering his questions, shouts from the outer reception area made my interrogator spin and—

Bang!

—the door swung open and in rushed Einstein, followed by Special Agent Kessler.

'Where is she—?' Einstein called before he saw me and rushed to my side, sweeping me up in his arms in a huge hug of relief.

'Oh, Hanna, my dear, are you all right?' He touched the cut on my forehead. 'Are you hurt?'

'I'm fine,' I said. 'It's just a scratch.'

My interrogator sat there, speechless.

The local policemen in the hallway outside stared slack-jawed at the most famous scientist in the world.

In their minds, they had more chance of flying to the moon than meeting Albert Einstein and yet here he was, the great man himself, in that small police station, embracing me.

Then, to their even greater shock, he addressed them. 'Gentlemen, please get these handcuffs off her.'

Stunned into silence, my interrogator unfastened the handcuffs around my wrists and took a step back.

I stood from my chair.

'Good God, you're freezing,' Einstein said, throwing his overcoat around me.

'I tried to tell them,' I said. 'I told them to call you, sir, but they wouldn't, they didn't—'

Agent Kessler shot Major Willis a look. 'Did she? Come on, Hanna. Let's get you out of here.'

Led by Kessler, Einstein guided me out of the concrete-walled room, draped in his overcoat, with one arm wrapped protectively around my shoulders.

He stopped in the doorway, turned to Major Willis.

'You should be giving this young woman a medal. She saved my life! She threw herself into the assassins when they tried to pull me into their truck.'

It was then that Major Willis found his voice.

'But . . . sir . . . who is she?'

Einstein said, 'She is my secretary!'

SECOND INTERROGATION
BERLIN, GERMANY
1942

> Heydrich [the head of the Gestapo] was
> so cruel that Hitler himself once famously
> described him as 'the man with the iron heart'.
>
> – From: *Germany and the Second World War*
> by Guy Longworth

REICH MAIN SECURITY OFFICE
PRINZ-ALBRECHT-STRASSE
BERLIN, GERMANY
JANUARY 1942, 2:45 A.M.

NINE YEARS LATER.

My second interrogation also took place in the dead of night, only this time in a cell inside Gestapo headquarters in Berlin.

It stank of fear and urine.

Its brick walls were pockmarked with bullet holes. Dried blood crusted their edges. The Gestapo didn't bother to take you outside to shoot you. They just did it right here.

I sat bound to a chair.

Beside me sat Gertrude Schneider, Bormann's secretary, mistress and informer. She was as committed a Nazi as you'd ever find as well as being a bitch.

She disdained me almost as much as she disdained Speer, my boss.

Gertrude liked her Nazis to be big, brutish and tough, like Bormann. Quiet and intellectual, Speer was not her type at all.

Speer was also a favourite of the Führer's, which meant Bormann saw him as a competitor, and since I was Speer's secretary, Gertrude damned me as a competitor-by-association.

Our interrogator entered the cell.

He walked slowly, like a cat circling a mouse caught in a mousetrap.

He was a sly-looking fellow with hollow cheeks and blank eyes. In any other normal nation, he would have been in jail. In Nazi Germany, he worked for the secret police.

He held in his hand a silver steel briefcase.

'Miss Schneider, Miss Fischer,' he said. 'Welcome to the Reich Main Security Office. I have a name but there is really no point telling it to you. You are probably wondering why you have been brought here.'

I wasn't wondering anything.

I knew precisely why.

They'd finally found me out.

Our interrogator smiled, glanced at his steel briefcase. 'My associate and I would like to ask you some questions, is all.'

It was then that the door opened and into the fetid cell walked a man in full black SS uniform. On his collar were the Totenkopf or 'death's head', the twin lightning bolts of the SS, plus some silver laurels.

I recognised him instantly.

So did Gertrude. She actually gasped.

In a regime of individuals who all provoked fear, he was the most feared. His face, with its long nose, high forehead and piercing pale eyes, was known to every German.

Even Speer visibly tensed whenever this man entered a room and Speer had Hitler protecting him.

He was Obergruppenführer Reinhard Heydrich, chief of the

Reich Main Security Office and Head of the Gestapo.

He was the man who had ordered the assassination of Einstein back in 1933.

And he was here, now, in the middle of the night, with Gertrude and me.

This was particularly disturbing.

Reinhard Heydrich didn't attend low-level tortures or random interrogations.

'Ladies,' he said pleasantly as he sat down opposite us.

His eyes never blinked, never left our faces. He was a predator searching for any sign of falsehood, fabrication or weakness.

'We have a lot to talk about,' he said. 'And it will take a while. A few days even. And I fear we are not going to let you sleep much during that time.'

Gertrude gasped again.

Heydrich held up a finger. 'Fear not, Fräuleins. Our methods are civilised, not like those of the Russians. Oh, goodness, no. They would be doing all sorts of horrible things to you right now.'

Gertrude almost fainted.

I found myself holding my breath.

Heydrich went on. 'But I fear that to do this correctly, to make sure I am not wasting my time with you both, I have to know that you are going to be honest with me.'

He nodded to his assistant who clicked open the steel briefcase to reveal inside it several rows of ghastly looking implements: knives, scalpels, pliers, a hammer and several horrific vice-like things.

'Now.' Heydrich smiled. 'Are you going to do that? Are you going to be honest with me? Remember, it could be worse. We could be the Russians.'

THIRD INTERROGATION

SOVIET COMMAND POST

BERLIN, GERMANY

MAY 1945

SOVIET MOBILE COMMAND POST
BERLIN
MAY 4, 1945

MY THIRD INTERROGATION IS *in a Red Army command post in the ruins of Berlin not far from the Reich Chancellery.*

Hitler is dead and Germany has apparently surrendered but here in Berlin, for those of us who have been captured by the dreaded Russians, the war is certainly not over.

This cell is a horror show. The blood on the walls is fresh. Clumps of human viscera lie on the floor. The stink is indescribable.

The Russians caught us three days ago.

They covered our heads with sacks and brought us here, a bombed-out building equipped with iron-barred cells that— amazingly—are still intact. It looks like a police station and suddenly to my horror I realise that I know this place.

It is Prinz-Albrecht-Strasse. Gestapo headquarters.

Only now it's under the management of the Russians.

Again, I am not alone.

Again, I wear handcuffs.

Only this time I am handcuffed to a man in a Nazi uniform with a bandaged leg.

But he isn't a Nazi.

He is an American agent.

A third prisoner is in the room. He is a Nazi. Stocky and bald, he was a very senior official in the former regime.

As I wake up, I see that his trousers are around his ankles and he is being vigorously raped by a gigantic Russian soldier. The fat Nazi whimpers at every thrust.

Three other dirty Russian soldiers hold him down. Soon after, they take their turns.

But for some reason, neither my American friend nor I are harmed.

With a shrill rusty squeal, the cell door opens.

Two Russian interrogators enter. They are both colonels.

They say nothing to the four dirty soldiers who continue to sodomise the whimpering Nazi.

They sit down.

'Hello, Hanna,' the senior interrogator says to me. 'My, my, you've been busy.'

FROM THE FIRST
INTERROGATION
NEW JERSEY, 1933

INTERROGATOR (MAJ. WILLIS, U.S. ARMY): Miss Fischer. You have to understand my situation here: finding you, a German citizen, in the vicinity of Professor Einstein at the same time as two German assassins.

FISCHER: I'm only *half*-German, sir. My mother came from Brooklyn.

INTERROGATOR: What were you doing at Princeton?

FISCHER: I told you, I work for Professor Einstein. I'm his junior secretary. I accompanied him to America for this three-month trip to Caltech and Princeton.

INTERROGATOR: How long have you worked for Professor Einstein?

FISCHER: About two years, not counting the time I assisted him at the Solvay Conference in '27. But I've known him much longer.

INTERROGATOR: How long?

FISCHER: Almost my whole life. When I was a child in Berlin, Albert Einstein was my next-door neighbour.

PART I

1912
BERLIN

There is always one moment in childhood when the door opens and lets the future in.

– Graham Greene

> Before he achieved worldwide fame, Albert
> Einstein worked out of a modest apartment in
> a very modest neighbourhood in Berlin.

– From: Einstein by Thomas McMahon

NO. 7 HABERLANDSTRASSE
BERLIN, GERMANY
JANUARY 1, 1912

FOR MY TENTH BIRTHDAY, I received a doll from my aunt, a bracelet from my father and a model of the solar system from my neighbour Mr Einstein.

I hated the doll, much like I hated my aunt Olga.

I adored the bracelet, much like I adored my father.

As for the model from Einstein, I thought it was simply *spectacular*.

My father looked on proudly as I lifted the enormous thing from its box, my eyes wide with wonder.

Those were the good years: before the first war, before the indignities we suffered during it, before Germany's humiliation at the end of it and before my father's death because of it.

In 1912, Germany was a nation on the rise, the most populous country in Europe, an industrial powerhouse, proud to the point of arrogant, a newly minted empire ruled by a bombastic and bellicose emperor, Kaiser Wilhelm II.

Being ten, of course I had no clue about international affairs or for that matter Einstein's intellectual reputation, although to be fair at that time he wasn't yet world famous.

His fame in 1912 was limited to the subculture of German-speaking physicists in European universities.

British physicists—still indignant at his attack on Newton's laws seven years earlier—did their best to ignore him, referring to him dismissively as a patent clerk.

I was aware enough to know that he was a scholar of note. But to me, he was just the quirky-looking little man who lived in the next building with his friendly wife.

Even then, his hair was a wild fuzzy mess, although it was shorter and less grey than it would become in his later days. His moustache, however, was the same. Droopy to the point of cartoonish, it looked like a cute bushy animal dozing on his upper lip.

But it was his eyes that got you.

Captured you.

Drew you in.

Glittering yet gentle, heavy-lidded yet alert, sharp yet kind, they possessed a singular welcomeness that made you feel like you had his absolute undivided attention.

Albert Einstein was the best listener I ever knew.

But back to his birthday gift.

Fully extended, Einstein's replica of the solar system was gigantic, four feet across. It was almost bigger than I was.

What made it extra delightful was the fact that Herr Einstein had built it himself. The image of him—kindly and gentle with his silly moustache—working away in some little woodworking studio making toys like a real-life Geppetto suited him.

Today, we would call it a *mobile*: the planets—from little Mercury to gigantic Jupiter—were wooden balls suspended on strings from a series of concentric brass rings that orbited a central sun.

To my ten-year-old eyes, it was magnificent.

28

Einstein had painted each little orb in colours that matched the planets' actual hues. Red for Mercury, pale blue for Venus, dull orange for Mars. Saturn—a much bigger orb—had dramatic sweeping rings made of translucent gauze.

I turned to my father. 'Papa, will Ooma also be getting presents, even if she is in hospital? It's her birthday, too.'

Ooma was my sister, my twin. Her actual name was Norma, but when I'd been very young I had mispronounced it 'Ooma' and the nickname had stuck.

'Why, yes, of course,' Papa replied. 'For now, though, your sister needs to rest a little.'

I didn't know the full details of my sister's latest trip to hospital. All I knew was that it had something to do with the incident the previous week when Papa had found her in the garden with the rat.

Alert to my father's discomfort, Einstein changed the subject.

'So, young miss?' he said to me. 'How are you coming along with your physics?'

He spoke with a distinctly German cadence: quick, clipped, efficient.

I did not reply. I was too absorbed with my new toy.

'Hanna?' Papa said. 'What do you say?'

'What? Oh, thank you, Herr Einstein, thank you very much.'

'No,' Papa said. 'What do you say to Herr Einstein's question?'

I blinked, trying to remember what he'd said.

Physics . . .

'Very well, thank you, Herr Einstein,' I said. 'I intend to become the greatest physicist in history, you know.'

Yes, I said that to the greatest physicist in history. I was in fifth grade and had only studied the most basic rudiments of science.

'And the greatest ballerina, doctor and football player,' I added.

Einstein chuckled.

I frowned glumly. 'But I'm in Fräulein Zoeller's science class and she's ever so strict. She assigns lots of homework. My friend, Wolfgang, he's in Herr Stuber's class across the hall and Wolfgang says Herr Stuber is constantly having fun and playing games with his students. And he gives practically no homework at all.'

'I see,' Einstein said. 'So you have the tough teacher, eh?'

'Yes.'

He leaned forward, looked me squarely in the eye. 'Young Hanna, trust me on this: *it's always better to have the tough teacher*. Because with the tough teacher, you learn. I'm sure Herr Stuber's students have a gay old time in his classroom, but it is Fräulein Zoeller's students who will change the world. Embrace the hard teacher, whether in science, literature or even ballet. Indeed, in any form of study, seek out the hard teacher. It will serve you well.'

I nodded, but said nothing. This was something that my ten-year-old brain would have to consider.

Einstein smiled. 'Your father tells me that your overall studies are going very well. I am pleased to hear it. Keep studying, keep reading, keep learning, and you will succeed at whatever you decide to do, scientist, ballerina or otherwise.'

'I will do that, Herr Einstein,' I said. 'May I ask you a question?'

'Certainly.'

'I have recently been reading about Madame Marie Curie and her work. She just won a second Nobel Prize, did you know?'

'I did know that, yes,' Einstein replied kindly.

'She is the first person *ever* to win two Nobel Prizes, did you know?'

'She is indeed.'

'Have you won a Nobel Prize, Herr Einstein?' I asked.

Einstein gave a little cough. 'Ahem. No, I haven't.'

'Is Madame Curie smarter than you?'

My father stifled a laugh. He glanced at Einstein and grinned. 'Oh, this is on you, Albert.'

Einstein turned to me. 'Without a shadow of a doubt, Marie is much smarter than I. She is a brilliant woman with an astounding mind.'

I frowned. 'But, Herr Einstein, my homeroom teacher at school, Fräulein Schmidt, says that men are smarter than women. She says that the male brain is larger than the female one and thus better suited to science and politics and business. She says women were designed by God to bear children and honour their husbands. If they are to work, then it should only be as nurses to the sick and as elementary school teachers. Should a woman marry, Fräulein Schmidt says she must resign from these occupations.'

When I stopped speaking, I saw that both my father and Einstein were gaping at me.

'Your teacher said that?' Einstein said.

My father's face was darker.

'Fräulein Schmidt really told you that?' he said quietly.

'Yes, Papa.'

'I think I shall have to pay your school a visit on Monday and have a quiet word with Fräulein Schmidt.'

I didn't know why he would need to do that, but I nodded anyway.

'Hanna dear,' Einstein said, leaning forward. 'I'm sure your teacher is correct about a good many things, but on this matter she could not be more wrong. Women are the intellectual equals of men. Many women, like Madame Curie, are actually far cleverer.

You keep reading about Marie Curie, young one. You will find no better role model than her.'

'Yes, sir, I will.'

My father turned to me. 'Hanna, did you tell Herr Einstein that you and I have been reading his special theory of relativity?'

'Oh, yes,' I said, excitedly. 'But I have a question, sir.'

'Go ahead,' Einstein said.

(I should say this about Einstein: he never condescended to anyone. He was always the most brilliant person in any room, but if someone had a question for him, he did his best to listen closely and answer it.)

'Your theory seems to be limited only to inertial systems where there is no acceleration,' I said. 'What happens when there *is* acceleration affecting time and space? I mean, like gravity?'

Again Papa threw a look at Einstein although this time there was no stifled laugh. This time, it was just a silent raising of his eyebrows.

Einstein said, 'Little Hanna, for one your age, your grasp of physics is remarkable. This is actually an issue I am grappling with in my studies right now.'

He turned to my father. 'Get her out of that school and to a science *Gymnasium* immediately, Manfred. The girl is gifted.'

'Believe me, I am working on it,' my father said.

I held up the mobile. 'Herr Einstein, thank you very kindly for this gift. I am ever so interested in the planets and their motions. This will spur me to read even more about them than I already have.'

Einstein smiled. 'Then it has served its purpose.'

I eyed my new toy.

'Papa. May I be excused to go to my room and play with my new solar system?'

'Of course, *Zaubermaus*. Off you go.'

I gave both Einstein and Papa quick hugs and scampered off to my bedroom.

I erected the mobile over my bed and lay on my back and gazed up at it, dreaming about planets and space and time and gravity.

I had been doing this for about ten minutes when I suddenly remembered Papa's gift.

The bracelet.

I hurried back to the living room, grabbed it, and raced back up to my room.

I call it a bracelet but it was actually two thin wooden bangles held together by a silver chain to form a single piece of jewellery.

It was a replacement for an older one I had outgrown.

Papa had painted one bangle blue and the other pink, just like the original. He had also reproduced the two inscriptions that had been on the original pair.

I smiled sadly as I read the two brief messages. One from Papa, and one from my mother, long since passed.

Being ten, I tossed the bracelet onto my dresser and promptly forgot about it, returning my attention to Einstein's marvellous solar system.

It's funny how children, so easily distracted by big shiny things, miss the important ones.

> The mind is like an iceberg. It floats with one-seventh of its bulk above water.
>
> – Sigmund Freud

MY RELATIONSHIP WITH MY twin sister warrants special mention.

From an early age, Ooma engaged in odd behaviour, behaviour that ranged from the mildly curious to the outright bizarre.

She lived with us off and on.

It was only when I reached my teens that I realised that the hospital she stayed at when she wasn't at home—down in the forests near Potsdam, about an hour south of Berlin by train—was actually an asylum run by the Protestant Church.

While our looks were identical, our minds were not.

Ooma's brain wasn't right.

Some days she was bright and gay, a smiling sprite who would dance in the middle of the street, making all the traffic stop.

Other days she was a dark and silent monster, her eyes downcast, her mouth downturned.

On those days, she might hear you, but she would not reply. She could stare at a wall for hours.

Ooma could read almost a year before I could. And she was naturally gifted at mathematics.

She could play the piano like a concert pianist, while I struggled to play simple tunes. She only had to hear a melody once and she could reproduce it perfectly.

Having said that, she could also sit at a piano all day, obsessively playing *the same tune* over and over and over.

She was able to show affection—in her way—but, again, that depended on her mood. On her good days, she showered us all with love. On her bad ones, she kicked and screamed and raged and broke things.

One time, when Ooma was seven years old—seven—and my mother forbade her and me from going to the park to play on the swings, Ooma had taken some scissors from the pantry and calmly walked into Mom and Papa's bedroom and proceeded to hack into their pillows in a crazed frenzy, causing a billowing snowstorm of feathers to fill the room.

Hence the asylum in the forest, where Ooma received treatment from a collection of doctors and Protestant ministers who specialised in disordered minds.

During her stays at the asylum, my parents would leave me with Mr Einstein—the most overqualified babysitter in history—while they took the train south to Potsdam.

They would disappear for the entire day and return well after dark, after I had fallen asleep on Mr Einstein's couch. Often were the times I recalled my father scooping me up, mumbling and sleepy, and carrying me back to my own bed next door.

When I reached the age of eight, Mom and Papa took me with them to visit Ooma, having determined that I was old enough to see my institutionalised sister.

(As I mentioned, Ooma had spent our tenth birthday—the one where I received Einstein's solar system—at the asylum after my father had discovered her in the garden vivisecting a live rat she had tied down with stakes.)

The asylum was a grim red-brick building with a forbidding arched entrance. It lay on a sizeable acreage that abutted a large forest with a stream running through it.

A very old church adjoined the main building—connected to it by a more recently constructed enclosed colonnade—for the spiritual needs of the insane.

The place stank of carbolic acid.

On my first visit there as an eight-year-old, however, what I saw when I beheld Ooma was a lean little girl, just like me only a little skinnier, who stared vacantly into the middle distance.

My father read to her, some tale from the Brothers Grimm. Ooma didn't seem to notice—staring at nothing, always staring—until he stopped and she cocked her head silently, as if to say, 'Why has this man stopped reading?'

Papa read on and she resumed her quiet listening pose.

When we made to leave, my mother tried—very gently, moving slowly—to hug Ooma.

Ooma received her embrace, but did not return it.

She stared forward over Mom's shoulder and whispered something that I could not hear.

My mother reacted instantly.

She squeezed her eyes shut and wept, her body shuddering.

On the train travelling back to Berlin, I heard Mom say to Papa, 'Did you hear what she said, Manny? She said, "I'm sorry I hurt you. I don't know what comes over me sometimes."'

Papa wrapped his arm around Mom.

I was confused. 'Mom? Papa? Is Ooma wicked?'

Mom said, 'Oh, no, Hanna, no. Not at all. Her mind simply doesn't work the same way ours do, so she needs a little help. Like a nice quiet place to live, away from the bustle and distractions of Berlin.'

Papa tousled my hair. 'Most of all, *Zaubermaus*, Ooma just requires us to have patience. She is our daughter and your sister, so it's our job to look after her.'

After he said this, he squeezed Mom's hand.

As the train swayed, Mom lay her head on his shoulder.

'She said she was sorry, Manny!'

My mother was murdered a few months later.

The memory of that train ride stirs another, this one from New York City in the 20s.

I clutch a child in my arms as I run frantically along the tracks of an elevated railway or 'el-train' as it was called then, pursued by men with guns.

They fire. Their bullets ricochet off the tracks at my feet, kicking up sparks as I round a bend behind a brick building, getting out of the line of fire while more bullets chew into the brickwork.

Another memory of trains.

Tens of thousands of deliriously happy Germans stride through the turnstiles of the railway station servicing the Reichssportfeld, the vast collection of sporting facilities in Berlin that will host the 1936 Olympic Games.

The fans converge on Speer's colossal Olympiastadion.

It has a capacity of 110,000.

Speer is very proud of it.

There is joy in the air, anticipation, expectation.

These happy Germans don't notice the many Nazi flags ringing the stadium.

Distracted by this circus, they ignore the country their nation has become.

1945.

I am loaded into the foul cattle car with all the other prisoners.

My mouth is covered by a leather gag, to stop me from biting the guards.

This train is going to Mauthausen, the worst of the camps.

> The person, be it a gentleman or lady, who
> has not pleasure in a good novel, must be
> intolerably stupid.
>
> – From: Jane Austen, *Northanger Abbey*

MY MOTHER DIED IN 1910.

She was a lecturer in physics at the Royal Prussian Academy of Sciences, a position that Einstein had helped her acquire after he had read a paper she'd written.

And she was American—from a place called Brooklyn in New York City—a fact which constantly grated on her German in-laws.

I once overheard my aunt Olga say: 'Like all Americans, she is vulgar and without manners. She forgets her place.'

Dr Sandra Rose Martin had come to Europe from Brooklyn with her brand-new Ph.D. in physics, to work with the greatest scientific minds of her age and had ended up in Berlin as Mrs Manfred Fischer.

She had met my father—a career bureaucrat in the government—at a party thrown by the American embassy and, to the astonishment of almost all who knew her, married him within a year.

My father's family were particularly perplexed by this.

My mother was a tall blonde beauty, lean and striking. My father was short and bookish and wore thick spectacles.

Aunt Olga again: 'She is as spritely as Manfred is dull. I can't imagine what she sees in him.'

She may have had a point.

My mother, it must be said, was never short of male attention. Workmen whistled at her as she walked down the street. Men in suits on the U-Bahn spontaneously offered to buy her drinks after work if she would join them.

But it was Papa she married.

And she only had eyes for him.

When I was four, I asked her what it was about him that made her marry him.

'Because the first time I met him at that party at the embassy, he glimpsed the book I was carrying in my purse and politely asked me what I was reading.'

I frowned. 'Why did *that* appeal to you?'

'He was the only man I'd ever met whose first comment to me was *not* about my appearance. Many men flatter women, and women who allow themselves to be flattered are fools betrayed by their vanity. They are lambs before the wolves.

'But here was a man who was curious—genuinely curious—about what I was reading. When I told him—it was *The Memoirs of Sherlock Holmes* by Arthur Conan Doyle—his eyes lit up and he said excitedly that he had read it himself and he asked what my opinion of it was.

'That was his second plus: he wanted to know what I thought of the book. Many men will happily tell you *their* thoughts on a subject. This man wanted to know mine.

'We chatted for the entire evening, on all manner of subjects, from novels to science to the state of the ascending German empire. And as I talked with him, I realised that Manfred Fischer—little Manny, with his soft voice and his round spectacles—didn't want to own me, to display me as his trophy. He saw who I was on the inside. He was in the purest sense a *gentle* man. A gentleman.

. 'You will be a very pretty woman one day, Mouse. Watch out for the charmers, the flatterers, the ones who admire you only for your looks. For what will they love when you are old and wrinkly?'

Then she had looked hard at me. 'Your father may not be great in size, but do not doubt his fortitude on the things that matter. A woman should marry a man like that and marry him right away. Which I did.'

I once asked my father to corroborate her story and he confirmed the details.

He added, '*Zaubermaus*, if you ever meet someone and you notice they are carrying a book, say "*Wunderbar!*" and rejoice.

'This is because books are the finest conversation-starters in the world and to discuss a book is to have a *real* conversation with a stranger and not banal small talk. Better yet, if that book is one you have read or by an author you yourself admire, then you immediately have something in common with that person to talk about—as I did with your mother.

'A book can also give you insight into that person's character: first and foremost, that that person is *curious*, because it is only the curious who read. The boorish and the arrogant do not read because they think they know everything already.'

He glanced over at my mother and saw that she had put down the novel she'd been reading and was observing our conversation.

'Oh, please, don't stop. You're on a roll, cowboy,' she said.

Papa said, 'Your mother, for instance, was reading a Sherlock Holmes book. This told me instantly that here was a lady who just enjoyed a good story, a grand mystery well told. Some readers turn up their noses at such books, considering them to be too lowbrow. But not I. One who reads such a book reads it for pleasure, for joy. That book revealed to me, in a single glance, that here was a woman who possessed a whimsy for pure joy. And I wanted to get to know such a soul.'

The smile my mother gave Papa after that comment stays with me to this day.

I remember her smell perfectly.

The one indulgence she allowed herself was a perfume called Californian Poppy.

It had a gorgeous citrus-like scent: fresh and vivacious. Like her.

'I just like the name, *Californian* Poppy,' my mother remarked as I watched her dab it on her elegant neck one evening. She only ever used it sparingly.

'Every time I put it on, it reminds me of home. You can take the girl out of America, but you can't take America out of the girl,' she added with a grin.

When I became a woman, I would wear this same perfume, to remind me of her.

> [Jews are a] nuisance that humanity must get
> rid of some way or other. I believe the best
> thing would be gas!
>
> – Kaiser Wilhelm II, Emperor of Germany

MY PARENTS' MARRIAGE ALSO explains how I came to be in possession of not one but two passports, one German and one American. Granted, passports in those days were not what they are today. They could better be described as travel papers and in those less suspicious times, they were far easier to obtain than they are now.

Still, many people—like Aunt Olga—saw only my parents' differences.

My mother was trained as a physicist. My father was a lawyer.

My mother danced in the rain. My father could hardly even shuffle.

My mother wore bright, modern outfits. My father always wore a dour grey wool suit.

My mother delved into the unknown of the universe. My father pored over every line of a government contract.

She was 'Mom'.

He was 'Papa'.

('I'll live in Germany,' she said, 'but damn it, I'll not be *Mama*. I'll be an American *Mom*, thank you very much.')

The only person, so far as I knew, who liked the match was our quirky neighbour Einstein.

He once told me that it was their very differences that made them such a fine couple. They complemented each other.

Later, he would say, 'Your father kept your mother's impulses in check, and your mother made your father have fun.'

Like the time she made him sit with me one rainy Sunday afternoon in 1910 when he said he had an awful lot of work to do, some government contract for something or other.

My mother was a whiz at concocting fun. She could keep me enthralled for hours.

It was her science experiments that I loved the most.

Once, to explain physics to me, she put a boiled egg in the mouth of a milk bottle and then lit a flame under the bottle: with a wet slurp, the ensuing suction pulled the egg into the bottle.

I was amazed.

'*That* is physics,' she'd said. 'And that is what Mom does for work.'

My eyes were wide as saucers.

'Do it again!' I cried.

On that rainy afternoon in 1910, while Papa had been working away at his desk, Mom and I did craft.

She'd bought several plain wooden bracelets along with glue, coloured paper and string. We were making bracelets for each other, personalising them in all manner of ways: painting them bright colours, gluing red paper hearts and yellow paper stars all over them, and dangling paper pendants from them with string.

After a time the kitchen bench was a wondrous mess of spills, paint, glue and offcuts of coloured paper.

I was having a ball.

Mom called Papa over just as we were putting the finishing touches to our bracelets.

'Come on, Manny,' she said. 'You must make a bracelet for Hanna, too. She should get one from each of us. Write a message on it. You can colour it with paint later.'

'All right,' he said, picking up a spare, unpainted bangle.

I presented the bracelet I had made to Mom.

It was very pink and, on reflection, truly hideous, wildly over-done. Like any eight-year-old, I had tried to cram too many stars, baubles and pendants onto it.

Mom put the childish pink bracelet straight on her wrist. 'This is now officially my favourite piece of jewellery. I'll wear it every day.'

'My turn!' I squealed.

They gave me their bracelets.

Mom's was elegantly covered in gold stars and loops of painted string. On it she had written:

I WILL <u>ALWAYS</u> BE PROUD OF YOU.

Papa's unadorned wooden bracelet read:

NO MATTER WHERE YOU ARE OR WHAT YOU DO, <u>YOU ARE AMAZING.</u>

I liked Mom's better.

But I gave them both hugs anyway.

As I hugged Papa, I heard him say to Mom, 'Thanks, Sandy.'

★ ★ ★

My mother was shot and killed two weeks later by a seventeen-year-old thug named Gunther Groethe while she was giving a lecture at the Academy.

Groethe hadn't come to the class to kill my mother. He'd come to kill the many Jewish students attending her lecture, the Academy being one of the few universities that allowed Jews.

Groethe was an angry barely literate unemployed Bavarian who had joined an anti-Semitic organisation in Munich that had told him—relentlessly—that it was the Jews who were to blame for his predicament in life.

In an economy that was second in size only to that of the United States, in a rising empire that had pretensions of ruling the world, Mr Groethe was a victim.

So he stole his older brother's army rifle, went to my mother's lecture theatre, randomly shot four Jewish students and my mother and then happily surrendered to the police, grinning like a fool.

In the pocket of his jacket was a German-language copy of *The Protocols of the Elders of Zion*, the notorious manifesto of Jewish world-domination-through-manipulation that would be debunked as a forgery in 1921.

Back in 1910, however, it was slithering its way across Europe, infiltrating anti-Jewish covens and validating their conspiracies and grievances.

Groethe was sentenced to thirty-five years in prison.

My mother had a doctorate in physics, a degree in chemistry and spoke three languages. She had been killed by a racist hooligan.

On the day she died, she was 39 years old.

And she was wearing the gaudy pink bracelet I had made for her.

★ ★ ★

When they returned the bracelet to Papa, along with her blood-stained dress, it bore the lingering scent of Californian Poppy perfume.

1933.

Another time.

Another Berlin.

Books burn.

The flames reach into the night sky as I hurry past the Royal Prussian Academy of Sciences, my head bent, trying not to be seen by the baying crowd.

The Academy is illuminated by the glow of the bonfire.

Angry students hurl books into the flames, works by authors now deemed un-German, indecent or immoral.

Brecht. Schnitzler. Marx. Hemingway.

And, of course, Einstein.

I am 31 now.

I have not lived in Berlin for the whole time since my mother's death. For many of those years, I lived away from Germany.

The man directing the book burning is an SA officer named Gunther Groethe.

The thug who murdered my mother is now part of the ruling regime.

1945.

Yet another time.

Yet another Berlin.

Another me.

All of Berlin is in flames.

Bombs land with monstrous booms as more whistle through the air, incoming.

Germans run and flee every which way, including those like us who were in the Führerbunker under the Chancellery.

We are desperate to get away from the Russian forces who have stormed across Eastern Europe to get here and wreak their vengeance on the nation that tried to seize their land for living space.

I run as fast as I can, close behind Bormann, out of the Führerbunker and across the Chancellery's inner garden.

I pass the small crater in the ground where Hitler and Eva Braun's corpses lie, charred and twisted.

The breakout has begun.

[Male grief] tends to be quieter and less
visible, less connected with the past and more
connected with the future.

– Thomas R. Golden, grief therapist

I WAS TOO YOUNG to really comprehend what had happened.

Mom had left for work—to suction more eggs into milk bottles, I supposed—and she hadn't come back.

My father grieved deeply, but he was determined not to do it in my presence. I would sometimes glimpse him in his bedroom, sitting on the end of his bed, quietly sobbing.

He continued to take me to visit Ooma at the asylum in Potsdam. I recall the first time we went there without my mother.

'Where is Mother?' Ooma asked.

'Ooma,' Papa said gently, 'your mother is dead.'

Ooma nodded coolly. 'Oh.'

Albert and Mrs Einstein would come over to our apartment with roast dinners and kind smiles. Einstein often stayed late into the evening, quietly talking with my father over a glass of port.

In the ensuing years, my father never so much as looked at another woman.

He just quietly went back to his work at the Reichstag, head bowed, the bookish lawyer in the grey wool suit who'd had his nine years of wonder with a goddess.

Once, about six months after my mother's death, when I had

ostensibly gone to bed, I overheard him in the living room confiding to Einstein.

'Albert, I don't know what to do. I try my best, I really do. Ooma is one thing, but Hanna is another entirely. I'm just not as good with Hanna as Sandy was. Sandy had an imagination that I simply don't have. She could turn a snowed-in afternoon into an adventure throughout the apartment. I literally ask myself, *What would Sandy do?*'

But, oh, did he try.

Outings to the zoo or the library. He even tried reading Jules Verne with me.

Amid all that, he still made time to venture down to Potsdam to visit Ooma.

On our birthday after Mom died, he gave Ooma and me a blank diary each, the kind one purchased from the newsstand.

I could picture him buying them. In his daze of grief, unable to think creatively, he probably saw the diaries at a newsstand and knowing he had to get his daughters some kind of gift, bought them.

Others might have said this was a terrible gift, but it turned out to be a wonder. I wrote my thoughts into it daily. In later years, when I finished one diary, I would buy another.

His most outstanding effort, however, at 'doing what Mom would do' was the bracelet he gave me on my tenth birthday in 1912—a replacement for my original and the gift that was, at the time, outshone by Einstein's solar system.

On that occasion, he had definitely channelled my mother.

Sensing a winning formula, he outdid himself on my sixteenth birthday.

Six years had seen me outgrow Bracelet Mark II, so my father updated it again.

'You are a woman now,' he said, 'so I think it is only fitting that your bracelet be a little more adult.'

It was a shining bracelet of silver, or to be more precise, two silver bracelets, stylishly intertwined.

I was speechless. They sparkled magnificently. In those days, silver was exceedingly rare. It must have cost him three months' pay.

Engraved on the inner side of the bangle were the two original phrases from my parents.

I put it on right away and hugged him tightly.

'Thank you, Papa! Thank you! It's wonderful!'

When he hugged me back, I knew he was crying.

On my next visit to the asylum in Potsdam, Ooma noticed the new shiny bracelet instantly.

She gripped my hand and gazed at it intently. 'That's *beautiful*, Hanna.'

She was wearing an almost identical bracelet. My father, wisely, had always tried to make sure that anything he gave to me, he gave to Ooma. Hers had different phrases engraved on the inner surfaces.

She was in a gay, even spritely, mood that day, jumping excitedly from topic to topic. She asked me about Berlin and school and science and boys.

Then she leaned in close to me and whispered, 'I snuck out of the asylum last week and met a local boy in the forest on the other side of the river.

'There's a secret exit in the church here. It was a Catholic church before the Protestants took it over, so there's a secret door built into the back wall of the confessional, so the Catholic priests could come in and out unseen. I slipped out through it and met Felix. I allowed him to touch my naked breasts and then—oh, goodness—I let him fuck me, Hanna. By God, it was simply delightful.'

I gasped. I wasn't experienced at all in such matters and to hear her speak so frankly about it startled me.

'You haven't been with a boy?' she asked.

'Well, no . . . not yet,' I stammered.

'Oh, Hanna. Grow up and start learning. You're a pretty girl and the sweet boys of Berlin will be wanting to pluck your flower very soon!'

Then her gaze returned to our matching bracelets.

'Aren't they sublime?' I said.

'I like yours better,' she answered coldly, her mood changing in an instant.

I frowned, not understanding the sharp change. Then it was gone, and she was fine again.

On the ride home, my father said that Ooma's doctors had told him that she'd been doing much better and was almost ready to come and live at home again.

I wasn't so sure, but figured such decisions were beyond my understanding.

A month later, Ooma came to live with Papa and me in Berlin.

A year after that, when I was seventeen, I saved Albert Einstein for the first time.

Front page of *The New York Times*
November 10, 1919

BERLIN, GERMANY
NOVEMBER 1919

I CAN REMEMBER THE exact date of the incident.

November 10, 1919.

For on that day, my neighbour became the most famous scientist on the planet.

He'd been mentioned on the front page of *The New York Times* as the man who had turned the universe on its head, or at least the Newtonian interpretation of it, and instantaneously become the most celebrated scientist on Earth.

In the years since Einstein had given me that model of the solar system, much had changed, both for me and the world I lived in.

I had grown into a young woman and I suppose you could say I was pretty—slim of build, with shoulder-length tawny-blonde hair—but like every seventeen-year-old girl I certainly didn't think so.

I had my mother's looks but my father's height, which is to say I was short, shorter than the other girls my age. Being seventeen and critical of everything, I fixated on this.

I wished I was taller, hoped for a growth spurt, and eyed the high-heeled shoes in Kaufhaus des Westens with longing. Every time I begged Papa to buy me a pair, he just shook his head sadly.

Papa had settled into a routine of work and managing Ooma and me, but he was not the man he'd once been. He seemed perpetually distracted, living in a daydream, inside his own reveries.

I did what I could to make his life easier: making dinner, ironing his shirts, keeping the pantry stocked.

Ooma was attending a standard high school in Berlin.

Music and mathematics were her best subjects, but I sensed that school gave her not a single ounce of joy.

It was different for me.

I attended a different school and I *lived* for it.

It was my sanctuary, my safe harbour, my delight.

I was now attending a special '*Gymnasium*' that only accepted students who had shown aptitude at physics and chemistry.

I *loved* the *Gymnasium*.

The teachers were smart and engaged—some were very demanding, but I knew, thanks to Einstein, that that was a good thing. The students, all studious types, were not bothered with the usual trivialities and banal social rituals of regular schoolyards.

My athletic limitations meant that my childhood goals of

becoming the world's greatest ballerina or football player were no longer realistic, but becoming a noted physicist still was.

After I completed my final exams at my specialised *Gymnasium*, I would, I was sure, attend the Kaiser Wilhelm Institute and study under the greatest minds in Germany, including Einstein himself.

From there greatness would follow.

I should add that around this time of my young life, I had also become friendly with a boy.

His name was Lukas—Lukas Hofstedter—and he was lean and gangly, boyish and freckled, with a floppy mop of dark hair that hung down over his spectacles.

The son of the local shopkeeper, he lived a few blocks from us with his parents in a flat above their store.

Lukas shared my love for science. Indeed, he was especially gifted at it. After high school, he too wanted to study at the Kaiser Wilhelm Institute. Almost all of our conversations were about life after school, which was then only a tantalising seven months away.

When he learned that I knew Einstein personally, Lukas almost died of shock.

One day in October, as we walked home together, he was behaving oddly, nervously.

Then suddenly he whipped out a flower and awkwardly shoved it at me and blurted, 'Hanna, will you accompany me to the winter dance in December?'

I had been hoping he would ask.

Thrilled, I accepted and threw my arms around him, squealing with delight.

It was around that time that I began to manage the levels of our pantry in such a way that I could contrive more visits to his family's store.

And, of course, I had my new silver bracelet which I wore to school every day.

In short, I had my studies, the attentions of a bright young man and my bracelet.

I was in heaven.

Men will not always die quietly . . . Who
can say how much is endurable, or in what
direction men will seek at last to escape from
their misfortunes?

– John Maynard Keynes, 1919

THE GERMANY IN WHICH I lived, however, was not.

The Great War had come and gone and it had been brutal on the German populace.

The Kaiser and his generals had actively misled the country about our fortunes in the conflict. Despite the food shortages caused by the British blockade of German ports, the ordinary German thought Germany had been winning the war. This, I confess, included me. The war existed at the edges of my consciousness. We ate less, sure, but my father still went to his job and my daily life continued.

So, when the armistice was signed inside a railway carriage in the Forest of Compiègne at the eleventh hour on the eleventh day of the eleventh month in 1918, the news was met in Germany with shock and disbelief.

Since no German general—all of them Prussian aristocrats who had happily sent two million young men to their deaths—would suffer the indignity of affixing their name to it, the government had sent a politician named Matthias Erzberger to sign the document and officially end the war.

(Three years later, in August of 1921, Erzberger would be assassinated by right-wing terrorists for that 'act of betrayal'.)

The nation was beaten, hungry and confused.

Kaiser Wilhelm II abdicated and with his flight into exile, the Second Reich, the German Empire, was no more. The fledgling Weimer democracy took its place.

It was hard to imagine how it could get any worse.

It got worse on June 28, 1919.

For on that day, in the Hall of Mirrors at the Palace of Versailles in France—ironically, the very same hall in which the German Empire had been born only thirty-eight years previously—two obscure German ministers, advised by my father, now a senior government lawyer, signed the Treaty of Versailles.

The treaty was punishing.

Under its terms, Germany lost 25,000 square miles—ten percent—of its immediate territory, was stripped of its overseas colonies and was hit with colossal reparations that it could not ever hope to repay.

More than all of this, the ordinary German hated Article 231 of the treaty: the notorious war guilt clause. It laid all the blame—all moral culpability—for the war on Germany.

The reparations crippled the already wounded German economy. Article 231 crippled Germany's soul.

In this already bitter environment, the Wehrmacht remained obstinately proud.

Despite the fact that its mainly Prussian commanders—haughty nobles who had attained their commissions not by any display of military skill but rather by virtue of their family names—had been roundly beaten by the Allied powers, the army successfully propounded the notion that it had never been defeated.

The war, it said, had been lost not by the army's ineptitude but rather by cowardly politicians at home like Erzberger. And, of course, by the obligatory Jewish conspiracy.

And thus was born the *Dolchstosslegende*, the stab-in-the-back myth.

The two German delegates who actually signed their names on the Treaty of Versailles—Dr Hermann Müller and Dr Johannes Bell—were spat on in the street and received death threats in the mail.

Someone wrote '*FEIGLINGE!*' on the door of my father's office at the Reichstag in pig's blood. ('COWARDS!')

A journalist who dared praise the treaty was shot dead in his home by masked thugs. They then burned his house down. The bodies of the journalist's wife and daughter were found in the ruins, their remains bound to chairs. They had been burned alive.

Despite all this, Berlin still stood, beautiful and proud.

In a war that extinguished 17 million lives, the German capital had not been touched by so much as a bullet.

Architecturally, it was like most old European cities: which is to say that most of its buildings stood five or six storeys tall, the limit one could reach with limestone brick structures.

Smoke billowed from chimneys, blackening the sky. The medieval streets had been steadily widened into grand boulevards— Paris-like—and along them trolleys mixed with horse-drawn carts and occasionally, rarely, since they were so expensive, an automobile.

Beneath it all, however, simmered a burning resentment that fed the rise of the nationalist groups like the Germanenorden and the death squad known as the Organisation Consul.

It was in the midst of all this national rancour that, on

November 10, 1919, there occurred a rare solar eclipse and my neighbour became an instant global celebrity and I would have to come to his rescue.

> Einstein published his two most famous papers on Special and General Relativity in 1905 and 1915 respectively. Worldwide fame, however, would not come until 1919 when his radical new theory was proved correct during a rare solar eclipse . . .
>
> – From: *Einstein: The Man Who Saw the Universe* by Lynda Marren

BERLIN, GERMANY
NOVEMBER 10, 1919

LET'S NOT GET MIRED in the physics.

Allow me to simplify it thus: according to Einstein's two remarkable theories, mass and energy are connected, and time and space are curved.

Regarding mass and energy, everyone knows the equation.

It is perhaps the most famous scientific statement in history:

$$E = mc^2$$

Energy = mass multiplied by the square of the speed of light. That it was correct was one thing, but that it was so elegantly and simply put was the real testament to Einstein's genius.

Even the average person on the street could, kind of, grasp it. Mass and energy were interchangeable: you could—at least theoretically—convert one into the other.

And if you multiplied something's mass by the square of the speed of light—an almost incalculably huge number—then the resulting energy must be simply enormous.

Those same average people in the street who kind of grasped the famous formula truly grasped it in 1945 when, utilising its principles, two atomic bombs were used to destroy the cities of Hiroshima and Nagasaki in an instant.

Einstein, however, didn't have to wait till 1945 for his theory regarding the curvature of time and space to be well and truly proved.

That was done in 1919.

For one way of measuring the curvature of space and time due to gravity is during a total solar eclipse, when the moon passes fully in front of the sun. This allows astronomers to observe the apparent movement of certain stars behind the sun—in effect, seeing how the light of those stars bends around the sun by virtue of its immense mass.

And in 1919 a total solar eclipse was due.

It was, ironically, an Englishman who turned my neighbour into the world's most famous scientist.

While Einstein had been largely rebuffed by the British scientific establishment, he did have a few select fans there, among them the Astronomer Royal of Britain, Sir Frank Watson Dyson.

It was Dyson who conceived the ingenious experiment that would prove for certain whether Einstein's theories really did supersede Newton's: he suggested they use the eclipse of 1919.

Dyson charged Sir Arthur Eddington with carrying out this remarkable experiment.

It was no small thing.

Eddington sent observers to two of the farthest corners of the world—to Brazil and to the remote island of Príncipe off the west coast of Africa—to observe the eclipse.

And in doing so, he proved that light did indeed bend around the sun in exactly the manner Einstein had described.

The Newtonian universe was dead.

The headlines on the front page of *The New York Times* on November 10, 1919, said it all:

LIGHTS ALL ASKEW IN THE HEAVENS
EINSTEIN THEORY TRIUMPHS

The press descended on Einstein's building at No. 5 Haberlandstrasse.

It was not just the local press. There were reporters from all over the world: from America, England, France and Italy.

They camped on the street, banged on his door, called out his name.

I heard the hubbub and looked across at Einstein's building from my bedroom window.

From my vantage point—across the narrow alley that separated our buildings—I could see into his apartment, and there he was, hiding, his eyes wide, looking not like a celebrated man of science but like a trapped animal.

So I opened my window and silently waved him across.

I'm sure many will find the image of a forty-year-old man climbing into the bedroom of a seventeen-year-old girl unseemly but it was nothing of the sort.

As he fell with an awkward thump onto the floor of my bedroom, Einstein looked up and said, 'Thank you, young Hanna. I am most appreciative of your aid in my time of need—aha, my solar system! You still have it!'

His gift still hung from my ceiling, although not over the bed, but over my desk. I still gazed at it when I wanted to ponder matters bigger than the Earth.

'It is one of my most treasured possessions, Herr Einstein,' I said. 'Why are all those people out there?' I did not yet know of *The New York Times* piece.

'It seems I am suddenly famous,' Einstein said. 'I had anticipated some attention, but not this. Now, hmmm'—his brow furrowed in thought—'I shall have to figure out how to handle it.'

That was Einstein. A problem required a solution. One just had to turn one's mind to it.

Then he looked at me and a look of horror crossed his kind face.

'My goodness, where are my manners? I have barrelled in here like a bull in a china shop and I have not once asked after you.'

And so, right then and there, he took a seat on the floor of my bedroom, crossed his legs like a schoolboy and said to me, 'So, young miss. How go your studies?'

We had a delightful conversation that day.

I told him about my upcoming high school exams in physics and chemistry and he asked me many probing questions that, upon reflection in later times, were woefully beneath him, but I couldn't tell. He seemed delighted to discuss science at *any* level.

'I hope to qualify for the Institute,' I said proudly.

'*Wunderbar!*' he exclaimed. 'Oh, that is just marvellous.'

'My plan is to become a physicist like you, Herr Einstein. I have already got a list of the required reading for the first semester.'

'Oh, you are a wonder, young Hanna. Gifted and yet also so

eager to learn. I have no doubt that you will succeed. The Institute will be lucky to have you. But mark me now.'

I paused at his tone.

'Yes?'

'Keep your joy.'

'My joy?'

'You have a spirit to you, Hanna Fischer, a spark that is most rare. Keep that spark, that joy in your heart. Physics are all well and good, but life must be *lived*.

'I am supposed to be this brilliant man. Well, here is the most important thing I know: retain your inner joy. If you do that, you will live a successful and happy life.'

'I will try to do that, Herr Einstein,' I said.

'And if you ever need help, you may always call on me,' he said. 'Always.'

'Thank you, sir.'

I would remember that day fondly: the day I rescued Albert Einstein and we talked about physics and life in my bedroom.

I recorded the event in my diary.

It was the last happy memory I would have for some time.

Four days later, I came home from school to find Ooma sitting on my bed reading my diary.

Apparently, she had been at it for some time . . . and tearing out the pages after she'd read them.

The floor was covered in them, my deepest thoughts and desires.

'Ooma! What are you doing!'

She looked up from the journal and tore out a recent page. 'In love with Lukas Hofstedter, are you? Honestly? Really? He's so dull.'

I rushed in and snatched the book from her, started raking up the pages scattered over the carpet.

'Ooma, that diary is private. It's my private thoughts.'

'Oh, please, Hanna. Maybe Lukas is right for you. You're just as fucking dull as he is. Look at this.' She held up the diary. 'It's so *banal*! The lovelorn pining of a schoolgirl. You're plain and boring and entirely unaware of how *ordinary* you are. Honestly, who could love you?'

'Ooma,' a voice said flatly from the door, making us both turn.

Our father stood there. 'Enough. Go to your room. Now, please.'

Ooma left, her head bowed.

The next morning I found her sobbing in the bathtub in a pool of blood, gripping a razor blade.

Two hideous cuts had been slashed across her left wrist.

I grabbed a towel and rushed to her side, wrapping the towel around her blood-smeared forearm, trying to staunch the flow.

'I'm so sorry, Hanna! So sorry! I'm a wretch! A witch! A worthless bitch! How can I be so horrible?'

Papa took her back to the hospital in Potsdam.

'How can she be like this?' I asked Papa when he returned. 'So gay one day and then so vicious?'

'It's not her. It's her mind. She'd been having issues at school, too. She bit a couple of other girls recently. *Bit* them. Sometimes her mind just throws a switch and this awful side of her is unleashed.'

And so the week in which I rescued Albert Einstein ended with Ooma returning to her asylum in Potsdam.

The next day my life would change forever and Einstein would rescue me.

> The cradle of the National Socialist movement
> was Versailles, not Munich.
>
> – Theodor Heuss, 1931

BERLIN, GERMANY
NOVEMBER 15, 1919

THE DAY BEGAN PLAINLY enough.

'Come on, *Zaubermaus*, we'll be late,' Papa said, appearing in my doorway, knotting his tie.

'I don't want to go,' I said petulantly.

'Neither do I, but Olga is my sister and it's her birthday and she invited us, so we're going.'

'But I shall have to sit with Cousin Gretel . . .'

'Gretel is a charming girl.'

'She is a miniature version of Aunt Olga and Aunt Olga is a witch,' I said.

My father's urgency vanished.

'Come now, Hanna. Don't speak like that. You mustn't say that of anybody, no matter how disagreeable they are.'

He never called me Hanna. He reserved it only for those occasions when he was particularly disappointed.

I bowed my head, chastised.

'But Aunt Olga *is* disagreeable. She says such horrible things,' I protested gamely. 'Especially about you, especially when she drinks.'

'I know she does, but she's family and when it comes to family, we—well—tolerate things like that.'

★ ★ ★

My aunt Olga lived about a mile away in Wilmersdorf, so we walked.

Olga was my father's younger sister by five years. They had both grown up in the same poor home, but whereas my father had worked three jobs to put himself through university, Olga had gone into menial work and never escaped from it.

Overweight and with a face naturally set in a dark frown, she complained a lot.

When we arrived, she was already halfway through a bottle of schnapps. Within an hour, as we sat down for dinner, she was ranting.

'They come here from Russia with their devious business minds and they take *advantage* of us! One of them just bought the factory where I work. Now *I* make *him* money with my labour!'

I had heard this before.

Ever since I was a child, Aunt Olga had raged about 'the Jewish Question'.

Even though I was seventeen, I sat at the children's table beside my four cousins, among them Gretel.

If it were at all possible, Gretel had become even more of a copy of her mother. Two years older than I, she had left school to work in a textile factory. She was fat, ugly and sullen.

Gretel added, 'They flee Russia because the Russians have discovered the solution to the Jewish Question. Remember Odessa? Perhaps we should have a little pogrom of our own in Germany.'

A little pogrom.

In 1905 in Odessa over four hundred Jews had been slaughtered by their Russian neighbours.

Aunt Olga smiled at her daughter. 'Now there's a thought.'

She shook her head. 'Germany shelters them from Russia and

what do we get in return? Lice in our hair and lies in the press that they own. Honestly, the Jew has no shame. Why, right now they happily profit from our national misery. The war wounded us and like jackals they pounce and bleed us of what little money we have left. Then they loan us more at usurious rates. What creature does that, I ask you? What kind of parasitic creature? I'll tell you: the Jew.'

'Olga . . .' Papa said gently. She had finally roused him to intervene.

'Don't you even speak, brother!' she shrieked, her voice breaking such was her fury. '*You* bear some responsibility for this! You helped craft the vile treaty that crushes Germany now. You capitulated at Versailles and in so doing you condemned your own people to ruin and left us naked before the gnawing jaws of the jackal Jews.'

'Jackal Jews,' Gretel agreed.

Aunt Olga glared at my father, as if daring him to respond.

The room fell silent.

Papa's response, when it came, surprised me.

He pushed back his chair and stood.

'Hanna,' he said softly. 'Come now. We're leaving.'

He took my hand and we left.

We walked home.

A light snow fell, backlit by the streetlamps. Berlin in the early winter.

'Papa, what exactly is *the Jewish Question*?'

Papa snorted. 'It is not a question at all. That phrase is just a veil to cover base prejudice against the Jewish people.'

'Why do people like Olga and Gretel hate them?'

Papa sighed heavily. 'This is a topic I have long pondered, *Zaubermaus*. In the end, all I can deduce is that humanity has a fatal flaw. Even the lowest, poorest soul wants someone or something to lord it over. The homeless vagrant beats his dog because it gives him power.

'Olga and Gretel have few prospects in life. Theirs will be hard lives, their days filled with repetitive labour. They need someone to blame for their lot and their gaze falls on the Jews.'

'But why the Jews?'

Papa said, 'Many Christians despise the Jews purely on religious grounds because the Jews do not accept Jesus Christ as the Son of God. They see Christ merely as a prophet. For these Christians this is a profound insult to their pride, for if the Jews are correct, then *the entire Christian religion* is based on an error and they are fools.

'But there is another reason and for me it is the main reason for centuries of European Jew-hating.

'The Jews prize knowledge. And it is this knowledge that for hundreds of years has made them shrewd businesspeople. Being landlords, owning shops and, most famously of all, lending money: these are all businesses in which *the money does the work*.

'Money-lending in particular. To lend out money for interest—an occupation intimately connected with Jewry since the time of Christ—is an ingenious enterprise because of the marvel of compound interest.

'Olga and Gretel, uneducated and uninterested in educating themselves, have only their labour to sell and human labour is cheap. They despise the Jews—like the Jewish gentleman who just purchased Olga's factory—because while Olga and Gretel toil and

72

sweat, the Jews are making fortunes with their minds. But to hate is cheap. One does not need any money to hate.'

I was silent for a long moment.

'Papa . . .?'

'Yes?'

'Why did you assist with that treaty when you must have known people would hate you for doing it?'

'*Zaubermaus*,' he said. 'Decision-making is a skill you learn over time. It's not easy. But in the end, I've found that every decision comes down to a choice: the right choice or the wrong choice. I always just try to make the right one.'

'A lot of Germans seem to think you made the wrong choice,' I said.

'Only because they don't know the full story. Our bargaining position in Paris wasn't just weak, it was hopeless. The Allied powers said that if we didn't sign, they would invade Germany *the next day*. The decision I made was the right one. The right choice is not always a happy one. Alas, sometimes the right choice can be a very bitter one.'

We came to an intersection.

Our home was to the left. To the right was the store owned by Lukas's parents and I knew that Lukas was manning the cash register that evening.

'Oh, Papa, we need bread and milk. I'd also like to get some sweets to give to Ooma on our next visit.'

'All right, *Zaubermaus*. See you back at the apartment.'

While he continued toward Haberlandstrasse, I diverted to the store, where I chatted with Lukas for about twenty minutes.

At length, I took my leave and headed home, strolling in the light-falling snow with a bag packed with bread, milk and sweets, under the cones of light given off by the streetlamps.

I saw the pulsing orange glow around the bend before I heard the people.

Quickening my pace, I rounded the corner onto Haberlandstrasse and saw a crowd massing outside my burning apartment building, pointing up at something.

Something on the front face of the building—

Strong hands grabbed me and pulled me back into the shadows.

'Hush!' a voice commanded and to my surprise I realised it was Einstein's.

'It is not safe for you here,' he whispered as he peered out fearfully at the street.

'What's going on?' I said, struggling against him. I wanted to see what was happening.

Einstein tried to restrain me. 'Hanna, please, you shouldn't see—'

But I broke free of his grasp and managed to look down the street and see my building.

I froze.

Backlit by the flames raging inside my building, the body of a man hung from the second floor like a broken doll, high above the ground, his neck bent at a grotesque angle, snapped by the noose.

It was my father.

WRITTEN IN BLOOD ACROSS the frosted-glass doors of our building were the words:

VERSAILLES VERRÄTER!

Versailles traitor.

Every part of me froze.

It was a vision from hell.

Einstein yanked me back out of view. 'Come with me, young one. Your father warned me about this and left instructions should it occur.'

Stunned and numb, I let Einstein lead me away.

I felt like I was in a cocoon. All sound was muffled. Einstein's voice was distant, even though he was right beside me. 'This way, child. Come now!'

Moving urgently, he took me to his apartment where his wife waited, her hand covering her mouth in horror.

'It was a gang of thugs,' she said. 'Maybe twelve of them. Yelling and howling, brandishing guns and pipes. They were waiting for him. Called him a pig of Versailles.'

'Get her some tea, please, Elsa,' Einstein said, while he set about rummaging through a drawer nearby.

In a faraway corner of my mind, I registered that even in his haste, Einstein said please. He always had manners.

Elsa Einstein added, 'They were looking for her, Albert. When they hanged him they said, "We hear you have a very pretty young daughter, pig. We will be sure to introduce ourselves to her." They were beasts.'

'Here it is.' Einstein pulled a white envelope from the drawer.

'What is that?' Elsa Einstein asked.

'Manfred gave it to me, to be opened in the event that something like this occurred,' Einstein said grimly.

I started babbling, 'Papa . . . it was Papa . . .'

Einstein tore open the envelope, pulled from it a thick handful of cash, both marks and U.S. dollars, copies of my U.S. and German papers, and a letter which he read aloud quickly:

> *Albert,*
>
> *I may not be safe. I have received numerous death threats since the Paris Conference in June. I hope they are just bluster, but in these dark times one cannot be truly sure. The Germany I once knew has gone mad.*
>
> *If the worst should befall me, please, my friend, you must help Hanna. If I should die unexpectedly, Hanna will be moved to my sister Olga's home and we cannot allow that. A girl as bright and gentle as Hanna should not be forced to dwell in such a hateful place.*
>
> *With this letter is a copy of her American citizenship papers*

and some money. Please use the money to buy Hanna passage to America, to the home of her mother's sister in New York. Her name is Mrs Penelope Carlson (née Martin) and she lives at 142 Garden Street, Brooklyn.

I also enclose with this note specific instructions regarding Norma and her situation. Moving her away is more complicated. Once Hanna gets established in America, she can send for Norma.

Please tell Hanna that I loved her with all my heart, even if these last few years I have been more silent. At least, I will be reunited with her mother again. We will be watching over her together.

With my heartfelt thanks,
Your friend,
Manfred

'Oh, my goodness,' Einstein breathed.

'But, but Ooma . . .' I said vacantly. 'I got sweets for her—and Lukas, he's taking me to the winter dance—and what about my diary, it's in my bedroom . . .'

But Einstein was having none of it. He looked sharply from his wife to me.

'We have to get you out of this country, child. We must go, *now*!'

Through the night we sped. First by taxi to the railway station, then by train to Hamburg and its port.

To me, it was all a blur. I was still numb with shock. The image of my father hanging there flashed constantly across my mind.

And then we were in Hamburg, in front of a giant white-hulled steamship. Einstein wore an overcoat. I wore the same clothes I had worn to my aunt's birthday dinner which thankfully included a winter coat.

Einstein haggled briefly with the purser and bought me a ticket.

He paid for it with his own money. The money from my father's envelope he stuffed into my coat pocket.

And then he was pushing me up the gangway.

'Take care, child. I wish I could take you in myself, but with my life right now—a new wife, my existing children and their problems, my newfound fame and constant travel—I just can't.

'Find a school of science. In America, there are many. I have no doubt one will gladly and promptly take in a student of your calibre.'

He hugged me tightly.

'Oh, child. Such a fate should not befall anyone, let alone one so young.'

And there we parted.

I strode up the gangway of the steamer with nothing but the clothes on my back and the address of my American aunt in New York City.

1934.

Berlin.

After a year of terror, it is now almost fully Nazified.

No other political parties exist. All the leftists, communists and trade unionists are either dead or at Prinz-Albrecht-Strasse or in a camp.

The camps have multiplied. First there was only Dachau. Now there are many. Germans walk by them as if they are gated parks.

I accompany my boss Speer on an inspection tour of the stadium at Nuremberg, walking behind him, my pad and pencil at the ready for any instructions he might have.

The biggest and final rally is this evening and Speer has been planning it day and night for months. He installed a cot in his office so he wouldn't have to go home to sleep.

A woman dressed in a brown Nazi uniform and who looks like a beachball with legs hurries up to him, clicks her heels together and performs a perfect Hitler salute.

'Heil Hitler!' she cries with all her heart.

'Heil Hitler,' Speer says more quietly. He never really got passionate about the Nazi salute. 'Report.'

'All the lights are in position, Herr Speer, and the banners, as you requested,' she barks.

This is quite an achievement. Speer's plans called for thousands of lights—all to be placed in very specific positions—and hundreds of swastika banners.

Speer looks off into the distance. 'And the U-Bahn station? Have you removed the turnstiles?'

They are expecting 700,000 spectators tonight and Speer has announced that all public transport will be free of charge. He wants the people to flow through the railway station with as little inconvenience as possible, hence removing the turnstiles.

'Yes, Herr Speer. They have been removed. Is there anything else you wish me to do?'

'No, thank you. You have done marvellously,' Speer says.

I bow my head, hoping she does not recognise me. My hair is different these days, darker. I also—I must admit—stand taller than I did as a teenager, more confidently.

The beachball woman is dazzled to be in the presence of a leader as senior as Albert Speer. For a worker-ant Nazi like her, it's like being in the presence of a god descended for a short time from Olympus.

She doesn't recognise me, thankfully. It has, after all, been over fifteen years since she has laid eyes on me.

She is my aunt Olga.

She loves this new Germany.

1945.

Berlin is the ninth circle of hell.

Bombs. Explosions. Slashing rain.

Running as fast as I can, I stumble toward Potsdamerplatz U-Bahn station, trying to beat the Russians to it.

The Reich Chancellery rises above me, a broken shadow against the firelit sky. Huge ragged voids slice through it.

It's raining hard and the ground beneath me is a slush of mud, water and blood.

Bodies lie everywhere, half-submerged in the pools that fill the bomb craters.

I reach the U-Bahn station and fly down the stairs.

←——————————

PART II

1919 AMERICA: THE UNDISCOVERED COUNTRY

The first day of school. The day when the countdown to the last day of school begins.

– Unknown

Yankee Doodle keep it up,
Yankee Doodle dandy,
Mind the music and the step,
And with the girls be handy.

– 'Yankee Doodle', second verse

NEW YORK CITY
DECEMBER 1, 1919

SIXTEEN DAYS AFTER MY father was murdered, I arrived in America.

I recall little of the voyage.

I spent most of it below decks, lying in a little cot, my back to the other passengers, crying my eyes out.

If I slept, my dreams were haunted by images of my father hanged from his own bedroom window, a rag doll, dead, lit by raging firelight.

Oddly, I do recall the smells of the voyage.

Cooked cabbage. The stink of old sleeping men.

After a few days, other consequences sank in.

There would be no more time with Lukas. No contrived visits to his family's store. No winter dance.

There would also be no graduation for me from the *Gymnasium*. I was still several months short of my final examinations.

I was not even a high school graduate.

★ ★ ★

My steamer arrived in New York Harbor with the dawn, the sun streaming over my shoulder as I looked out from the bow at this strange land about which I had heard so much.

Of course, everyone in Europe spoke of America: the upstart nation that had grown so large so swiftly. For a thousand years, the various European powers had been fighting among themselves, waging wars over religion, slights or contested borders.

But in the last century, as they continued to bicker, this curious country—with its limitless land, its welcoming policies of immigration and its lack of a social hierarchy—had been growing into a behemoth.

Imagine Europe's shock when, after its royal brawling reached its apotheosis in the war of 1914–1918, it had been America who had intervened decisively.

And now I was here.

The Statue of Liberty loomed above me, reaching for the sky with her torch, impossibly tall.

The towers of the financial district rose before me, somehow taller.

'Skyscrapers,' someone next to me said in awe.

It was an apt term.

I'd never seen structures so high. The notion that they might scrape the sky was perfectly believable.

Off to the right I saw not one, not two, but *three* gigantic suspension bridges, the Brooklyn, Manhattan and Williamsburg Bridges.

I had thought Berlin to be a true 20th-century metropolis, one of the most modern cities in the world.

New York existed on another scale entirely.

To compare it to Berlin would be like comparing a full-size motor car with all its many moving parts to a toy car pulled along by a string.

In size, complexity and sheer energy, it dwarfed Berlin.

With its bridges, lights and relentless activity, it was like some city from the future made real.

Most striking were the skyscrapers. Their steel skeletons allowed them to far exceed the six-storey limit of Old World masonry.

The buildings before me were easily *forty* storeys tall.

And there were dozens of them, with more being built.

Lording it over this forest of towers, stretching almost 800 feet into the sky, was the tallest one of them all, the mighty Woolworth Building. It was sixty storeys high.

It all made Berlin look positively quaint.

While Europe had been distracted, America had sprinted ahead of it and left it behind.

After disembarking and using my U.S. papers to enter the country, I found my way to Brooklyn and knocked on the door of 142 Garden Street.

A woman wearing an apron and with a cigarette dangling from her lips answered the door.

My aunt.

That it was she, there could be no doubt. She was an older if slightly fatter doppelganger for my mother.

I can't imagine what she thought of the sight that met her: a teary-eyed girl of seventeen freshly arrived from Germany with not even a suitcase by her side.

She stared at me, completely and utterly flummoxed, put her hands on her aproned hips and said, 'What the actual fuck?'

BROOKLYN, NEW YORK
DECEMBER 1, 1919

MY AMERICAN AUNT, IT turned out, was not as progressive or adventurous as her sister.

Penny Carlson (née Martin) had not exactly been in favour of her younger sister prancing off to Europe in pursuit of her dreams in the world of modern physics.

Two years my mother's senior, she looked like a worn version of her: older, wider, more wrinkles. They had the exact same blue eyes. I had them, too.

After I stepped inside and told Aunt Penny—in tears—what had happened to Papa, she just pursed her lips and shook her head.

'You have got to be fucking kidding me,' she muttered in a coarse voice.

'Oh, no, I assure you, I'm not kidding,' I said earnestly.

She waved away my protest. 'Sorry, kid. I didn't mean it that way. It's just an expression.'

She sighed deeply. Gruff she may have been, and swear like a sailor she did, but there was a heart inside her somewhere. 'Well, shit, kid. Take a seat and let's get some decent food into you.'

Discussions with her husband—Uncle Michael, an insurance salesman—ensued when he arrived home that evening to find me in his living room.

They already had four children, ranging in age from twenty down to twelve.

I had been deposited in the room of the youngest child and I listened as my aunt and uncle talked about me in not-so-hushed whispers in the kitchen.

(Their kitchen, I should add, had its own stove, oven and icebox: modern amenities that only the richest in Germany could afford. And yet they didn't strike me as rich among Americans.)

'We can't afford her,' Uncle Michael said. 'Another goddamn mouth to feed. I'm struggling to make ends meet as it is.'

'What do we do?' Penny said.

'She's seventeen, she can get a job.'

'She's my sister's daughter, Mike. I'll not have her working in some rag mill or steel factory.'

Shell-shocked as I was, I was glad to hear that.

'In his letters, Manfred always said she was good at school, especially science.'

'Jesus, what fucking good is that?' Uncle Michael spat.

'Mike . . .'

'And what about the other one? The retard? Is she gonna come over here, too? Fucking hell.'

He took a deep breath.

'Okay. All right. Listen,' he said. 'We just hired some girls from that secretarial school downtown. I actually saw an ad for it the other day. They offer student loans and dorm accommodation. I'll take her down there tomorrow. She can take out a loan, learn some skills, and get a nice clean office job. Once she can support herself, she can figure out what to do about her sister. How about that? Would that satisfy you?'

'Yes,' Aunt Penny said.

> The city seen from the Queensboro Bridge is
> always the city seen for the first time, in its first
> wild promise of all the mystery and the beauty
> in the world.
>
> – From: F. Scott Fitzgerald, *The Great Gatsby*

NEW YORK CITY
DECEMBER 1919

THE FOLLOWING MORNING, ESCORTED by my ill-tempered uncle and still wearing my German clothes, I caught a subway train into New York City.

If the skyscrapers of Manhattan had looked colossal from my steamship, up close they looked positively gargantuan.

And the people!

I had never seen so many in one place.

Men and women, all bustling this way and that, going somewhere or other.

Buses rumbled, trolleys tooted, newspaper boys shouted, and if I dared stop for a moment to look up at one of the towering glass-and-steel buildings above me, someone would shove me and say, 'Hey, yokel, don't stop here! Welcome to Noo Yawk!'

At length, we came to an older building that wasn't as tall as the others.

It was a great sturdy granite thing from the previous century with pillars flanking a high doorway. It looked like a stately country mansion that had been plonked down in the middle of this lively city.

Stencilled on its translucent front door were the words:

THE GRAHAM-COULSON
SECRETARIAL SCHOOL FOR LADIES

My uncle yanked open the door and—without offering to hold it open for me—went inside.

For a moment I just stood there on the doorstep of the building on that busy New York street.

Then I hurried inside.

In less than three weeks, my world had been turned completely upside down.

My dream of a life lived in physics in Germany was suddenly gone, replaced by this, admission into a school for secretaries, based on a hurried decision made by a harried uncle who didn't know anything about me and cared even less.

It would turn out to be the most pivotal decision of my life.

> If you can smile through the whirl of a busy
> day . . . *you're a SECRETARY!*

– Vintage advertisement for
Underwood typewriters

THE GRAHAM-COULSON SECRETARIAL SCHOOL FOR LADIES
NEW YORK CITY, 1919

I WALKED INTO THE front office of the secretarial school.

After my uncle spoke with some people, I was led into a side office.

A whirl of paperwork followed.

In the presence of an officious young gentleman wearing a vest and tie and a *very* stern-looking older secretary, my uncle Michael filled out a battery of forms that sought among other things my name, age, height, weight, hat size and dress size. For my glove size, my handspan was measured.

The officious young gentleman said to my uncle, 'Your timing is excellent. We are literally just starting a new intake today for our winter semester.'

My uncle snorted in reply.

All the while he grumbled at the time it was taking, checking his watch constantly. He hurriedly filled out some loan forms and shoved them in front of me to sign, which I did.

The young man in the vest smiled as he took them, tapped them on the desk and slid them into a file. 'I think you'll find our student-loan rates to be very competit—'

'Whatever,' my uncle said, pushing back his chair.

And then it was over and he patted me on the back—'Good luck, kid'—and he was gone.

The young man in the vest turned to me. 'Miss Bomback here will show you to your accommodations.' Then his interest in me vanished and he returned to other work.

The stern secretary appeared in front of me, her eyes hard. She was a short round woman, perhaps fifty and not very attractive.

She shoved two folded sheets, a blanket and a pillowcase into my hands, plus a toiletry bag, a leatherbound notepad and a pen.

'Follow me,' Miss Bomback said. 'The other girls have already chosen their rooms and school's about to start.'

Miss Bomback waddled at a fast clip and I struggled to keep up with her.

She led me to the third floor where a collection of small dormitory-style rooms branched off a long corridor.

Young women—ranging in age from seventeen to perhaps twenty—mingled in the doorways.

They all looked at me as I walked past, led by Miss Bomback.

At length, we came to the farthest end of the corridor where a window looked directly out over an elevated train line not five paces away. It was an ugly iron thing: hard, black and soot-stained.

Next to the window was the very last room, its door open.

Two beds, two desks and two dressers were inside it. Sitting on one of those beds was a rather large girl with shiny pink cheeks, a frizzy ball of red-brown hair and a hopeful smile.

Miss Bomback said, 'Hanna Fischer, this is Fanny O'Toole. She'll be your roommate while you're here at the school.'

Then the little round secretary marched out in her officious way.

I entered the room shyly, cautiously.

The plump girl's smile widened. 'It's ever so nice to meet you, Hanna.'

Fanny O'Toole's accent was as thickly Irish as mine was German. She shook my hand with a giant, chubby paw.

'It is nice to meet you as well,' I said.

I laid my few possessions on the empty bed by the window, on its bare grey mattress—

Suddenly, explosively, a train rushed by outside.

The roar was deafening.

The scream of wheels-on-track was like fingernails on a chalkboard. A half-dozen silver carriages blurred by at speed, rushing past the window, three storeys off the ground but outrageously close to me.

And then it was gone and blessed silence resumed.

Fanny smiled grimly. 'Doesn't pay to be last ones to the dorm. All the other rooms were taken when I got here. Now I know why. The trains are loud and the lock on the window doesn't work. It don't even close properly. Where you from? Germany?'

'I am, yes.'

I stood there, trying to think of something else to say, but I was still reeling. My world was moving too fast.

I scanned the little room.

Fanny had already unpacked. On the desk beside her bed was a teetering stack of paperback books.

Books. I heard Papa's voice in my head: *Wunderbar! The best way to start a conversation.*

I scanned the titles:

The Complete Oz by L. Frank Baum.

Pollyanna by Eleanor H. Porter.

The Lone Star Ranger by Zane Grey.

The War of the Worlds by H.G. Wells.

I could not have gleaned a better summation of Fanny O'Toole's personality had I interrogated her.

That pile indicated a sensibility that delighted in high adventure and pulp fantasy: faraway lands, sweet girls, handsome outlaws and grand conflicts with Martians.

Except for the final book on the pile.

The Economic Consequences of the Peace by John Maynard Keynes.

I had heard about this book but not read it. Keynes was the famed British economist who had stormed out of the Paris Peace Conference in protest.

He had argued that the terms of the Treaty of Versailles were far too harsh on Germany—a 'Carthaginian Peace', he'd called it.

I nodded at the final book. 'You are reading the Keynes book? How are you finding it?'

Fanny's face brightened instantly, delighted, it seemed, to be asked.

'Oh, it's swell! Absolutely swell. I just love reading about economic topics and Mr Keynes is so very modern. Keynes is a big-picture guy and, ooh, he doesn't like the treaty, not one bit. He says it'll lead to hyperinflation and the impoverishment of Germany. He says the French were right arseholes during the peace conference. They just wanted to *crush* Germany. He says Germany will be like a wild dog backed into a corner: when it's had enough of being kicked, it'll strike back hard.'

She paused, catching herself. 'But I guess I don't have to tell you this. You've probably seen it.'

'I have. But it is still very interesting to hear nonetheless.'

'It is, isn't it?' Fanny said. 'I've always been fascinated by the way money works: price inflation, stocks and bonds, loan spreads. Why, just look at this place and their student loans.'

'What about them?' I asked, having just blindly signed one.

'Oh, they make great money on them loans. An eighteen-week course here costs $600, including bed and board. But if you take one of their loans and pay it off over the standard term of ten years, you end up payin' $1,161. That's almost double. *Double!* Mrs Graham-Coulson isn't running a school. She's running a money-lending business and money-lending is the best business in the world.'

A faint chill ran up my spine.

I had practically no money. Now, it seemed, in this strange and foreign land, with the stroke of a pen I was already in a financial hole.

I said, 'Hopefully by attending this school, one will garner a well-paying job with which to repay the loan . . .'

Fanny shrugged. 'That's the theory. It's also the hook they use to suck you in. If you have one of them loans, my pretty skinny friend, I'd find a way to pay it off early. Then the tables are turned and *you* get the benefit of using *their* money now and they don't get the interest.'

'How did you learn about all this?' I asked.

Fanny said, 'Me dad ran a gambling den—cockfightin' and bettin' on the cocks. He taught me all about the spread. Trust me, if you're bettin' on *any*thing, the house is winnin' no matter what.'

'He sounds like a very clever man,' I said.

'He was'—Fanny's face fell—'till Baby Face Mancino's goons came round to shut down his little gamblin' den. They shot him full o' holes with a couple of them German spray guns. The house always wins . . . until a bigger house decides to shut it down.'

'I'm very sorry to hear about that—'

A shrill whistle cut me off.

'*Ladies!*' Miss Bomback's voice barked from the corridor. '*Main classroom! Five minutes!*'

Fanny and I gathered our notepads and pens and scurried out to our first class.

Urge your boss to buy you an Underwood . . .
and you'll *always* have his letters looking
their best!

– Vintage advertisement for
Underwood typewriters

ALONG WITH TWENTY-THREE OF our classmates, Fanny and I arrived
in the main classroom of the Graham-Coulson Secretarial School
for Ladies.

Twenty-five chairs were arranged in front of a small stage, on
which stood a table. On the table sat an object mysteriously covered by a purple-and-gold tablecloth. Behind it stood a blackboard,
currently blank.

The room was abuzz with girlish chatter.

Most of my fellow students stood on their own or with their
newly acquired roommates.

One cluster of four girls, however, stood together.

They were all blonde and shapely—narrow in the waist and pert
of bosom—and all immaculately groomed and made up.

I would learn their names later—Stella, Thelma, Lorna and
Beatrice—but it was Stella who was their leader. Taller, blonder
and slimmer than the others, Miss Stella Lang was a genuine
beauty.

She also—somehow—seemed to already know her way around
the school.

'Don't sit in the front row,' I heard her whisper to her friends as

Fanny and I walked past her. 'She always picks someone from the front row . . .'

Taking this snippet of free advice, Fanny and I took seats in the second row just as a door closed loudly behind us, silencing the room, and the *click-click* of fast-moving sharp-heeled shoes echoed off the marble walls.

We all turned . . .

. . . to see a striking dark-haired woman striding confidently into the room, passing us in our chairs before she took her place on the stage and glared down at us.

I had never seen a woman like her.

Or an outfit like hers.

She wore a dark navy suit, only it had a skirt as the bottom half. A skirt!

The suit was ever so stylish and it fit her like a glove. A pair of towering high-heeled shoes completed her look.

She was perhaps forty, tall and athletic. Her long brown hair cascaded over her shoulders, perfectly curled.

Her make-up was discreet yet apparent. Her lips were blood red.

In all of twelve seconds, she had taken command of the room.

'Good morning, ladies. My name is Katherine Graham-Coulson and I am the owner, head teacher and headmistress of this establishment. I was once the principal private secretary of Mr John D. Rockefeller, to this day the richest man in the United States.

'In the nine years that this school has existed, I have produced over two hundred of the finest secretaries in America and placed them in the offices of some of the most influential men in this country, from chairmen and chief executives, to the New York City Mayor's office and even one ex-president.

'I charge a high price but I guarantee results,' she said as her eyes found every one of us. 'A few months from now, you will walk out of here knowing everything you need to know about the modern office and its management. Because in the end, ladies, *my* reputation rests on *you*. If a businessman employs a Graham-Coulson secretary then he is entitled to expect the best personal assistant money can buy.'

She turned to the table beside her with the object on it covered by the purple-and-gold cloth.

Like a magician, she whipped the cloth away, revealing a typewriter.

It looked sturdy, heavy, all brass and cast iron.

Its four rows of keys glistened.

The word 'UNDERWOOD' blazed in large letters on its top.

'Ladies,' Mrs Graham-Coulson said, 'meet the Underwood Number 5 typewriter. It is a front-stroke type-bar four-bank single-shift, ribbon-ink typewriter and it is, without doubt, the finest typewriter ever built.

'It is almost indestructible and it is *fast*. By the time you're done here, you will know it like the back of your hand. You will be able to type a letter on it at seventy words per minute with one hundred percent accuracy *in the dark*.'

A buzz rippled through the audience.

Mrs Katherine Graham-Coulson smiled knowingly.

'But we're going to do more than that. We are going to transform *you*, too. Here you will not just learn how to take dictation or answer a telephone. You will learn etiquette. How to dress, how to eat, how to carry yourself and converse with titans. How to apply foundation and curl your hair. You have entered this school as girls. You will leave as polished, cultured and capable ladies. You will leave as *Graham-Coulson secretaries*.'

She had reached her crescendo, but then her voice softened to a whisper.

'You may not know it yet, but you are all very lucky ladies,' she added, 'for you have enrolled at this school at a special time. As the premier school in the nation for secretaries, at the end of every term, the top-placed student from this school receives an offer of employment with the chairman or chief executive at a leading company in New York City.

'Well, in these heady post-war times, business is booming and I have an extraordinary placement for the first-placed student of this class. In the coming weeks, when the time is right, I shall inform you all of that company, but let me assure you, it is an incredible opportunity. Ladies, let us begin.'

With those words, Mrs Katherine Graham-Coulson turned to the blackboard on the stage and flipped it over on a hinge, revealing its rear side.

On that side was written the following:

THE RULES
TO BECOMING
A GREAT SECRETARY

RULE #1: Your job is to help <u>your boss</u> to do <u>his job</u>!

RULE #2: Always look <u>immaculate</u>!

RULE #3: Always be <u>on time</u>!

RULE #4: Spelling, punctuation and grammar are the markers of <u>sophistication</u>!

RULE #5: Fast and wrong is still wrong. <u>Be correct</u>!

Over the next eighteen weeks, those five rules would be drilled into us, over and over again.

Mrs Katherine Graham-Coulson gave that first class herself—and just as Stella had foretold, she selected some poor girl from the front row to demonstrate her presently inadequate typing skills.

Other classes on specific topics—from typing and stenography to spelling and grammar—would be taught by her staff.

While she didn't teach beyond that first day's class, she was always a presence at the school.

Almost every day I would see her guiding some gentleman in a suit around the premises—a prospect I guessed, from some major company.

For ultimately, in addition to her apparently lucrative money-lending enterprise, she was herself a businesswoman creating a product to sell: us.

1927.

Einstein never cared about my appearance when I was his assistant.

Or about punctuality for that matter.

He rarely wore a watch. Lost in his thoughts, he existed in his own time. And everyone happily waited for him, even kings and presidents.

He only cared about Rule #5: Fast and wrong is still wrong.

Be correct.

1933.

Speer was different.

A graduate of the Graham-Coulson School was tailor-made for him, since he insisted that all five rules be adhered to.

His first comment to me was: 'I need you to be on time and precise. I do not have time to wait for you or to correct your mistakes. If I have a meeting with the Führer at 7 a.m., then I need you to be in the office at six, to have my coffee ready and all pertinent documents at hand. Wear little make-up but have your hair in place. The Führer expects everyone in his presence to have a professional appearance.'

'Yes, sir,' I replied.

He took his own advice. Speer was always perfectly turned out, even when he was touring Auschwitz for the first time, selecting the locations for the ovens.

1945.

Bormann didn't care about any rules.

He just wanted power, which is why he always stayed so close to Hitler.

The 18th Amendment to the Constitution prohibited the manufacture, sale or transportation of 'intoxicating liquors' anywhere inside the United States.

It went into effect at 12:01 a.m. on January 17th, 1920.

Prohibition was a law created by rural puritans and it was roundly despised by city sophisticates. It is remembered as one of history's greatest failures because all it did was send liquor underground and create a new class of criminal: the gangster.

– From: *Guns, Gangsters and Rum Runners: The Roaring 20s* by George Paris

PRESENTATION AND BEAUTY (MISS DECKER)

MY FIRST MONTH AT secretary school went by in a blur.

Days were spent in classes.

Like *Presentation and Beauty* with Miss Decker. Exercises included creating perfect curls in our hair, applying lipstick, powdering one's face, altering and tailoring one's clothes (Rule #2), and the correct way to iron clothing, both my own and my boss's (Rule #1).

The best student in this class was easily Stella, not least because she was beautiful already.

Stella.

Where to start?

For one thing, she was blonde, tall and nineteen. For another—and this was very important—she'd had an older sister come through the secretarial school two years previously, so Stella—and her clique of three friends whom I shall just call the Fawning Triplets—had something that the likes of Fanny and I did not: a roadmap for what lay ahead.

Once at breakfast during the dizzying first week, I overheard Stella instructing her friends: 'Now, listen. There will be a surprise typing exam on Monday of week two, and a stenography test . . .'

(I was thus prepared for that first surprise typing exam—thank God—but many other tests caught me unawares.)

I also heard Stella on one occasion say to her friends, 'Ladies, through my sources, I also happen to know the name of the company that will employ the first-placed student in this class. It is Bentley & Sons.'

One of her friends gasped. 'Clay Bentley? The millionaire?'

'The *multi*-millionaire,' Stella said. 'Who works side by side with his very handsome son, Clay Jr.'

When I heard this, I sighed. I didn't know what kind of company Bentley & Sons was, let alone who the Bentleys were.

It was just another thing Stella knew and I didn't.

In any case, Stella was always prepared in advance for any snap test or exam and right from the get-go, she shone.

Forewarned and forearmed, she instantly became the leading student in the class, whether it was in *Presentation and Beauty* or *Typing and Stenography*, or *Spelling, Punctuation and Grammar*.

She was also a born ringleader and her advanced knowledge of the curriculum at the Graham-Coulson Secretarial School only added to this.

What did she make of me? Did she treat me poorly, like every archetypal leading girl in history has done toward the new foreign girl?

To be honest, I don't think she cared.

She was aware of me, of that I am certain. I was the quiet German girl. But I don't think I was anything more than a presence at the edge of her consciousness, at least not until I became a threat.

Stella also had one other string to her bow that made her the clear leader of our class.

She shone *after* class, at night, because she was a local—Brooklyn born and bred—and thus she knew all the best bars and cafés in and around our school.

Days were thus spent in classes.

Nights were different.

They were spent, whenever possible, on the town, using all the techniques we learned in *Presentation and Beauty*.

> **Prohibition only drives drunkenness behind doors and into dark places.**
>
> – Mark Twain

IF NEW YORK CITY with its ceaseless energy shook my senses during the day, then at night it rattled me completely.

After night fell, Berlin was quiet and serene, but New York came *alive*.

It was as busy and bustling after dark as it was during the day, a glittering circus of music and dancing and—especially that December—drinking to outrageous excess.

With their faces perfectly powdered, their lips perfectly painted, and their skirts perfectly altered to cling to the curves of their hips, Stella and the Triplets went out on the town every single weekend, Friday through Sunday.

Unsure, shy and, quite frankly, frightened of the many night-time noises of the pulsating city, I did not go as often, but I confess I went with them several times.

And oh, what I saw!

I must say, I was lucky, because I saw New York's bars and nightclubs both before and after the foolishness of Prohibition.

On my first such outing that December, with Fanny at my side, I followed Stella and her gang into a bar lined with red velvet walls and filled with well-dressed young men who worked for the Wall Street banks and finance companies.

(Forgive me, but I must repeat what was happening here: a group of women—*unaccompanied* young women—were strolling without a care in the world around the night-time streets of the world's largest city. They had no concerns for their safety. They did not need chaperones. They were independent women and no-one cared a whit. America was so modern.)

At the bar, Stella's friends went straight for the young men in their sleek suits.

Stella did not.

I asked her why.

She smiled wanly. 'Hanna, these are boys. Sure, they're smartly dressed and have a little greenmail in their pockets, but they're still boys. I call them "tykes": wannabe Wall Street tycoons. They're good for a little bit of fun, but that's all. I'm looking for a *man*, a very particular kind of man.'

She did not elaborate on what that meant.

The second time I went out with the girls was New Year's Eve.

As everyone knows, the turn of a decade always makes a New Year's Eve celebration extra enjoyable, but that final night of 1919 had an extra element to it: it was the last New Year's Eve before Prohibition was to come into effect on January the 17th, 1920.

I have never seen a more decadent night of drinking and outright debauchery. It was like everyone in the city was inebriated.

I saw a drunk girl, her skirt hitched up around her hips, having sex with a man down a side alley off Times Square. Further down the alley, I saw another sucking on a man's penis. One of Stella's group drank so much she was sick. I heard her retching in the bathroom for hours.

Seventeen days later, Prohibition took hold and everything changed.

★ ★ ★

The bars vanished. The nightclubs, too.

Of course, they hadn't ceased to exist. They just went underground, into the alleyways, into the speakeasies.

In an instant a whole new kind of nightlife was born.

And Stella and her gang—dressed up and made up—simply started going to these new off-the-books establishments.

Curious and wanting to be included, I went along with them one night.

The contrast was immediate.

Down a back alley, into a storeroom, through a curtain . . .

. . . and suddenly I was in a dark smoky bar, with a black woman crooning sensuously, ringed by the same young Wall Street tykes drinking bootlegged beer.

But the mood was different here.

Darker, more menacing.

Even the tykes knew it and kept their voices down.

It wasn't for fear of the police bursting in. That wouldn't happen. For the police were there, too—drinking to their hearts' content— happily bought off.

No, it was due to the gangsters sitting in the booths in the more shadowy corners of the establishment, sipping whiskey in the half-darkness, the pistols in their shoulder holsters visible for all the world to see.

Stella loved it. So did the Triplets.

I must confess that I felt it, too.

The thrill of illegality, of proximity to dangerous men. The rush of rebellion created simply by having a drink.

It was something the champion of Prohibition, Representative Andrew Volstead of Minnesota—rural, religious, and utterly naïve when it came to human nature—had never anticipated.

Banning alcohol made it more exciting.

Stella selected the local speakeasy that the girls of our school would attend most regularly: a place known as Pearl's.

Of course, none of the illegal bars and clubs had actual names. This one was called Pearl's simply because it was located off Pearl Street in the shadow of the Brooklyn Bridge, among all the warehouses there.

It was run by Douglas 'Baby Face' Mancino.

Mancino was young then and he really did have a baby face. In a few short years, he would become one of the most feared gangsters in New York City.

But in early 1920, he was just starting out like the rest of this new criminal class and Pearl's—with its illegal booze and gambling tables—did very nicely.

Pearl's was also conveniently located within easy walking distance from our school, down an alley behind a warehouse marked Bentley & Sons Trucking and Shipping.

I noted that fact instantly.

'I like Pearl's,' Stella said, 'because it's close to Wall Street and the tykes are cashed up enough to buy us plenty of drinks while also mannered enough not to be too pushy when it comes to all the other stuff.'

And also, I soon discovered, because Mr Clay Bentley Jr—one of the 'Sons' in Bentley & Sons and thus an heir to one of the wealthiest men in the city—frequented Pearl's.

It's strange now that I look back on it.

That choice, Stella's choice of an illegal bar, would have a profound effect on me.

It would bring four men into my world, four very different men who for four very different reasons would alter the course of my life.

Mr Clay Bentley Jr, wealthy, young and reckless.

Mr Clay Bentley Sr, his stoic father.

The gangster 'Baby Face' Mancino.

And Special Agent Dan Kessler of the U.S. Treasury Department.

> Doubts raced through my mind as I considered
> the feasibility of enforcing a law which the
> majority of honest citizens didn't seem to want.
>
> – Eliot Ness

TYPING AND STENOGRAPHY (MISS CARLING)

BY DAY, MORE CLASSES.

Typing and Stenography with Miss Carling was the most important class. Fifty percent of our final passing grade would be based on our performance in it.

'Fast typing is good typing,' Miss Carling called over the clatter of our Underwoods. 'Fast is good, but fast *and wrong* is ultimately slower! Because you will have to start all over again! You must be fast yet also accurate!'

I took this to heart.

I was a good typist, quick and efficient, but not the fastest in our class.

That was also Stella. Not only had she come to the school knowing the curriculum, she had already practised her typing for six months.

We hammered on our keys, transposing a business letter of some kind or another.

I was bent over my Underwood when Miss Carling suddenly called, 'Ladies! Cease typing!'

I looked up, blinking.

Mrs Graham-Coulson stood before us.

'Hello, ladies,' she said, holding up a sheet of paper. 'The class grades. With only three weeks to go till graduation, there are many of you who can still win the top spot and the position of executive secretary to Mr Clay Bentley Sr at Bentley & Sons Trucking and Shipping.'

She pinned the sheet to a corkboard by the door and left.

When that class was over, we all rushed to look at it.

Stella was at no. 1.

I was in fourth place, quite close and within striking distance so long as (a) I topped every coming test and (b) Stella made a mistake.

She had not made a single one yet.

By night, Pearl's and other illegal dance halls.

Stella and her gang would lead the way to Pearl's and on a few occasions I joined them.

One night, as a pretty black woman sang one of the new 'jazz' songs that were popular then, I sat with Stella. She was eyeing a tall man at the craps table with curly blond hair, a giant dimple in his chin and gorgeous blue eyes.

He wore a dapper grey suit that shimmered slightly and laughed like someone who did not have a care in the world.

'Who is that?' I asked.

'Oh, dear me,' Stella said, 'I forget sometimes that you're not from around here. That is my future husband, Mr Clay Bentley Jr.'

'Oh,' I said. 'From the company.'

'Which is why I *must* come in first place in our class,' Stella said.

'If I can enter into the Bentley family's orbit as Bentley Sr's executive secretary, I have no doubt I can catch Junior's eye and snare him as my husband. Then I shall promptly retire and live the life of leisure that I have always aspired to.'

I frowned. Innocent I may have been, but I had eyes, and they spotted the wedding ring on Clay Bentley Jr's left hand.

'Stella, he's married.'

Stella snorted. 'Oh, Hanna, Hanna. A man like Clay Bentley Jr spends more of his waking hours with his secretary than he does his wife. And no wife, sequestered at home with some wailing brats while her husband works downtown, can *ever* match his secretary for influence. Or, better yet, match the secretary of her husband's wealthy *father*. No, if I can get into that company, I am sure I can steal Junior away without too much trouble at all.'

And in that moment, I saw Stella.

Beneath all her swagger, all her confidence, all her insider knowledge of the tests at the secretary school, her primary goal was to marry out of her current station and into a better one, no matter who got damaged in the process.

In response I said nothing for I was literally speechless.

Later that night, a frisson of excitement rippled across the bar.

Baby Face Mancino had arrived.

I have to give this to Mancino. He looked like a gangster before gangsters even had a 'look'.

He wore a black pinstripe suit under a huge fur-lined overcoat and a white felt fedora with a black band. He was flanked by four sizeable men, his bodyguards.

He must have been thirty then. He was a big man, burly and he had a round pasty face that seemed to have a perpetual sheen of sweat on it.

But it was his eyes that grabbed you.

They were wider than most men's, so that you always saw the whites.

The eyes of a psychopath.

———————————▶

Himmler has those same eyes.
Heydrich does, too.

———————————▶

As we flee from the Führerbunker together, Bormann's eyes are wide, the whites showing.

They say psychopaths care for nothing, but this is not true.

The only thing a psychopath truly cares about is self-preservation.

◀———————————

Baby Face held out his hand and a whiskey was placed in it and without losing a step he went over to chat with Clay Bentley Jr at the craps table.

They huddled close as they whispered, Bentley Jr nodding quickly.

This was one of the unintended consequences of Prohibition and one of its most remarkable features: here was the scion of a prominent New York family chatting with a known gangster while a black woman sang an entirely new kind of music and a German woman, me, watched.

While Stella and the girls loitered with intent around the gaming table where Bentley Jr now chatted with Mancino, I moved to the back wall near the restrooms, nursing the same drink I'd bought an hour before.

'I wouldn't get too goo-goo-eyed over young Bentley,' a voice said suddenly from behind me.

I turned.

A handsome man stood there, also watching the interplay between the gangster and the young executive.

My new companion had a pleasant face. He was only a few years older than I, maybe twenty-four. He had dark hair, stubble on his square chin and his eyes were brown and serious, older than his years.

He wore a white fedora and a flashy white suit. Another gangster, albeit a good-looking one.

'What do you mean?' I said.

'I mean, he's in deep with Baby Face. Owes him money. A lot of money. Gambles too much, does young Bentley. Trust me, you don't want to owe Baby Face Mancino anything.'

I glanced at the pair at the craps table again. 'But he has a wealthy father. Daddy could pay.'

'I don't think Daddy knows about these debts,' my companion said. 'We're talking eighteen thousand dollars, here.'

My jaw dropped. That was an astronomical sum of money back then, more than any of the Wall Street tykes made in a year, in five years. 'Clay Bentley Jr has lost *eighteen thousand dollars* gambling?'

'Yuh-huh,' the man in the white fedora said. 'A bunch of these Wall Street boys are in the hole, too.'

'And how do you come to know this?' I gave his white suit a once-over. 'Are you Baby Face Mancino's accountant?'

'Something like that.'

'What do you mean? Something like that?'

He gave me a long evaluating look, as if he were deciding what to say next.

Then he surreptitiously flipped open his wallet, revealing an I.D. card inside. It read:

THE UNITED STATES TREASURY DEPARTMENT INTERNAL REVENUE SERVICE

THIS CERTIFIES THAT
Daniel J. Kessler
OF *New York, N.Y.* **IS DULY EMPLOYED AS A**
Federal Prohibition Agent

AND IS HEREBY AUTHORIZED TO EXECUTE AND PERFORM ALL THE DUTIES DELEGATED TO SUCH OFFICERS BY LAW.

He held out his hand. 'Dan Kessler. Federal agent.'

Frozen mute, I shook it.

'And you are?' he prompted.

'Hanna Fischer. I'm absolutely nobody.'

My fear must have shown on my face.

He chuckled but not in a mean way.

'It's okay, Hanna Fischer. I'm not gonna bust you or anybody else tonight,' Dan Kessler said. 'I'm just looking into Mr Mancino, that's all. Trying to figure out a few things.'

'Like what?'

'Like how he gets his liquor into New York City undetected,' he said, eyeing Mancino across the smoky room.

'So, where are you from, Hanna Fischer? By that accent, I'm guessing not from around here.'

'Berlin. Germany.'

'And what brought you to New York?'

'Do you always ask this many questions, Mr Kessler?'

'It's my job.'

'I'm at secretary school,' I said. 'It's not far from here.'

'But that ain't what *brought* you here, is it,' he said, looking at me closely.

'No,' I said softly, bowing my head.

He seemed to sense my discomfort and let it go.

'Maybe you can tell me about that some other time,' he said.

'If I'm not mistaken, *Kessler* is a German name, Agent Kessler,' I said. 'Where has your accent gone?'

He smiled again.

'Christ, I oughta give you a job with those deductive skills. My parents caught a boat here from Germany thirty years ago, back when Kaiser Wilhelm wanted to gas Jews and Bismarck was building the Second Reich. They were from Munich. Me, though, I was born here. Hundred percent American.'

'*Sprechen Sie Deutsch?*' I asked. *Do you speak German?*

'*Ja,*' he replied. 'My dad insisted on it. Said it was part of my heritage. I speak it fluently.'

'Have you ever been back to Germany?'

'Nope. Was too busy getting my law degree and my badge at Treasury.'

'I imagine it would be hard to go back to Germany after living here.' I gestured at all of New York around us.

'I imagine it would be,' Dan said. 'This has been one of the nicer chats I've had in a long while, Hanna Fischer from Berlin, Germany. You have a pleasant evening now. And if any of these slick young assholes in silver suits asks you out on a date, you might want to check with me first about their financial situation. I can let you know if they're in debt to any gangsters—'

'Yo, Kriegler,' a huge hand landed on Dan Kessler's shoulder.

Kriegler? I thought.

The hand belonged to Baby Face Mancino's tallest bodyguard, a gigantic Italian who also wore an expensive pinstripe suit. He had a nose that was both wide and long. He was not exactly handsome, but he had a magnetism that was unmistakable.

Everyone knew who he was: he was Charles Luciano, or 'Lucky'.

Dan said, 'Hey, Lucky. How you doin'?'

'Good, yeah good. Listen, keep the 31st free, okay? Gonna be a big meeting at Dobson's fish warehouse.'

'I'll be there,' Dan said.

'Gonna be historic,' Lucky Luciano said. 'You don't wanna miss it.'

'Like I said, I'll be there.'

Lucky gave me a once-over, smirked approvingly, and left.

'Is it Kriegler or Kessler?' I said, giving Dan a look.

'Hardest thing about being undercover is remembering all the fake names. Sorry, Miss Fischer, but I gotta go now. You take care of yourself, okay.'

He tipped his fedora, smiled and left.

I liked that smile.

Be careful who you call your friends.

– Al Capone

OVER THE NEXT FEW weeks, I ran into Dan Kessler at several speakeasies.

It was fascinating to talk with him. The government wasn't really enforcing Prohibition so much as observing its effects and what he was seeing on the ground wasn't good.

'You wouldn't believe how fast the criminal element moved to fill the void of alcohol,' he told me once as he smoked a cigarette in the alley outside Pearl's. 'It's a new kind of criminal element. Collective, united, organised.'

'Smarter?' I asked.

'More cunning. And we're seeing new players, young guys, mainly Italians, who are making names for themselves quickly, often by cooperating, *teaming up*. Like Baby Face Mancino and his pal, Lucky Luciano. The Treasury Department's watching them all. Getting the lay of the land. It's no use rushing in and busting the small-timers now. We'll move soon, though, after the big players establish themselves.'

'What about the gangsters and their alliances? Will they last?'

Dan snuffed a wry laugh. 'Sure, they'll last. So long as there's honour among thieves.'

★ ★ ★

At this juncture, I should mention Fanny.

Fanny sometimes joined the girls when they went out on the town. Most of the time, however, no matter how much pressure they applied, she demurred, preferring to stay in the dorm.

I really liked Fanny, in particular, the way she could withstand the powerful entreaties of the other girls.

I said, 'I've never really had friends who are girls, so I find it very hard to say no when they invite me to go out on the town with them. I guess, I don't know, I want them to like me. How do you do it?'

Fanny shrugged. 'What do I care what Stella or her band of followers think of me? Our final exams are in a fortnight. After they're done, we'll all scatter and, chances are, I'll never see Stella or any of those girls again. So why try to please them now?'

'Fair point,' I said.

'It was the same for me at school,' Fanny said. 'I was good at math and the other kids used to tease me. They'd say, "Why do you study, Fanny?" "Why do you try so hard?" But then I realised. By studying and working hard and scoring well in my tests, *I was making them look bad.*

'Hanna, I don't pretend to know much. But I know a few things. I know what I'm good at: numbers, spreads, patterns. I also know I'm fat and not that pretty—'

'Don't say that, Fanny. Never say that. You're beautiful!'

'—and I know when I see a good person. You're a good person, Hanna. And we all like to have friends, sure. But be careful when you venture out on the town with those other girls, especially Stella. She might cajole you into going out, but she's not your friend. She's only ever looking out for one person, herself.'

I was a little taken aback by her candour.

I'd never heard her speak so forcefully about anything.

Fanny looked out the window. 'School is a funny thing. Not just secretary school, any kind of school. Middle school, high school. It brings us together every day, so we think our classmates are our friends. But they're not. School *forces* us to see them every day. But that's not how real friendships work. Real friends stay by your side when they're *not* forced to be there.'

That said, Fanny also had her secrets.

One night, after I drank a peculiar-tasting brand of moonshine at a new speakeasy and felt unwell, I returned to the dorms within an hour of leaving.

As I walked down the hall toward the room I shared with Fanny I heard them.

Faint grunts and joyous gasps.

The door was ajar and I peered inside our room to see Fanny, naked, sitting astride the school's janitor, Raymond, riding him furiously. Both participants were enjoying the act immensely.

As soon as I saw them, I crept back from the doorway, giving them their privacy.

I fell asleep on a reading chair in the library.

A couple of days later, I said to Fanny, 'So, Fanny, is there anything I should know about you and Raymond the janitor?'

She threw me a look.

Then she started gushing. 'Oh, Hanna! He's such a sweet young gent. He's from Poland, you know. His actual name is Rajmund, Rajmund Wozniak, but he goes by "Raymond" here and I just call him Raymey. He's ever so smart, but his English isn't so good. He came here from Europe a few years ago with the clothes on his back and not speaking a word of English.

'But he loves mathematics and we got talking one day about gambling and odds. I told him I've started tracking the stock market, which—let's be honest—is just another form of gambling, only it's legal. Raymey doesn't like stocks so much. He says it's a tool used by the capitalist class to get rich while the workers suffer.'

'The workers?'

'The working class. Raymey reads a lot about that stuff. He wants to join a union some day.'

'Have you kissed him?' I asked, even though I knew she'd done much more than that.

'Kissed him? Hanna, I've fucked his brains out and he's fucked mine, mostly when you've been out with the girls. But, *please*, don't ever tell my brothers. God, can you imagine what my Irish brothers would say if they found out I was letting a Polack into my bed?'

She laughed uproariously.

Then she leaned forward conspiratorially. 'Hanna. Raymey asked me yesterday if I would be his girlfriend. I said yes. Oh, Hanna, I've never had a boyfriend before.'

As Fanny said this, I thought about Lukas back in Berlin. I missed him terribly and planned to write to him, to tell him about all that had happened to me. At some point—someday, somehow, when I earned some money—I would have to figure out a way to get back to him in Germany.

But I just said, 'That's wonderful, Fanny. I'm so happy for you.'

The next two weeks went by in whirl.

Classes and homework, speakeasies and booze, all in the presence of gangsters and their undercover observer, Agent Dan Kessler.

At length, my final week at secretary school arrived.

Our final exams were scheduled for Friday, yet on the Wednesday night of that week, I found myself at Pearl's.

Stella had convinced us all to go out for one last night, only a night that was not too close to our final exam. Fanny refused to go and, in a whisper, counselled me not to go ('Stella only ever thinks about Stella'). But I didn't have her strength and went with them.

At first I was glad I went because I bumped into Dan Kessler. But it turned out that he was on his way out, not in.

'Leaving so soon?' I said.

'Wish I could stay, but it looks like my little act as a bootlegger has worked. I'm going with a bunch of other gangsters to a big meeting at midnight tonight down at Dobson's fish warehouse on the docks.'

Then he was gone.

An hour or so later, I found myself sitting in a booth with Stella.

All the other girls had left, but Stella—desperate to stay close to Clay Bentley Jr—had begged me to stay with her until he took a break from his gambling and she could sit with him.

After what felt like an eternity, Clay Jr finally stepped away from the craps table and we found ourselves in a booth on either side of him.

He was losing at the tables that night because he was drunk, and because he was losing, he was in a foul mood—although he didn't refuse when Baby Face's barman sent over a round of free drinks for all three of us. He threw back his whiskey in a single gulp.

I was tired and bored.

I wanted to go back to the dorm and get some sleep. I didn't need to be here while Stella flirted.

But then Bentley Jr and Stella started talking about his father, Clay Bentley Sr, and how the prize for being the first-placed student at the secretarial school was to be *his* executive secretary.

Junior laughed. 'Ha! First prize is working for my father! Fuck, what's second prize? Polio? The old man's a straitlaced curmudgeon who hasn't changed how he does things in years. He also hasn't got the first damned clue how the new economy works. This decade, the twenties, it's all gonna be about information, investing in the right companies. My father just doesn't see that coming. He's old, both inside and out. His ideas are old, his suits are old. Good luck to the girl who wins that booby prize.'

Stella snuggled close to Junior. 'If I won it, you could ask him to get me to work for you. Imagine all the things we could do working late.'

Junior stared straight at her breasts and snorted approvingly. 'Gotta say I like the sound of that.' He was slurring openly now.

God, I wanted to leave.

But then he said something that caught my attention.

'You want a hot tip, ladies? Later tonight, down by the docks, things are gonna get nasty.'

Stella was only half listening.

'What do you mean?' I said.

Junior grinned smugly, happy to be the possessor of secret knowledge. 'You want to know how to do business in the 1920s? Baby Face Mancino is about to show everybody how it's done. Tonight, he's gonna take over *all* the illegal liquor and gaming businesses in the downtown area. He's called a meeting of all the speakeasy owners in downtown Manhattan, plus all the bootleggers who supply them. They're gonna gather down at Dobson's fish warehouse at midnight. Biggest gathering of gangsters you've ever seen. And when they get there inside that warehouse, Baby Face and his boys are gonna kill 'em all.'

> **If you don't like action and excitement, don't go into police work.**
>
> – Eliot Ness

MY BLOOD TURNED TO ice.

Dan, posing as a bootlegger, was going to Dobson's fish warehouse at midnight.

He was walking into an ambush.

For some reason—I don't know why—I found myself worried for him. Was it because of our shared German heritage? Or because he was a federal agent, one of the good guys? Was it his smile? Whatever it was, I didn't want Dan Kessler to die.

I stole a glance at my watch.

11:40 p.m.

I could get to Dobson's warehouse in maybe ten minutes if I ran.

I had to get out of there. But Clay Bentley Jr was still rambling and I didn't want it to look like what he'd just said had caused me to dash out.

Precious minutes ticked by.

11:45.

I slipped out of the booth. 'Stella, I have to go to bed. I need some sleep before our big exam on Friday morning. Good evening, Mr Bentley.'

He just waved me away.

Stella mouthed the words, *Thank you*.

Then I was outside, running.

Racing through the empty streets of New York City, dashing for the docks.

The darkened city loomed above me.

At 11:57, I burst out of a side street and beheld the warehouses that lined the East River, saw one marked '9B: DOBSON'S FISH AND SEAFOOD' in giant black letters.

About ten automobiles were parked in front of it, beside three insulated trucks backed up to roller doors. Dobson's Fish and Seafood used those trucks to transport fresh fish from the wharf to restaurants in the city on beds of ice.

The air was damp, misty, cold. A fog was rolling in.

Two of Baby Face Mancino's thugs guarded the door. They wore thick overcoats and dark expressions.

I walked quickly across the street to the warehouse, in full view of the two guards, looking for Dan.

I didn't see him anywhere.

Either he hadn't arrived yet or he was already inside.

11:58.

I walked up to the guards.

'Who are you?' one of them asked.

'I'm . . . Mr Kriegler's secretary,' I said. 'He was told to bring all his delivery ledgers to the meeting, but he left them in his office. Have you seen him yet?'

'Yeah,' the bigger guard said. 'He's inside.'

The guards swapped knowing looks. They knew that whoever

walked into that warehouse was going to die.

'You think you could go and get him for me?' I asked. 'Seriously, I don't want to get fired.'

'Sorry, toots. We got instructions. Once somebody's inside, they stay inside till the meeting's done.'

I froze, swallowing. Damn. What could I do?

And in that moment, I heard my father's voice inside my head. *Every decision comes down to a choice: the right choice or the wrong choice. Just try to make the right one.*

Unfortunately, as he'd told me, sometimes that choice could be an unpleasant or bitter one. For me, now, it was something else again: a dangerous one.

I took a deep breath as I made my decision.

'All right, then,' I said. 'Let me go in and give these ledgers to him.'

'Go on in, sweetheart,' the big guard growled, smirking knowingly to his partner again as he stepped aside and allowed me to pass.

My heart pounding, I entered a long vast space that reeked of dead fish.

Aisle upon aisle of large hooks and chains stretched away from me down the length of the warehouse, creating rows of thick metal curtains.

Dozens of pens with ceramic floors, grated drains and hoses lined the right-hand wall: for hosing down the fish and cleaning off the guts.

The whole assembly line of fishworks ended at the roller doors to my right, where the finished product was loaded onto the ice trucks.

It was, I had to admit, the perfect place for a mass murder. You could just hose away the blood.

I saw a group of men about a hundred yards away, all wearing overcoats.

A hierarchy was instantly apparent: the bosses sat on folding chairs while their goons stood behind them.

Baby Face Mancino and his chief henchman, Lucky Luciano, shook hands with the various gang lords. Baby Face looked like a politician: all smiles and charm as he exclaimed, 'I'm so glad you made it!'

And then I saw Dan, lingering at the edge of the wide circle, over by a row of fishhooks.

I hurried over to him and touched his shoulder.

He turned and in a single instant saw me, recognised me, and tried to process my presence there in the fishworks, his expression transforming from confusion to alarm.

'Wait, Hanna—'

'You have to leave *right now*,' I said. 'Don't question me. Come now.'

He processed that quickly, too, and immediately followed me out of sight, behind the rows of fishhooks.

'What's going on?' he whispered.

'This is a trap,' I hissed. 'Baby Face is going to assassinate all his rivals and take all of southern New York City for himself.'

'How do you know this?'

'Just trust me.' I grabbed his hand and guided him behind the many fishhook chains, out of Mancino's sight and back toward the entrance—

Boom.

The two goons who had been guarding the door slammed it

shut, extracted their Tommy guns and stood in front of it, blocking the way out.

And then gunshots.

Great resounding booms.

In the vastness of the warehouse, their volume was terrifying.

My heart almost stopped.

I thought the massacre had begun.

But just as suddenly as it had started, it stopped.

It wasn't the sound of a firing squad. It was Baby Face's men surrounding the assembled gangsters and firing their shotguns into the air to get their attention.

Dan and I peered back through the curtain of chains and hooks to see Baby Face's men, led by Lucky Luciano, brandishing shotguns, surrounding the assembled gang lords, bootleggers and their bodyguards.

Baby Face addressed the trapped gangsters.

'Gentlemen! Thank you for coming! I told you that tonight would see a reconfiguration of the trade in illegal vices in this town! And I did not lie. This is how it's gonna change: your businesses are now mine! Lucky!'

That was when the real gunfire started.

That was the firing squad.

1939.

A camp for the disabled, mentally ill and homosexuals has been set up in the old jail at Brandenburg, in outer Berlin.

I am there with Speer on another inspection tour.

They bring out the crippled first.

Line them up in front of a wall.
The waiting firing squad shoots them.

———————————————————➤

1945.

As I race from the river into the government district, I spy a
Russian firing squad in a side alley.

Six Red Army troops have cornered a lone German corporal,
whose pants have been removed.

The Russians cackle as they form a semi-circle around the cor-
poral and shoot him dead.

◀———————————————————

As Dan and I watched in horror, Lucky Luciano and the other thugs
opened fire on the gang lords of New York City.

In moments, they were all dead, lying in a great pool of blood.

I searched for an exit, some form of escape. But the two gun-
toting door guards were still covering that way out. Going the other
way—to the river end of the warehouse—meant passing Mancino
and Luciano and the armed men there so that wasn't going to
happen.

'There's no way out of here,' I whispered.

'We need to hide,' Dan said.

We both saw it at the same time: an ice truck parked up against
the roller doors at the landward end of the warehouse.

We raced to its box-shaped rear cargo hold, cracked open the
insulated doors and slid inside.

A waist-high mound of melting ice lay inside the truck's hold, left over from the previous day. We buried ourselves in the ice, going fully under it, huddling close to stay warm—

'Lucky!' Mancino called. 'Get rid of 'em. Not a trace, you hear.'

'You got it, boss.'

A few moments later, the door to our truck was yanked open and my heart raced at the thought that we had been discovered—

The first body landed inside the ice truck with a dull thud.

Then a second, and a third, landing on the ice on top of Dan and me.

Mancino's men were loading up the truck—our truck—with the corpses of their victims!

The grim loading took another fifteen minutes or so, until the whole icy hold was filled with bloody bodies.

Blood seeped downward, dripping onto my face.

I wanted to scream.

Dan's face was pressed up close to mine. He gripped my hand tightly.

Then someone shut the rear doors of the truck and with a rumble, its engine started and abruptly it began moving, driving away from the warehouse, into the night.

IT WAS A SHORT trip, barely five minutes.

We didn't go far from the docks.

The reason why became apparent very quickly.

Still lying hidden in the ice in the back of the truck, Dan and I jolted as the vehicle squealed to a halt.

Then we were thrown forward as the truck switched into reverse.

And then—with a sickening lurch—*the whole truck tilted vertically*, its rear end dropping away.

Dan and I fell for a second or two—straight down, with all the corpses and the ice bouncing around us—before our truck slammed into something, something that gave a little with the impact, and then water started flooding in through the gap between the truck's rear doors and I realised . . .

. . . whoever had been driving our ice truck had backed it *off* the riverside boardwalk, letting it fall into the river, and now it was sinking to the bottom.

The truck flooded fast.

When it had hit the surface of the water, Dan and I had been thrown downward and we landed on the foul pile of bodies now lying in a jumbled heap against the closed rear doors.

As it sank, the truck righted itself a little.

If I could have seen it from the outside, I would have seen the ice truck floating half-submerged in the East River a short way out from the seawall at an extreme angle: its whole rear end entirely below the surface, its cab and front grille just above the waterline.

Inside the sinking truck, incoming water rose fast, roiling and bubbling as it did. Once the whole truck was full, it would sink like a stone to the bottom of the river, never to be seen again, with us in it.

'There's no way out!' I gasped.

'The doors at the back are the only exit!' Dan agreed.

Right now, however, those rear doors were blocked by the mound of corpses.

I bit my lip, thinking.

I said, 'If we wait for the truck to fill some more, the bodies will start to float. *Then* we can move them out of the way, open the doors and swim out of here. But it'll mean waiting till the truck goes fully under.'

Dan gave me a look.

'Hope you can hold your breath,' he said.

The water kept rising—to my waist, to my chest—at which point it began *lifting* the pile of bodies off the floor and we shoved our way downward, moving between the corpses to get as close as we could to the rear doors.

The water was up to my neck by the time we reached them.

Dan pushed against the doors, but the weight of water still rushing in was too strong.

The waterline was near the ceiling now.

We craned our necks, straining to breathe in the shrinking space available to us.

And then the entire hold filled and we took matching deep breaths and went under.

Underwater silence.

Corpses floated all around us.

Dan pulled them away then started kicking against the doors with great powerful blows.

His fourth kick broke them open and we swam out as fast as we could, searching for the surface, desperate for air.

We broke the surface together and sucked in great gasping breaths.

New York City rose above us. The harbour stretched away to the ocean. I could even see the Statue of Liberty.

Somehow we'd got out alive.

Dan bobbed in the water beside me. 'I owe you a serious debt of gratitude, Miss Fischer. Thank you.'

We swam to the shore, scaled the seawall and fell onto our backs, heaving for breath.

'Would dinner be out of the question?' he asked.

'Not for a couple of days,' I said.

'Why?'

'I have my final exam at secretarial school to take.'

I never let my schooling interfere with my education.

– Mark Twain

THE CLOCK TICKED LOUDLY in the exam room.

'Ladies. Your time starts . . . *now*!' Miss Bomback called.

Instantly, the clatter of typewriters filled the room as we all started hammering on our keys.

The final exam: typing.

It was between Stella and me now.

After all the other tests—stenography, memory, note-taking, all of them—we were level at the top of the class. Curiously, I found myself *wanting* to come first, so that I could get the best job and thus earn the most money and thus get back to Lukas and my old life back in Berlin.

And so it came down to typing a long letter that had been written out by hand by Mrs Graham-Coulson.

I couldn't make a mistake, but this was also a timed test.

If you didn't finish the letter, you got zero.

So I had to type fast and get everything—everything—right, knowing that in all our time at the school, Stella had never made an error in a typing test.

After ten minutes, Miss Bomback called, 'Time! Cease typing!'

Everyone leaned back from their Underwoods.

Knowing that we were the two contenders for the first prize placement, Miss Bomback came over and collected Stella's and my letters and with Mrs Katherine Graham-Coulson herself, they graded the two typewritten letters then and there.

The whole room was on tenterhooks.

Miss Bomback read Stella's letter while Mrs Graham-Coulson read mine.

Both held red pens poised to mark any errors.

Then they switched.

Now, Miss Bomback was reading mine. I watched her, frozen. She lifted her red pen to make a correction, but then thought better of it.

And then Mrs Graham-Coulson frowned as she examined Stella's letter.

'There's a mistake here,' she said and the crowd of girls gasped. 'You used a period instead of a comma after *Yours sincerely*.'

Stella had made an error. One error. Her only one during her whole time at secretarial school.

A period instead of a comma.

Is it not strange how one's life can turn on the smallest of things?

A single keystroke on a typewriter.

The class leapt from their chairs and surrounded me with congratulations. Stella burst into tears.

Mrs Graham-Coulson watched it all with a studied gaze.

I was crowned the number one student and awarded my prize: I was expected at Mr Clay Bentley Sr's office on the 52nd floor of the Woolworth Building at nine o'clock sharp on Monday morning.

And thus my time at the Graham-Coulson Secretarial School for Ladies came to an end.

I don't know where I would have ended up had Stella not made that mistake.

All I know now is that her one errant keystroke would initiate a chain of events that would set the course of my life down a long and winding and very dangerous path.

FROM THE FIRST INTERROGATION
NEW JERSEY, 1933

INTERROGATOR (MAJ. WILLIS): So, let me get this straight, in 1919, after your father was murdered in Berlin, you were shipped off to America to live with your aunt, your mother's sister?

FISCHER: That's correct.

INTERROGATOR: And once here, you attended secretarial school and became the secretary of Mr Clay Bentley, the millionaire industrialist?

FISCHER: Yes. The older one, not the younger one.

INTERROGATOR: Tell us about that.

PART III

1920
MR BENTLEY'S
SECRETARY

The parties were bigger. The pace was faster, the shows were broader, the buildings were higher, the morals were looser, and the liquor was cheaper.

– From: *The Great Gatsby*, by F. Scott Fitzgerald

> You never get a second chance to make a first
> impression.
>
> – Advertising slogan for a suit company

BENTLEY & SONS TRUCKING AND SHIPPING
52ND FLOOR
WOOLWORTH BUILDING, NEW YORK CITY
APRIL 1920

THE FOLLOWING MONDAY MORNING, I arrived at the reception area of Bentley & Sons Trucking and Shipping at 8:50 a.m., dressed in a grey skirt-suit with my hair tightly bound.

(RULE #2: Always look immaculate!)
(RULE #3: Always be on time!)

(My suit had been purchased from the secretarial school, the cost of it added to my existing loan. The school also fronted me some money to pay a month's rent on a tiny apartment—of course at the same interest rate.)

I announced myself to the receptionist sitting behind a large counter and went to sit in the waiting area—

Someone I knew was already there.

Stella.

She was sitting on a couch, waiting patiently.

I'd never seen her look so good. Her blonde hair was curled to perfection. Her bright red lipstick was a work of art. Her skirt-suit was an eye-catching sky-blue and didn't have a single crease in it. It looked brand new. Honestly, she looked like a secretary in a poster.

'Oh, hello, Hanna,' she said, feigning surprise. 'Looks like we're both starting work here today.'

'Stella, hi . . .' I said, not understanding.

My confusion was answered a few seconds later as, from the inner offices, Mr Clay Bentley Jr appeared.

He bounded across the reception area, bursting with energy. I realised then that I'd only ever seen him at night—late at night—in the liquor and gambling dens when he was drunk and tired and not at all this chipper.

'There she is!' he called. 'My secretary! Newly minted from the finest secretarial school in the land!'

He danced over to Stella and shook her hand with mock formality. I alone saw the sly wink that accompanied it.

He said, 'We are gonna have such a swell time working together—'

'Clayton,' another voice said, softly but firmly cutting him off.

A second man stood in the doorway to the inner offices, having entered the reception area unnoticed behind Clay Jr.

Clay Bentley Sr was sixty years old then. He had a wide face, wide glasses and a wide jaw. He wore his snow-white hair parted neatly on the side.

'Miss Fischer?'

I stood, ramrod straight.

'Yes, Mr Bentley, sir, yes.'

'Come on, we have a meeting to attend across town. Do you have your pen and notepad? It's time to get to work.'

Within twenty minutes, I was standing with Mr Bentley Sr inside an elevator inside the Empire Building at 71 Broadway, travelling rapidly upward.

'All right, Miss Fischer,' Mr Bentley Sr said crisply. 'Here's how we're going to work. You attend every meeting I do. You stand behind me, you utter not a word, and you take down notes of *everything* of importance that is said. Then when we return to the office, you advise the appropriate departments of what transpired at said meeting and what they have to do. You insert follow-up meetings in my calendar. Indeed, you control my calendar in its entirety. When I come into the office on any given day, I expect you to tell me where I have to be and when. Do you understand?'

'Yes, sir.'

'And young lady. Pay attention. Because I do not repeat myself.'

'Yes, sir. I understand,' I said, terrified.

The next thing I knew I was in a gigantic office standing silently behind Mr Bentley as he spoke with executives from U.S. Steel, the largest company in the world.

It was a dizzying meeting, with shipping quantities and dates and prices thrown about.

'—Sixty tons of steel girders, coming by rail from Pittsburgh on the 9th of June.'

'—Another seventy from Allentown, which will need to be brought overland by truck and be in New York by July 4th.'

'—A building boom is coming, Mr Bentley, and we need

unimaginable quantities of steel to do it. Mark my words, within ten years, your Woolworth Building is going to be regarded as *small . . .*'

I scribbled down what I could, trying desperately to keep up.

And then it was over and Mr Bentley and I stepped into the elevator and rode back down to the street.

'All right, young miss,' he said. 'Let's get back to the office. I want you to pass on all those details and dates to Mr Dawson in Logistics. Bentley & Sons doesn't miss a delivery date!'

That was his mantra.

Bentley & Sons doesn't miss a delivery date!

If I heard that line once, I would hear it a hundred times. It was the unbreakable rule that Mr Clay Bentley Sr lived by.

'Now, what were those Pittsburgh and Allentown dates? The 4th of June and the 9th of July.'

'No, sir,' I said. 'The Pittsburgh shipment is due on the 9th of June and the Allentown one on July 4th.'

He froze.

And looked at me.

His eyes searched for my notepad, but I didn't have it in my hand. It was in my bag.

'You remembered that?'

'Yes, sir.'

He regarded me silently and said nothing more.

I don't think it's overstating things to say that working for Clay Bentley Sr was absolutely exhausting.

He didn't stop.

And he didn't expect me to stop either. The man had limitless energy and a razor-sharp mind and he expected me to keep up.

It was also a crazy time for business.

It was a boom time in America.

Great office towers were being built. Automobiles were becoming commonplace, along with their honking horns. New York City was lit up every night. Flush with their post-war earnings, men and women were buying clothes, hosting parties and living large.

Iron girders, fur-lined coats, automobile parts: America of the 1920s was awash with sellable products and someone had to ship it all.

And that was Clay Bentley Sr's business.

Which meant that Mr Bentley Sr's attentions on any given day could be drawn in a dozen different directions—from how to ship certain goods, to maintaining his fleet of trucks and railcars and ships—all requiring fast yet considered decisions. After he made those decisions, I was to put them into effect, conveying his resolutions to the departments who would enact them.

My first few weeks, it was all I could do to stay upright and not collapse at the nonstop rush of it all.

It was only by the end of the first month that I figured out how to pace myself—to assign time for breakfast and other meals, and to make sure I got to bed at an hour that allowed me to recharge my energies for the onslaught of the following day.

Many were the evenings when I returned to my little apartment, kicked off my shoes and fell flat onto my bed, spent.

When the Fourth of July holiday came a few months after I'd started working for Mr Bentley Sr, I slept till noon.

On that blissfully quiet day off, I tabulated my savings. Since I had started working, I had tried to be thrifty and to save as much of my salary as I could—while also following Fanny's advice and paying off my student loan as quickly as possible—all so that I might eventually afford the price of a steamer ticket back to Germany and return to Lukas.

I had done some research.

A third-class ticket on a steamer to Hamburg cost a whopping $142 plus taxes.

With rent payments, loan repayments, and the various other costs of living—plus the fact that I would only get two weeks of vacation per year and would thus have to wait a year to combine *two sets* of vacations—it would take me some time to reach my goal. But I was determined.

I did another thing that July 4th.

I wrote to Lukas in Berlin, at his parents' store. For the past six months, I had been meaning to write a letter to him, a long and detailed explanation of my abrupt departure from Berlin and my time in America and on that sunny Fourth of July afternoon in 1920, I wrote it.

It turned out to be a long letter, twelve densely-crammed hand-written pages that came pouring out of me in a rush.

I even asked if he could find out what had happened to Ooma after my father's death. I'd hardly even thought about her during those months and I felt terrible about it.

I also asked Lukas to let Mr Einstein know that I had arrived in New York City safely and to thank him for helping me on that terrible night in Berlin. I would have written to Einstein separately but postage to Europe was far too costly for me to send two letters.

Mail travelled slowly in those days, carried as it was by ship, and I returned to the nonstop tornado that was Mr Bentley's daily routine. But as the months ticked by and I thought about Lukas receiving my letter and tearing it open and reading about my tragic flight, I received no reply.

STELLA'S EXPERIENCE AT BENTLEY & Sons Trucking and Shipping could not have been more different from mine.

Many were the times as I toiled away at my desk that I saw her and Clay Jr leave early for lunch, giggling and laughing—heading not to a restaurant but to a nearby hotel and often never returning to the office.

On the days he did attend meetings with his father, Clay Jr clashed with Clay Sr.

'Father, you're a dinosaur!' he shouted one day in the board-room in front of me, Stella and several department heads. 'You waste hours every day solving problems like greasing our trucks or renting railcars. I, on the other hand, have been investing in stocks. Why, in the last month, my investments in the market have returned 22 percent. In one month! I didn't need to grease an axle or book a railcar. The money did the work.'

There was actually more to it than that.

That evening, Stella invited me to accompany her and Clay Jr to a local speakeasy for dinner and a show, and after a few drinks, Clay Jr got started talking.

'I've actually been investing my trust fund money,' he said. 'I'm now worth six million dollars.'

'Six million dollars!' Stella gasped.

'Well, on paper,' Clay Jr said. 'You see, darling, it only becomes real money when I sell my options.'

'Options?' I asked. 'I thought you bought and sold stocks on the market?'

Clay Jr smiled at me condescendingly. 'It's all right, Hanna, I wouldn't expect a woman to know about such matters. It's all frightfully complicated. Gosh, I'm not even sure I understand it myself. My broker put me onto them. Options are something sophisticated investors deal in. Only chumps buy basic stocks these days.'

He snorted and threw back another whiskey.

Stella gazed at him adoringly, no doubt thinking just how much money six million dollars was. She curled up closer to him, nestling in his arms.

Thirty minutes later, Clay Jr hit the roulette table out the back and I took my leave and went home to bed.

On those occasions when I had the opportunity to go out for lunch, I would meet up with Fanny at a café near the Woolworth Building.

After graduating from secretarial school, Fanny had been placed as the secretary to a senior executive at a mid-sized brokerage on Wall Street.

She had been placed there by Mrs Graham-Coulson herself, who, to my surprise, had been aware of Fanny's interest in such matters.

It was a perfect placement for Fanny and, for the most part, she loved it.

'Although the damned men in the office laughed in my face

yesterday when I had the temerity to suggest a stock,' she said to me at lunch one day.

'They laughed?'

'They thought it was cute that a *secretary* might offer a tip. But I read the *Journal*, I watch the ticker and the Dow Jones. I've even created a trading account for myself, to invest my salary in, I have.'

'Good for you, Fanny,' I said. 'I bet you're better than all of them put together.'

'Damn right, I am.'

'Would you, maybe, I don't know, consider investing for me?' I asked. 'Just a little bit of my salary each month?'

'Would I?' She smiled broadly. 'I'd love to! You trust me, you hear, and I'll turn your little salary into a nice nest egg, I will.'

'Thanks, Fanny. Say, tell me, what are options?'

She looked at me askance. 'My, you might be savvier at investing than I thought. Options are what's called a derivative and they can make you a lot of money real fast. Because, you see, you don't actually buy a stock up-front. Rather, you make a promise to buy or sell a stock *at a future date*. You can make a lot of money.

'You can lose a lot, too. That's the problem with options and why I steer clear of them. Basically, an option is a bet. A bet between you and some other guy about the future price of a stock: whoever wins the bet, wins big; whoever loses, loses big. In my firm, it's the cocky cowboys who deal with options—they strut around like high-stakes gamblers, which I suppose is what they are.'

'Oh, okay,' I said. 'Sounds complicated. How is Raymond?'

'He's just swell!' Fanny beamed. 'God love him, he joined the local union a couple of weeks ago and it's already become his life.

He gets all worked up about workers' rights and the like. Said he's gonna stand for city council at the next election. He's feisty, my sweet little Polack. I just love him to death.'

I always enjoyed seeing Fanny.

WHILE CLAY BENTLEY JR drank, bought options and gambled—and played around with his secretary three afternoons a week—Mr Clay Bentley Sr worked.

Hard.

Which meant I worked hard, too.

It was only after I was there three months that the receptionist told me that the reason he'd needed a new secretary was that he had burned out the last four. None had lasted more than two weeks. Which was why he'd gone to Mrs Graham-Coulson and stumped up a lot of money to acquire her top-placed student. Me.

But I was also adapting. I trained myself to wake an hour earlier and with that extra hour of the day available to me, I gradually got on top of his brutal schedule.

And just as Mr Bentley Sr had ordered me to do on my first day, I became the unchallenged keeper of his diary.

All meetings with him went through me, plus all lunches, dinners, weekend brunches and even wedding invitations.

Throughout those early months, I learned a lot about my boss.

He was a widower. His beloved wife—Clay Jr's mother—had died of tuberculosis back in 1912. He did not date and, when the matchmaking wives of his male friends asked him if he wanted to, he professed no interest.

'I loved my wife,' he would say. 'I do not think I shall love or marry again.'

(That said, at the wedding reception for his nephew, I did see him chat for an exceedingly long time with Mrs Henrietta Henderson, a very handsome woman from Long Island who had herself been widowed the previous summer.)

He didn't drink.

He didn't smoke.

He didn't gamble or go to speakeasies.

He just worked.

I began to realise, however, that he didn't work for the money— and he made a lot of money. He seemed to genuinely enjoy doing business and making deals and, surprisingly, seeing his employees flourish.

'See Freddy Dawson in Logistics,' he whispered to me once, during a rare break as we waited for some deliveries to arrive in the loading dock and watched Dawson very competently managing things. 'He started out as a truck driver for me, you know. I promoted him to Head of Logistics two years ago and look at him now. He's grown into a brilliant foreman, a real leader of men.'

It was a rare insight into my gruff boss.

Another glimpse came when he arrived at work extra early one Monday morning to find me already there, reading *The New York Times*.

'Why, hello, Hanna,' he said, surprised. 'I didn't know you'd be here so early.'

'It gives me time to read the news, sir.'

He again regarded me with that look of his.

'How long have you been doing this? Coming in early to read the newspaper?'

'About a month, sir. It's the only time I have to do it. I don't just read the newspaper. Sometimes I read novels and at other times, books about physics. I think it's important to keep up with the news and when I was younger I was quite good at physics, you know.'

He sat down opposite me. 'Really?'

I said, 'I was actually neighbours with Albert Einstein. He was a close friend of my father's before, well, my father passed away. It was Einstein who inspired me to study physics.'

'Albert Einstein himself. Goodness me,' Mr Bentley said.

'He is a kind and decent man, sir,' I said. 'And brilliant, of course.'

Mr Bentley nodded. 'Tell me, Hanna, what you think about the news.'

'I don't understand.'

'About these heady times. These so-called roaring twenties. I'm an old man. You're young. I like to know what the young make of these things.'

I thought for a moment. 'Well, it seems to me, sir, that the world is moving too fast. As the populace emerged from a grim and terrible war and the worldwide pandemic that followed it, they are now too energetic in their glee. They do business with money that is too freely available. They drink and dance and carouse with abandon. It all has to come to a head sometime. I mean, for want of a better comparison, it's basically like Newton's third law of motion.'

'Newton's third law? What is that?'

'That for every action, there is an equal and opposite reaction,' I said. 'It is, so far as I can tell, a law that applies to people as well as motion. If you drink too much and have a gay time, you suffer a hangover the following morning. If business booms based on unsustainable levels, it must also correct itself eventually. If the world moves too fast for too long, it becomes inherently unstable and flies off into chaos. At least for a time.'

I stopped my blathering.

Mr Bentley Sr was staring at me, his face blank.

'I have heard speeches from economists and politicians and even philosophers about these unusual times, but that, my dear Hanna, is the best description of them that I have ever heard.'

I just bowed my head.

He stood.

'Reading time is important. But not at the expense of sleep, which is even more important, my dear. I tell you what, let us block out an hour from our diary every Tuesday and Thursday morning, from nine till ten, just to read. Anything. The newspaper, a physics book, a novel. Anything.'

'That would be wonderful, sir,' I said. 'But, er, why?'

'I work hard, Hanna, which means you work hard, too. Trust me, I know that. I see it every day. Consider this your reward.'

And in that moment, I saw Clay Bentley Sr.

Beneath his taciturn exterior was a genuinely sweet man who actually saw his employees.

'Thank you, sir,' I said. 'Thank you very kindly.'

Clearly uncomfortable, he mumbled something and bowed his head, spun on his heel and shuffled into his office and closed the door behind him.

A few days later, he burst out of his office, his face beet-red.

'Miss Fischer!' he bellowed. 'What is this meeting you've set for me at 9:30?'

'It's a coffee meeting, sir. At a café down the block.'

'I know that! I can see that!' he stammered. 'But it's with . . . with . . . during *business hours*.'

'Yes, sir,' I said. 'I know, sir. Since you put me in charge of your diary, I took the liberty of calling Mrs Henrietta Henderson to see if she was available and she was. She was also, I might add, most pleased to be invited to have coffee with you.'

'Are you telling me that you—'

'Yes, sir. I did. I arranged to send you on a date. And you're due there in one hour.'

'But I can't—I mean, I could—she *is* a delight—'

'Consider this your reward, sir,' I said.

As 1920 BECAME 1921, I truly became Mr Bentley's secretary.

We both worked long hours and in doing so we developed a rapport. On a few occasions I even saw him smile, like when he noted that I had scheduled a second coffee date with the widow Henderson.

Other things happened, too.

Fanny married Raymond in St Michael's Catholic church in the Bronx.

It was a delightful day.

The ceremony at the church went off without a hitch, but the reception afterward on the roof of her uncle's pub in Brooklyn was another story.

It all began rather tensely as Fanny's Irish brothers and cousins faced off against Raymond's Polish ones.

Glares and stares were exchanged, as only young lads can do, easily offended as they can be. On any given weekend, these lads would probably have been fighting each other in the backstreets of the city, but there at Fanny's reception, in their ill-fitting suits and poorly knotted ties, they behaved impeccably.

I later learned that Fanny had insisted on this in her customary way: 'If any of you larrikin arseholes start up a fistfight, I swear before Jesus, God and Mary that I will creep into your bedroom one night and cut off yer fuckin' balls!'

There was no fighting during her wedding day. Indeed, as the beer flowed and the music played—first, Irish dancing music and then its Polish equivalent—the evening became a most festive one.

I danced a little, but mostly I watched from my table, a literal wallflower.

And thus Miss Fanny O'Toole became Mrs Fanny Wozniak, and that made me very happy.

Another marital incident occurred around that time.

In January of 1921, Clay Bentley Jr announced that he was leaving his wife, filed for divorce and promptly moved in with his secretary, Miss Stella Lang.

Stella's plan to wrest Clay Jr from his wife had succeeded.

Within a few months, they would be engaged and when I saw Stella on her last day in the office, packing her things—as Clay Jr's fiancée, she would, of course, no longer be working for him—she smiled at me.

'Enjoy working, Hanna,' she said breezily. 'Ciao, bella!'

And she was gone.

As for me, I kept diligently saving my salary, ever desirous to return to Berlin and reunite with Lukas. I had continued to write to him, but despite including my home and work addresses, I still had not received any reply.

I didn't quite know how to feel about this. Had my letters gone missing in the mail? This was very possible. Or had Lukas received them and ignored them? Had he moved on and forgotten about me? The thought of that broke my heart.

Sometimes, in the evenings, alone in my small apartment, I would think of my old life in Berlin—of my father, of Lukas, of my studies at the *Gymnasium* and my dreams of a life in physics.

When I thought of physics, my mind would naturally turn to my old neighbour, Einstein, and I wondered if, when I returned to Berlin, he would still be living on Haberlandstrasse, even if he was now the most famous scientist in the world.

And then, in March of 1921, during one of my reading hours with Mr Bentley Sr, I saw an article in *The New York Times* that made me gasp out loud.

'Whatever is it, Hanna?' Mr Bentley asked, concerned.

'He's coming here. To America.'

'Who?'

'Einstein. He's to do a speaking tour in the United States. He'll be arriving in New York by steamer next month.'

I didn't need to go back to Berlin to see my old neighbour.

He was coming to me.

NEW YORK HARBOR
APRIL 3, 1921

ALBERT EINSTEIN'S ARRIVAL IN New York Harbor on April 3, 1921, on the steamship *Rotterdam* was a celebration of colossal proportions.

The citizens of the largest city in America lined the docks at Battery Park and the streets of downtown, cheering wildly, waving flags and kerchiefs, craning their necks to see the wizard of science whose insights into the inner workings of the universe—insights that none of them could ever hope to comprehend—had changed the world.

They came out in droves to see him. The sidewalks were so filled with crowds that it resembled a tickertape parade.

I watched it all from a fifth-storey window of the Woolworth Building, seeing Einstein standing in the back of an open-topped automobile, waving to the people of New York.

Even though he was some distance from me, I could see he still had his trademark wild hair and drooping caterpillar moustache.

I longed to talk with him again—to inform him of all that had happened to me after my departure from Berlin; if nothing else, to tell him that I was still alive. I called out to him from my window, but there was no hope that he would hear me above the noise of the cheering throng.

I heard that he was to be presented with the keys to the city at a reception that night and that he had a full schedule of dinners and speaking engagements with the politicians and prominent citizens of New York.

Still, I was happy to see him.

My old neighbour in my new city.

But there was still work to do and I had to manage my boss's travel and accommodation arrangements for the most important meeting of his life: a meeting at the White House with President Harding on April 26.

The meeting had been arranged by the head of U.S. Steel, Mr John Pierpont Morgan Jr. President Harding hailed from Ohio—steel country—and Morgan, as one of his main backers, had unfettered access to him.

The meeting would be followed by a dinner at the White House and Mr Morgan had invited Mr Bentley Sr to attend as his guest.

When word got out about the Presidential meeting and dinner, I received an unexpected call.

'Hanna, darling, it's Stella.' Stella had acquired a languid edge to her accent since she and Clay Jr had become engaged. She also wore furs and minks and the latest fashionable dresses.

'You must include Clay Jr and me in that White House dinner. We simply have to come. It'll be the society event of the season.'

'I'll see what I can do, Stella,' I said.

'Don't *see* what you can do, dear. Make it happen. Or I'll have you fired.'

Click. She hung up.

And so I made some calls and got her and Clay Jr invited to the White House dinner.

Stella and Clay Jr would catch the train to Washington, D.C., a week before the dinner, so that they could sample the nightlife of the nation's capital.

Mr Bentley Sr, typically, intended to work all the way until the day of the dinner, the 26th. He asked me to book him on the last possible train that day. He would travel in his tuxedo.

By the time it came for Mr Bentley Sr to leave, I had arranged everything for him and as he emerged from his private office, I stood by the door holding his train ticket.

'I must say, you are looking very dapper, sir,' I said.

He smiled, one of those rare grins.

Indeed, this smile could even be described as cheeky.

It was then that I saw the object he held dangling from one finger: a dress on a hanger, in Bloomingdale's wrapping.

'Forgive me, Hanna, but I asked one of the other secretaries for your size.'

He handed me the dress, removing the wrapping.

It was the single most gorgeous dress I had ever seen: a vision of red with glittering sparkles, elegant yet refined. An evening gown.

'What is this all about?' I asked.

'I got my friend, J.P., to get an extra seat at our table at the White House dinner and I booked a room for you at the Lafayette Hotel.'

'But I—'

He smiled, more broadly this time. 'I was informed only yesterday that there is going to be a special guest at this dinner, someone you know, so I took immediate action and got you an appropriate dress. I hope you don't mind.'

I was still catching up, dumbly holding the red gown.

'Wait, what? A special guest? Who?'

'Why, Professor Einstein, of course. Consider this your next reward.'

THE WHITE HOUSE
WASHINGTON, D.C.
APRIL 26, 1921

AND SO THAT NIGHT, after changing into my dress and travelling to D.C. on the train—Cinderella-like, with Mr Bentley—I attended a fabulous dinner at the White House in honour of Albert Einstein.

Clay Jr and Stella were there when we arrived, but at a faraway table.

I was seated at J.P. Morgan's table, about as close to the official Presidential table as one could get.

And then in walked Einstein with his wife Elsa and the President and his wife and everyone stood and applauded.

The President waved.

His wife nodded.

Elsa Einstein took in the vast room, with its many guests and elaborate table settings.

Albert Einstein saw me and stopped dead in his tracks.

Then, to the astonishment of all, he broke away from the President of the United States—crying 'Hanna! *Zaubermaus!*'—and raced to my table and embraced me with unconcealed joy.

I cannot even begin to imagine how it looked—me, a nobody in a red dress, surrounded by the most distinguished and powerful people in America, all dressed in their best finery, in the grand ballroom of the White House, twenty feet from the President himself, being hugged by Einstein.

I glimpsed Stella watching in stunned astonishment as Einstein held me so emotionally and familiarly.

I didn't care.

In his embrace, I felt warm and safe, a child again. I noticed that he was wearing aftershave—it was, I guess, a special occasion.

And in that moment as he held me, I burst into tears and cried away two years of pain.

As I wiped away my tears, Einstein whispered in German, 'My goodness, Hanna, there has not been a day since that dreadful night that I have not thought of you! I have long wondered what became of you after I put you onto that steamer in Hamburg. And here you are, of all the places!'

I could barely speak.

I gripped him tightly.

'Come, little one,' he said in that calm voice of his as he gently extracted himself from my grasp. 'I fear I am the prize ox this evening and I must go and be put on show. Let us find a quiet moment to talk later.'

I HAD ATTENDED POLITICAL functions with Mr Bentley Sr before, but at much lower levels: dinners with the Mayor of New York, lunches with state senators. That sort of thing.

It was strange, then, that even though this event took place at the White House—with all its pomp and ceremony, white tablecloths, fresh flowers and sparkling silverware—it was, in the end, no different from the little ones.

Speeches, toasts, pleasantries.

President Harding was a handsome and elegant man, but from his speech it was clear that he—and his speechwriters—knew nothing about physics.

In the end, like all politicians he just wanted a photograph with a highly regarded visitor, hoping that some of that regard would rub off on him.

After dinner and the speeches were done and the President took his leave—no-one could go until he left—Einstein found me and in a quiet corner of that glittering ballroom, we sat down together and I told him about everything that had happened to me in America: secretary school, gangsters, falling into the river inside an ice truck with a government agent, and, finally, working for Mr Bentley.

We spoke in German, for in those days Einstein's English wasn't very good and he appreciated conversing in his native tongue.

As I prattled on, he listened patiently.

When I was done he said, 'Oh, Hanna, look at you. It would be too glib to say you have landed on your feet, for it is nothing of the sort. In the face of unspeakable tragedy and the total upheaval of your young life, you have persevered and ended up standing. Your dear father was right. You truly are a *Zaubermaus*: a Magic Mouse. I am so proud of you.'

I bowed my head modestly.

'How are things in Germany?' I asked.

'Germany is descending into ever greater madness by the day,' Einstein said. 'What happened to your father was just the beginning. Germany has become a nation of thugs, thugs who despise knowledge and who rule by the fist. And they target Jews more than ever. It will not end well. Let us not dwell on such nastiness. Tell me, have you had any chance to further your studies in physics?'

'Oh, no, Herr Einstein, I have been too busy repaying my school loan, paying my rent and working for Mr Bentley. One day, I hope to resume them. One day.'

Mr Bentley was standing a short distance away, chatting with his friend, J.P. Morgan.

Einstein called to him. 'Good sir, are you aware that your secretary is one of Berlin's finest students of physics?'

'I was not,' Bentley said, coming over. Morgan did, too. 'But I'm not surprised. She's a clever one, a brilliant secretary who finished at the top of her class. She is also, I might add, a remarkable and kind young lady. I'm lucky to have her managing my life and affairs.'

'Indeed,' Einstein said. 'Say. My tour of America is to last another month and I have found that managing *my* life and affairs—as I

travel and speak and meet all manner of dignitaries—is most difficult. Would it be possible, perchance, for you to loan Hanna to me
for the next month, to act as my assistant for the remainder of my
tour?'

Mr Bentley Sr blinked, surprised by the sudden and most
unusual question.

Beside him, J.P. Morgan burst out laughing. 'Oh, Clay! You
bring the lass to the ball and you lose her to the guest of honour!
Ha! Well, old man, what do you say? I mean, how many of us can
say we loaned our secretary for a short while to the smartest man
in the world?'

Mr Bentley Sr seemed to think about it for a moment.

Then he turned to me, his expression softening.

'It's not for me to decide, J.P.,' he said. 'It's for Hanna. Hanna,
what do you say, would you like to accompany Professor Einstein
for the remainder of his trip? I'm perfectly fine with it and your job
will be waiting for you when you return.'

I looked from him to Mr Einstein and back again. 'Will you be
all right without me?'

Mr Bentley Sr said, 'Oh, I'm sure I can bumble along without
you for one month. I might even take a short vacation. Henrietta
has been urging me to spend a week or two in Westhampton with
her. Go, child. It'll be good for you.'

I'd started that day in New York as Mr Clay Bentley Sr's secretary. I finished it in Washington, D.C., as Mr Einstein's.

THE EINSTEIN TOUR

MAY 1921

IT TURNED OUT THAT working for Mr Clay Bentley Sr was nothing compared to working for Albert Einstein.

Working for Mr Bentley was hard.

Working for Einstein was ten times harder and twenty times faster.

The demands on his time and attention were astonishing.

The poor fellow. No wonder he needed help.

But as Mr Einstein himself had told me on my tenth birthday, the hard teachers serve you the best and my whirlwind secretarial education in Mr Bentley Sr's office had prepared me well for the nonstop juggernaut that was Einstein's American tour.

Over the course of his trip, Einstein spoke at universities in New York, Chicago and Boston but his most professionally important appearance was a series of four lectures he gave at Princeton University in New Jersey where he outlined his Theory of Relativity in brutal mathematical and scientific terms that would have sounded like gibberish to the lay observer.

He attended charity dinners and balls; he was feted by tickertape parades. And all the while, he was chased and harangued by journalists wanting his opinion or academics wanting his endorsement for their own papers.

Everywhere he went, he was asked to explain relativity.

It became a burden reducing his masterwork—the result of over a decade of study and thought—to a bite-sized phrase that the layperson could understand.

He often tried this version with reporters: 'Consider this, right now, you and I are both travelling around the sun at thirty kilometres per second, and yet neither of us even notices. Our speed is relative.'

When he tired of this and said nothing, the journalists would ask for his opinions of America: very dangerous ground.

As it turned out, Einstein was fascinated by America. By its relentless forward motion, its glorious dismissal of Old World traditions, but most of all, by its astounding standard of living.

He was amazed that even young women of my age and modest means dressed 'like countesses'.

In our quiet moments at the end of a given day, he would say to me, 'Hanna, this country is astonishing. It is not held back by foolish and antiquated European notions of class, birthright and aristocracies. Anything is possible in America.'

There were also more secretive moments.

One occurred at Princeton.

During his stay at Princeton for the lecture series, Einstein was sought out by an American physicist by the name of Arthur Compton.

A Princeton graduate, Dr Compton was the head of the Physics Department at Washington University in St Louis. When he introduced himself to Einstein after one of Einstein's lectures, Einstein—who had shaken the man's hand wearily, expecting some mention of a paper or an invitation to speak—came to life.

'Why, Dr Compton! It is a great pleasure to meet you! Please, let us find a quiet room to talk. I am most interested in your work on the particle-like momentum of photons.'

Like I said, what was gibberish to the layperson was code to people like Einstein, Compton and me.

This was significant.

Einstein's own work on the photoelectric effect had touched on this and Compton had brilliantly taken it many steps further.[*]

Einstein was not a man easily impressed and he was very impressed by Compton.

They talked deep into the night.

And then, just as quickly as my American adventure with Einstein began, it was over and he was gone, back on a steamer bound for Europe and home.

The next year, he would be awarded the Nobel Prize in Physics.

Curiously, he won the prize not for his work on relativity, but for his work on the photoelectric effect, and in the years following the award, few—even Einstein himself—could explain why this was so.

And so, again Cinderella-like, my carriage had become a pumpkin and I returned to New York City to my job as the personal private secretary to Mr Clay Bentley Sr.

I must admit that after the stimulation of travelling and engaging with Einstein and his scientifically minded acquaintances, my life seemed dull, grey, banal.

---

[*] Arthur Compton would win the Nobel Prize in Physics in 1927 for his discovery of the particle-like nature of electromagnetic radiation, which came to be known as the *Compton effect*. During World War II, he would be a key figure in the Manhattan Project.

Einstein was challenging the very basis of our existence. Changing the world. I was managing bills of lading and shipping charges.

But I kept working and, importantly, kept paying off my loan and putting money away, building my savings toward the magic amount of $142 plus taxes, the price of a steamer ticket to take me back to Lukas.

1921 BECAME 1922.

Clay Jr and Stella were married in a magnificent ceremony on the lawn of their splendid Long Island mansion. The Mayor was there, as was J.P. Morgan and some of Mr Bentley Sr's older friends.

Mr Bentley Sr didn't seem exactly pleased with the whole thing: Clay Jr divorcing his wife and then marrying his secretary/mistress.

I did hear J.P. Morgan, however, whisper something to his wife about the matter that I shall never forget.

'Whenever a man marries his mistress, he leaves a vacancy,' Morgan said wryly.

It was an extravagant wedding to the point of being unseemly.

Stella was brought out onto the lawn, in her wedding dress, on the back of a blazing white stallion, flanked by riders from Clay Jr's polo team. The crowd gasped and applauded vigorously.

The party *after* the wedding ceremony was a truly decadent affair, with much dancing, music and champagne—despite Prohibition still being very much in effect—with the last drunken guests not leaving till seven the following morning.

I left early.

I'd had a better time at Fanny and Ray's little Irish–Polish wedding in Brooklyn, and they didn't have any horses there.

Weddings, horses. Horses, weddings.

August 1936.

Horses at the Berlin Olympic Games.

I sit with my boss Albert Speer beside SS-Sturmbannführer Hermann Fegelein, an ambitious pig of a man who is in charge of the equestrian events at the Olympics. We are watching the dressage.

German riders—most of them hailing from the cavalry school in Hanover—are winning in every discipline, so Fegelein is thrilled. They have been doing so well, Hitler himself came to watch them yesterday, he tells us.

Speer tells me later that Fegelein gave the layout of the courses and the heights of all the jumps to the German team months ago, so they and their horses would know every detail in advance.

German riders will win all the gold medals in the 1936 equestrian Olympic program.

June 3, 1944.

Mirabell Palace, Salzburg, Austria.

I am at another rowdy drunken wedding.

Eva Braun's sister is marrying Hermann Fegelein.

The war has been good to Fegelein.

Now a Brigadeführer, he is one of the highest-ranking members in the Waffen-SS.

He is a Nazi's Nazi, a highly decorated officer who oversaw the killing of tens of thousands of Jewish civilians on the Eastern Front.

My boss Speer is there even though he despises Fegelein. 'The man is a psychopath, one of the most disgusting people in Hitler's circle,' he says. 'And now he is getting what he desires most, marrying into the Führer's family.'

While the war is not going well for Germany, Hitler, Himmler and Bormann are also all present at this lavish affair literally taking place in a palace.

Hitler doesn't drink.

Nor does Himmler.

Speer checks his watch a lot.

Bormann drinks so much he passes out.

But not before he caresses my buttocks and slurs in my ear, 'Come, little darling, if you let me fuck you in the kitchen right now, I'll get you anything you want. Jewellery, dresses, money.'

I politely decline. Later, I help his secretary carry him to his car so she can drive him home, as she has done many times before.

In three days, on June 6, 1944, the Allies will invade Europe.

150,000 troops from America, Canada and the U.K. will storm the beaches at Normandy in northern France.

I know this is coming.

The Nazis do not.

Eleven months from now, in April of 1945, Hitler will personally order his brother-in-law's execution for the crime of desertion.

Fegelein will be taken out of the Führerbunker to the garden of the Reich Chancellery and shot.

WITHIN A YEAR OF her glittering wedding, Stella produced a bouncing baby boy who was promptly christened Clayton Charles Bentley III.

The birth of Clay III—who would come to be known by his middle name Charlie—was greeted with parties and gifts for the happy couple.

The birth of her son, however, was a source of much consternation for Stella.

This was because a new form of crime had been rising around that time.

Known as 'kidnapping', it had become a frightening new phenomenon in the well-to-do neighbourhoods of greater New York: the children of wealthy families would be taken from their homes in the dead of night and then held for ransom.

In two notorious cases, those involving the Coughlin child and the Verotta boy, the criminals followed through with their threats and murdered the poor babes.

Thinking that her palatial mansion on Long Island might be an alluring target for kidnappers, Stella insisted upon higher fences and sturdier gates for the compound, and even night guards.

I was not concerned by any such issues. First, I had no children and, second, I had little money. I just continued to work and save, work and save, determined to return to Germany and Lukas.

1922 became 1923.

Prohibition continued.

Baby Face Mancino maintained his dominance of the illegal liquor trade in downtown New York City.

(I confess I frequented some of his speakeasies myself, including the occasional visit to my old haunt, Pearl's, down near the Graham-Coulson Secretarial School.)

President Harding died of a heart attack in San Francisco and was replaced by Calvin Coolidge.

During my reading hours, when I wasn't reading about kidnappings, I began to focus with increasing concern on the news out of Germany.

Things were not good.

Indeed, if it were at all possible, matters had deteriorated since I had left there at the end of 1919.

Since France continued to insist upon punishing reparations, the German government foolishly tried to solve the issue by printing money.

The result was runaway inflation.

In 1919, after the war had ended, it required 48 marks to buy one U.S. dollar.

In 1923, it required 4.2 trillion marks.

The numbers were so large as to be ridiculous and as I read about this financial disaster in *The New York Times*, I could hardly believe it, let alone imagine what it would be like handing over a five-million-mark coin.

Then, in early 1923, when Germany failed to make another round of crippling reparations payments, French and Belgian forces occupied the Ruhr, the locus of German heavy industry.

Life in Germany had been hard. Now, Germany had been humiliated again.

After that, the *Times*'s German correspondent increasingly began to report on the angry speeches, marches and riots of a new anti-Semitic party in southern Germany that was openly hostile to the new German government.

It was known as the National Socialist German Workers' Party, or the Nazis. Its leader was an angry if charismatic war veteran by the name of Adolf Hitler.

Hitler spoke passionately in the beer halls of Munich to larger and larger crowds, stoking their resentments and laying all the blame at the feet of the Treaty of Versailles.

On November 8, 1923, this Hitler character fired gunshots into the ceiling of a beer hall in Munich and declared a 'national revolution!' The following day he and his thugs marched on a Bavarian government building, only to be met by security forces. Gunfire was exchanged and sixteen Nazis were killed.

Hitler fled the chaotic scene and hid in an attic. Two days later he was arrested and charged with high treason. That, all the commentators agreed, would no doubt be the end of the matter.

For my part, I continued to marvel at America.

New York City was growing. More construction. More automobiles. And thousands more people filling the bustling streets every day.

The curiously and yet wonderfully egalitarian nature of America also struck me constantly.

Like the Sunday two days before Christmas in 1923 when I accompanied Mr Bentley Sr and the widow Henderson to church in the city.

Mr Bentley was not particularly given to religion, but he had been invited by the Mayor who had been invited by the Archbishop, so we attended mass.

There, in the front row of the cathedral, his head bowed in prayer, was the gangster, Baby Face Mancino, with his beautifully dressed wife, Carol. Seated between them was a cute little boy of about four, dressed in a miniature suit and tie.

Only in America, I thought, could a known gangster attend church in the presence of the Mayor of New York City and the Pope's most senior representative in the whole of the United States.

(It turned out that like many Italian–American gangsters, Mancino was very Italian in his faith. Throughout his murderous reign, he was a regular churchgoer and, it should be noted, one of the single largest donors to the Catholic Church in New York.)

Seeing Baby Face there in the cathedral, I wondered something and looked around—

—and saw him, sitting inconspicuously in the back row.

Special Agent Dan Kessler of the United States Treasury Department.

When the service ended and the members of the congregation rose from their pews to depart, I sidled over to Dan.

'Good morning,' I said from behind him, 'I didn't know you were such a pious fellow.'

Dan turned. 'Well, hey there. For me, this is an occupational requirement. Didn't know you were so holy either.'

'I'm here on business, too. Haven't found your way into any ice trucks lately, I hope.'

'Couple of close calls, but none as close as that one. Oh, gosh, I still owe you dinner from that night. I'm so sorry, I got busy.'

'Don't worry, I did, too,' I said. 'Still on the Mancino beat?'

'Ooh, yeah. He's built himself quite the empire. As far as illegal liquor, speakeasies and prostitution is concerned, he owns the entire south end of this island. Guns down anyone who tries to intrude on his turf and he has almost every major city official on his payroll.

'Although word on the street is that his loyal lieutenant, Lucky Luciano, is champing at the bit. Lucky wants to go bigger—take the *whole* of Manhattan and then the boroughs, too. I've heard him say to some of the other young bucks that Mancino is too conservative, too small in his thinking.'

I laughed. 'Sounds like illegitimate business in America isn't that different from legitimate business: someone is always trying to innovate, do it better.'

'Hey, you still living downtown? I'm gonna be in your old neighbourhood tomorrow night, down by the train station. Can I buy you that dinner?'

I paused. I liked Dan, but I was still resolved to return to Lukas.

'As friends,' I said.

'Sure,' he smiled. 'Of course. As friends.'

We arranged to meet the next evening at a new little Italian place called Luigi's near the Pearl Street el-train station.

LUIGI'S RESTAURANT
DOWNTOWN NEW YORK CITY
DECEMBER 24, 1923

I MUST SAY I enjoyed having dinner with Dan Kessler at Luigi's that Christmas Eve.

It was a cosy little place, dimly lit, with red checked tablecloths and wood-panelled walls. Romantic even.

Our table by the window looked out at the street and the sturdy iron stairs leading up to the elevated train station above. Only one other table was taken, another couple, dining quietly. And the food was great.

Dan asked me many questions: about myself, my youth in Berlin, and, after I told him about my short stint working for Einstein, my connection with the great man.

'Einstein is just a marvellous, wonderful fellow,' I said. 'His mind is simply extraordinary.'

Dan shook his head. 'The newspaper printed some extracts from one of his theories once. I tried to read them but they just bamboozled me. Energy, mass, the speed of light, bending space and time. I mean, it doesn't seem to make any sense.'

I laughed. 'Understanding that this new physics doesn't quite make sense actually means you're halfway toward getting it! Take the speed of light, for instance. If you travelled for 1,000 years at the speed of light, according to Einstein's calculations of a thing called "time dilation", you will actually have travelled for 1,005 years.'

I scribbled an equation on my napkin:

$$T = \frac{T_0}{\sqrt{1 - \frac{v^2}{c^2}}}$$

'This is a formula from Einstein's theory of special relativity, where c is the speed of light . . .'

I prattled on for two more minutes before I looked up to find Dan just staring at me.

I stopped, embarrassed. 'Sorry, I just get carried away when I think about all this.'

He laughed. 'That's okay. I like seeing you get carried away. It's very charming. So, let me get this straight. You're telling me that if I travel for 1,000 years at the speed of light I will have actually travelled for 1,005 years?'

'Yes,' I said brightly.

He rolled his eyes. 'I think I'll stick to chasing bad guys.'

He nodded at my silver bracelet. 'Tell me about that? You're always wearing it.'

'It's a long story,' I said. 'It was a gift from both my parents at first and then my father updated it twice. It's engraved on the inside with messages from them. By wearing it, I feel like I carry them with me.'

'Nice,' Dan said.

The main course arrived and our conversation turned to Dan's life.

'I'm not going to be in New York much longer,' he said.

'Where are you going?'

'I've been recalled to D.C. The Army asked the Treasury Department for the names of some agents who could speak German. Something about a new agency. My name got thrown up, so I leave next week.'

'What about your work here with Mancino and the gangs?'

'My bosses are gonna let me finish it,' Dan said, 'with a bang. I got a major operation planned in a few days' time. Treasury and the New York P.D. are working together. We're gonna make a lot of arrests, including Baby Face himself.'

'Be careful,' I said.

'I will,' he said as a shadow fell across our table.

Baby Face Mancino stood over us.

'Hello, Agent Kessler. Mind if I join you?'

DAN'S FACE WENT WHITE.

Large men in dark hats and black overcoats appeared in the back and front doors, guns in their gloved hands.

The waiters and the maître d' had all vanished. The other couple were led away.

The first thing Dan said to Baby Face was, 'Let her go. She's got nothing to do with any of this.'

'The broad stays,' Baby Face Mancino said. 'So, Agent Kessler— Special Agent Daniel Kessler of the Department of the Treasury, Federal Prohibition Agent—a little birdie told me that you're planning to take me down later this week.'

Dan remained dead calm. 'How'd you know?'

'I have my sources.'

'N.Y.P.D.?'

Mancino nodded. 'The chief himself. You should be more careful who you confide in. You Feds are all fine upstanding boy scouts, but the local police, seriously, they're all dumb Irish chumps. Half the cops in this district are on my payroll and the other half drink my booze and gamble in my bars when they're off duty.'

'What do you want from me?' Dan said.

'Oh, nothin'. I just wanted to meet you before I had you and your lady friend taken out back and shot.'

As he said this, I searched for an escape, but there was no way out.

I saw a black Packard limousine parked outside, with Mrs Carol Mancino and four-year-old Douglas Jr sitting in the back and a driver poised at the wheel.

I had to hand it to Baby Face. He was such a cool customer, he could do his deadly business inside the restaurant while his family waited outside in a car with the engine running.

He waved a finger and two of his goons moved in and grabbed Dan and me, ready to yank us from our seats.

When it happened.

A fusillade of deafening gunshots shattered the window beside me, causing an explosion of glass to rain down around us.

We all ducked: Dan, Baby Face and me.

The two goons didn't duck fast enough and their heads were torn open, exploding with blood, and they fell.

The squeal of tyres cut through the air as three black cars, all with armed men standing on their running boards, skidded to simultaneous halts outside the restaurant.

The men brandished Thompson submachine guns: the new weapon of choice for the gangster class, with its high rate of fire, its trademark forward handgrip and circular bullet magazine.

One of the men standing on the side of the lead car fired furiously with his gun, sending a tongue of fire blazing from its muzzle and more bullets whipped over our heads.

I got a brief look at him.

It was Lucky Luciano.

Baby Face Mancino's loyal lieutenant was no longer very loyal. He was staging a takeover, a very hostile takeover.

What happened next happened very fast.

Lucky's men leapt off their cars—some raining gunfire on the restaurant while others raced for the limousine containing Mancino's wife and son.

And I realised.

This wasn't just an assassination attempt on Baby Face's life.

It was also a kidnapping.

And Dan and I were caught in the middle of it.

Pinned between Mancino's surviving men in the restaurant and Lucky's attackers outside—who were all now exchanging booming gunfire with each other—we did the only thing we could do.

We dived out through the shattered window onto the pavement outside and scurried for cover behind a nearby shuttered newsstand.

'This way!' Dan pulled me left toward the safety of a side alley.

I was about to follow him when I heard a scream—from Mrs Mancino—and turned and saw them.

One of Lucky Luciano's thugs had just yanked young Douglas Mancino Jr from his mother's grasp, hauling him out of the limousine as she fell out of the car into the gutter, shrieking in protest.

As he was manhandled away, the struggling boy shouted, 'Mama! Mama!'

To this day, I'm not sure what made me do it.

Maybe it was the cry of a mother losing her child, maybe it was the cry of the child, or maybe it was the thought of what had happened to those other recently kidnapped children. I don't know.

But in that moment I freed myself from Dan's grip and raced toward the gangster holding the boy.

I tackled him bodily, with my shoulder, knocking him against a lamppost.

He lost his balance, but he was far bigger than I was, and so didn't fall. He raised his pistol at me and—*bang!*—the back of his head exploded with blood and he fell, releasing the boy, and I turned to see Dan with his M1911 Colt pistol levelled and smoking.

He'd shot the gangster dead.

And suddenly I was moving, grabbing Mancino's son by the hand and with Dan by my side, we raced up the stairs of the el-train station, trying to get the lad clear of the gangsters on the street still firing their guns into the restaurant, pinning Baby Face down.

Lucky saw us flee and pointed to three of his men. 'Get the boy! And kill those two!'

DAN AND I POUNDED up the iron stairs, pulling the little boy with us, running as fast as we could.

Bullet sparks chased us, pinging off the girders.

Dan fired back with his pistol, striking the iron uprights of the staircase as Luciano's three thugs reached the bottom.

We rose onto the station's platform just as a train pulled in.

We were high above the street now, three storeys off the ground, and we could still hear the gunbattle raging below.

'Go! Go! Get inside!' Dan urged and we raced forward along the platform and dashed inside the open doors of the train's second carriage.

Then the doors began to close—but not before the three goons came bounding out of the staircase and dived into one of the rear carriages behind us—and the train pulled out and suddenly we were moving, on the train, with Mancino's four-year-old son, and three heavily armed gangsters on the train with us, a couple of carriages behind.

It was after eight and Christmas Eve so there weren't many passengers on the train, maybe four in each carriage.

Who knows what they thought as Lucky Luciano's men opened

fire with their Tommy guns down the length of the train, shattering the windows of the connecting doors between the carriages.

Dan gamely fired back with his Colt pistol, and hit one of them, throwing his head back and the man fell.

The train picked up speed, shooming along its elevated rails between the warehouses, tenements and buildings of lower Manhattan.

The two remaining goons leapfrogged their way forward, moving from their carriage to the third one. They were only one carriage away from us now.

'How long to the next station?' Dan asked hurriedly.

'Too long,' I said. 'We're not gonna make it before those guys reach us.'

The train hit a curve, rumbling along on its raised tracks.

'Damn it, what can we do—' Dan started to say when I did it.

I yanked on the Emergency Stop cable hanging from the ceiling.

The response was immediate.

The train's wheels shrieked as they locked up and the train skidded to a halt high above the streets.

The two gangsters were thrown to the ground, landing on their faces.

'This way,' I urged Dan, guiding him to one of the side doors.

I threw it open and jumped down to the tracks. Dan handed the boy down to me and followed as I ran down the tracks in front of the stopped train, high above the dim streets of southern New York City, dancing across the wooden slats of the tracks.

'Where are you going?' Dan yelled.

'Just move!' I called back. 'We have to get there before they get out of the train.'

Thirty seconds later, Lucky Luciano's two thugs emerged from the stationary el-train, their Tommy guns firing, their bullets strafing the brickwork of a building as we raced around the corner, taking cover behind it.

The two thugs charged down the tracks, gripping their deadly submachine guns, searching for the couple who had taken Mancino's boy.

They rounded the corner, guns up . . .

. . . only to see empty railway tracks stretching away in front of them.

They made it all the way to the next station, but found nothing.

Confounded and confused, they ran off as police sirens began to sound from the direction of Pearl Street.

Dan and I—with Baby Face Mancino's four-year-old son wedged between us—crouched tensely underneath the window of my old dorm room at the Graham-Coulson Secretarial School for Ladies.

As the two gun-wielding thugs had walked past us on the tracks outside the window—not five yards away—we had held our breaths.

Luckily, it being Christmas, there was no-one sleeping in the dorm room at that time and we had managed to open the window—its lock still unfixed—and dive inside before they'd rounded the corner.

For a long while after the thugs passed, we didn't dare move.

In fact, we ended up sleeping in the dorm room for the remainder of the night and woke on Christmas morning in the same lumpy beds that Fanny and I had slept in a few years before while we'd been at secretary school.

When we woke, the little boy was fast asleep, his thumb in his mouth.

DAN AND I RETURNED the boy to Baby Face the next morning.

There was no fieldcraft, no subtlety.

We just walked up the steps of his brownstone townhouse and Dan knocked loudly on the door.

Baby Face answered the door himself and when he saw us, his eyes boggled.

Then Mrs Mancino brushed past him and scooped up the lad and, sobbing, held the boy tightly in her arms and hurried back inside, leaving the two of us standing there on the doorstep, staring at her gangster husband, the man who only twelve hours earlier had ordered us to be killed.

'You two saved my son,' he said.

He turned to face me. 'You. Miss. What's your name?'

'Don't tell him—' Dan began.

'Hanna Fischer,' I said firmly.

'I saw you run from cover *into* a gunbattle to rescue my son. Saw you tackle one of Lucky's men and wrench my boy from him. Why?'

At first, I said nothing. Oddly, I felt no fear under Baby Face's gaze.

Then I said, 'He's just a kid. Whatever business you're involved in—illegal or otherwise—it shouldn't ever involve him. Your enemies were wrong to try and take him.'

'Even though a couple of minutes before, I was gonna kill you?' Baby Face said.

'Didn't make it any less wrong.'

Beside me, Dan inhaled sharply.

Baby Face's wide mouth broadened into a knowing grin. 'I like you, Miss Hanna Fischer. I don't know where you learned it, but you got a fine sense of honour.'

He nodded at Dan. 'You too, Special Agent Kessler of the Treasury Department. Given what you did for my son last night, as of today, I'm gonna consider our differences settled, our ledger squared. Thank you. Thank you, both of you.'

A week later, Dan would leave for D.C. to start work at the government's new agency.

His raid on Mancino's operation never happened. The Christmas Eve Gunfight, as it became known, had raised the temperature on everyone concerned and Mancino and Lucky Luciano—now bitter enemies—cleared out all their illegal booze stashes and shut down their speakeasies for a while.

They reopened after Dan left, safe in the knowledge that the local New York cops were bought off.

As for me, shortly after that time, I hit my savings target, applied for four weeks' leave and bought a third-class steamer ticket for Hamburg.

I was finally going back to Germany.

I was finally going back to Lukas.

> **There is no such thing as high treason against the traitors of 1918.**
>
> – Adolf Hitler, 1924, during his trial
> after the Beer Hall Putsch

GERMANY
1924

My STEAMER DOCKED IN Hamburg on March 31, 1924.

I found a country in chaos.

Inflation was out of control.

Ultranationalist gangs roamed the streets.

And the trial of Adolf Hitler in Bavaria on charges of high treason was causing a national sensation.

Far from being a humiliation of the man, the judges in Hitler's trial—all of them Nazi sympathisers—had allowed him to rant and speak at his pleasure. They even let him cross-examine witnesses.

He turned the trial into his own national—nay, international—propaganda vehicle and far from fighting the charges against him, Hitler happily admitted that he wanted to overthrow the fledgling Weimar government.

When I arrived by train in Berlin on April the 1st, one day later, Hitler was sentenced by the pliant court to five years imprisonment, but he would be eligible for parole in a paltry six months.

The political and journalist classes were horrified.

The Nazi gangs in the streets rejoiced.

It was impossible for me not to notice all this as I arrived in Berlin, but I honestly didn't care.

Bounding off the train, I raced toward Haberlandstrasse and my old neighbourhood to find Lukas.

I stood in front of my old building.

I'm not sure what exactly I had expected to find, but it was not this.

The building had been repaired during the past four years, but in the crevices of its façade, one could still make out dark char-marks from the bonfire that had raged on the night of my father's death.

Another family was living in our apartment.

They were new to Berlin, having only arrived the previous year, and knew nothing but vague rumours of what had transpired here in 1919.

I was told that all of my family's furniture and possessions— those that hadn't been burnt in the fire—had at some point been taken away and disposed of, including my clothes, my books, even my diary. Damn.

I had to locate Lukas.

I went to the Hofstedters' store a few blocks away.

There I found Lukas's father, Herr Hofstedter, at his usual post behind the counter and I breathlessly asked where I could find Lukas.

He looked at me oddly.

'Why, young Hanna, where else but at the Kaiser Wilhelm Institute? Where he always is.'

I registered the strangeness of his reply, but didn't dwell on it.

Thirty minutes later, I dashed through the front doors of the

Kaiser Wilhelm Institute for Physics and asked the receptionist for Lukas's whereabouts, whereupon I was directed to some offices in the physics department on the second floor.

I bounded up the stairs as though my life depended on it and swung into a small office, breathless.

Where I found him.

My Lukas.

He didn't look a day older than when I had left.

He'd always been boyish in that way; slight, lean and bespectacled.

He was sitting at a small desk, reading some research paper when I barged in, my eyes wide, my heart full.

To my great bewilderment, he showed no surprise.

He just frowned.

'Hanna, goodness, whatever is the matter?' he said.

'Lukas!' I said. 'By God, I'm glad to see you! It's been so long—'

'So long? Hanna, are you feeling all right?'

This was not going the way I had planned.

It was like some kind of twisted dream.

And then I saw it.

On his left ring finger.

A gold wedding band.

'You got *married*?' I blurted.

'Uh, yes . . .'

'To who?' I demanded, incredulous.

'Why, who else, Hanna,' Lukas said. 'To you.'

My mind spun.

He had married me?

But how?

Lukas made the connection a moment before I did.

He frowned darkly, stood from his desk, and glared very sternly at me.

'Oh, I see what's going on,' he said. 'Hanna said this might happen. Norma, it's very wrong for you to do this, to arrive out of the blue and impersonate your sister. I'm going to call security and have the guards detain you. Then I shall call the sanitorium and have them come fetch you.'

Now my mind spun even more.

It took all of my will to remain standing and not faint then and there.

'*Norma?*' I said. 'You think I'm Norma. No, I'm Hanna—'

Lukas brushed past me into the hallway outside and called, 'Can I have security here, please!'

I didn't know what to do.

This was a nightmare, a surrealist nightmare.

For four years, I had been trying to work my way back to Berlin, to Lukas, to my life.

But it seemed that my life was no longer mine. In my absence, my sweet love, Lukas, had married someone claiming to be me.

There could be only one suspect.

My brilliant yet troubled twin.

How she had done this, I didn't know. What I did know that day in the Kaiser Wilhelm Institute for Physics was that Lukas thought *I* was *she*, trying to impersonate *me*. And Norma had warned him that I might do this.

I heard their heavy footfalls before I saw them.

Two burly security guards, coming to detain me.

Even though my mind was still reeling, I still had enough wits about me to grasp that whatever scheme Norma had contrived here, right now it was going to end with *me* being taken away to an asylum.

I turned to flee the other way, only to see two more guards appear there.

Before I knew it, the four guards were on me, holding me down as I screamed and protested, kicked and struggled.

And then one of them clubbed me with his nightstick and my world went black.

I AWOKE IN A frightening white-walled room, bound to a wooden wheelchair.

It was a dank little room with a cold tiled floor, a metal sink, a bench and a rolling bed. The white walls were soiled with rust and grime.

I was in a hospital of some sort, an asylum.

The odour of carbolic acid mixed with nastier human smells filled the air.

With a jolt of fear, I recognised the place.

This was the same asylum in Potsdam where Ooma had resided on and off during her youth, the one that I had visited with my father several times.

A gruff fat nurse stood near me, unloading the contents of my shoulder bag onto a counter while a second nurse noted them in a ledger.

'One hairbrush, red,' the first one said briskly.

'Hairbrush, red,' the second nurse said, writing it down.

'One pair of stockings, brown.'

'Stockings, brown.'

'One wallet . . .' The fat nurse paused, frowning. 'Well, well. Our little miss has some real money.'

I saw the first nurse extract my wallet from my bag and open it, revealing a thick wad of U.S. dollars.

In a country being overwhelmed by hyperinflation, this was hard currency.

'The little devil must have stolen it from an American tourist,' the second nurse grunted.

After a time, they departed and I was left alone in the room, bound to the wheelchair.

I fell asleep again.

When I woke, the sky outside the barred window was orange with the sunset.

And someone was sitting in front of me.

Ooma.

'HELLO, HANNA,' SHE WHISPERED. 'But to keep up appearances, I will call you Norma from now on.'

'Ooma!' I struggled against the buckled leather straps binding me to the wheelchair. 'What are you doing? What have you done?'

She looked at me as if I were the one who was insane.

'You *left*, so I assumed your life,' she said.

I tried to absorb this. Such a thing wasn't easy to do. I mean, how could she convince Lukas that she was I—

'Given I had no life of my own, it was only fair, really,' Ooma added. 'Four years ago, I got out of this very asylum and returned to Haberlandstrasse to find our father dead, the family apartment abandoned and you nowhere to be found.

'The neighbours told me what happened, how the lynch mob hanged our sweet father and how you—I—had vanished afterward.

'The apartment had been sealed up while a magistrate had prepared the official declaration of abandonment. That declaration was only a day away when I arrived so I broke in and grabbed as many useful things as I could find—clothes or shoes that had survived the fire—and also . . .'

'My diary,' I said.

'Your diary,' Ooma said. 'It was fun to read it again. Only this time it would probably be better to say that I was *studying* it.'

And so it had flowed from there.

From my diary, she'd learned everything about Lukas, my schooling and my life.

And so she had become me.

'I deflowered your Lukas,' Ooma said. 'Such a sweet boy he was back then. So innocent. But he came around pretty fast when I wrapped my mouth around his cock. The innocent ones are such good fuckers, you know. Earnest.

'He's come along so well with his studies, too. Got his degree in physics and went straight to the Kaiser Wilhelm Institute. We were married soon after he started there. I kept up your physics studies for a while, but they were so tiresome, I got bored. I preferred a life of domesticity paid for by sweet Lukas. I fuck him a couple of times a week and he's happy. He doesn't know that when he is at work, I go to the city and fuck the men at a bar. Life is good as Mrs Hanna Hofstedter.'

I reeled. 'My Lukas . . . how could you . . .?'

She smirked. 'And then you wrote him that letter from New York! That nice long letter which I quickly snatched up when it arrived in the mail at his parents' store. Seriously, you went to secretary school? *Secretary* school? With your brain? Christ all-fucking-mighty.

'I intercepted the other letters that you wrote, too. I must say, they gave me wonderful insights into who you are, which meant I could become even more like you with Lukas. By that I mean: a simpering fool. So, thanks for that.'

She stood. 'Well, I must be going, but don't fret, I've asked the authorities here at the asylum to be kind to you. You're not bad, just mad. I promise I'll visit.'

And then she was gone.

Leaving me in that asylum in the forest near Potsdam, known to all who worked there as the insane Miss Norma Fischer.

That evening, two more nurses came to take me to a dormitory, one that would be locked at night.

By then, however, I had my full wits about me again.

'Would you mind, please,' I said gently to the nurses, 'if I could stop by the church and say my prayers to the good Lord?'

The two nurses swapped looks and shrugged.

We stopped at the old Catholic church connected to the main building by its enclosed colonnade and they waited outside as I knelt in the back row of pews and bowed my head.

Some time later, aware that I hadn't emerged, one of them must have pushed open the doors and peered inside to see me gone and to eventually find the secret door in the back of the confessional, cracked open.

I had already doubled back and snatched my bag from the intake room and was sprinting through the forest, fleeing from that dreadful place.

AT LENGTH I STOPPED running and, in a darkened park on the edge of Potsdam, I sat down on a bench and opened my bag.

I gaped in horror.

All of my money was gone. My prized American money.

No doubt, the nurses at the asylum had taken it, as they probably did from the luggage of all the poor wretches who were imprisoned there.

My return ticket to America *was* still in my bag, though, probably because it was written in English and the nurses had not been able to determine what it was.

My mind raced. I was penniless. In Germany. With nothing but the clothes on my back and a steamer ticket to New York. I didn't even have my own identity.

There was only one place I could think to go.

The next morning, I knocked on the door of 5 Haberlandstrasse.

'Herr Einstein is not taking visitors!' a muffled woman's voice barked from within.

'Please!' I called. 'Tell Herr Einstein that it is Hanna Fischer, daughter of Manfred Fischer, his old friend—'

The door flew open and Einstein appeared, his eyes wide with surprise.

'Young Hanna!' he exclaimed, wrapping me in a delighted embrace. 'Oh, my! Come inside! Come inside!'

Later that day—after I had washed, eaten and slept—I told him my tale, everything that had happened over the previous few days.

When I was finished, he leapt to his feet, all energy.

'This is unacceptable! We must fix this at once!' he exclaimed.

Within an hour, we were in the office of the Director of the Kaiser Wilhelm Institute with the Director himself, Lukas and Ooma.

After Einstein had explained the situation, the Director said, 'Professor Einstein, I'm sorry, but this is most irregular.'

'You,' Einstein jerked his chin at Ooma. 'Your left wrist. Show it to us.'

Ooma hesitated, her eyes darting to mine.

Oh, Einstein, I thought. *You are far cleverer than I.*

Einstein said, 'Manfred Fischer had two twin daughters, Hanna and Norma, known as Ooma. At the age of seventeen, Ooma tried to take her own life by cutting her left wrist twice with a razor blade.'

Ooma made to hide her wrist but before she could, Lukas grabbed it, lifting aside the bracelet that ringed it.

'Good Lord . . .' he whispered, gazing at her exposed wrist.

Ooma's two scars were clearly visible.

And in that moment, I saw a universe of emotions cross Lukas's face. He had been duped—for years—in the most manipulative and callous of ways: his love for me, pure and genuine, had been abducted by another.

His eyes swept from Ooma to me, awash with confusion. He blinked, as if trying to comprehend the lie that the last few years of his life had been.

'Lukas . . .' I reached for his hand.

'No.' He snatched it away. 'No, I have to . . . I can't . . .'

He stormed out of the room, leaving Einstein and me and the Director of the Institute staring at Ooma.

She just shrugged, then smirked. 'Oh, well, it was good while it lasted.'

The police were called.

Before they arrived, Ooma excused herself to go to the ladies' room. The two security guards went with her, but when she didn't emerge after ten minutes, they went inside to discover that she'd slipped out a window and vanished.

The next week went by in a blur.

I stayed with Einstein since I had no money to stay in a hotel of any kind.

It turned out that, in order to fund her profligate lifestyle, Ooma had taken out four different loans in my name, happily defaulting on each one.

To make things worse, she had used Lukas's property as collateral on two of the larger ones, meaning that while she had fled, Lukas and I were left with the debts.

For days, Lukas would not hear my pleas to meet, but eventually we did meet on the grounds of the Institute at lunch on the fourth day.

'I thought she was you,' he said softly. 'I mean, sure, she did some things differently, but she knew things, things that only you and I had discussed.'

'She stole my diary,' I said. 'She knew all of my innermost feelings, especially about you.'

In addition to the financial damage she had inflicted on him, Lukas had also discovered the second life Ooma had been living—under my name—during the day: her frolicking and fornicating in the bars and dens of the city, paid for with the various loans. She even had a secret apartment in the city for her liaisons.

Heartbroken, confused and furious, he had already spoken to a lawyer to initiate an annulment of their sham marriage.

'She used me,' Lukas said. 'Used me like a fool.'

'Lukas, I'm sure we can—'

'No, we can't, Hanna. I can't see you.'

'What?'

'Don't you understand? *I can't even look at you!* Every time I see you, all I see is her, not just cuckolding me but cuckolding my feelings for you.'

He stared off into space. 'Please, Hanna. Just go. Leave me be.'

I went back to Einstein's home on Haberlandstrasse, my mind reeling.

My return to Germany had been an outright disaster. Ooma had destroyed my love, my life and my reputation. Lukas, far from welcoming me back into his arms, had banished me.

I might have had my identity back, but what was it worth?

Beyond the financial frauds, I couldn't begin to imagine what other horrid things Ooma had said or done while she'd acted as me.

And on top of that, all my money had been stolen.

I literally had nothing.

'Herr Einstein, what should I do?' I asked Einstein one night.

He frowned. 'Child. Even with my imaginative mind, I can hardly fathom what has happened to you here and how you must be feeling.

'But Germany is a hard place right now. Jobs are difficult to find and money, if you can earn it, is worthless. And Germany itself grows angrier by the day. It is not a place for you to live, let alone to find your feet again. I am earning more money now, but only through ceaseless appearances and speaking engagements, and it is not enough to be of help to you.

'This will sound terrible, child, but you have in your pocket a solution. A ticket back to America. From what I saw when I was there and from all that you've told me, you have fashioned a life in New York. And in these strange and difficult times, America has promise and potential. My advice to you, Hanna, is to go back there.'

And so I did.

I boarded a train for Hamburg that night and then a steamer the next morning and for the second time in my life, I sailed to America in a stunned daze, wondering what would become of me there.

I RETURNED IN MY melancholy to a buoyant America.

Everybody seemed to be having fun and getting rich.

As I worked away for the stern and reserved Clay Bentley Sr, I watched as Clay Bentley Jr—flush with the paper winnings from his investments—became more lavish in his spending, more outspoken in his political opinions and more openly critical of his father.

With many of his white-shoed gentlemen friends, Bentley Jr became a member of the local Ku Klux Klan coven. The bloodline of the white race, he said, was under threat from the bloodlines of negroes and Jews.

Stella remained in New York City with their son when Bentley Jr attended a Ku Klux Klan march in 1925 in Washington, D.C.

More than 30,000 Klansmen, all dressed in their ghostly white robes—but with their hoods worn brazenly open so that their faces could be clearly seen—marched proudly down Pennsylvania Avenue.

I overheard Bentley Jr, on his return, remark to one of his drinking friends that he had bedded four prostitutes while he had been in D.C. for the march: 'Two of them were negroes and, my oh my, I did enjoy them ladies.'

By 1926, a year later, my life had reacquired some semblance of normality.

I worked. I saw Fanny. I worked some more. I paid my final student-loan instalment to the Graham-Coulson Secretarial School for Ladies: paying off the loan in six years and not ten. Fanny was very proud of me for doing that.

In 1927, along with seemingly all of Manhattan, I celebrated the news that Charles Lindbergh had completed a flight across the Atlantic Ocean from New York to Paris.

Only 25 at the time, Lindbergh became instantly famous and the embodiment of those heady times. He started a thriving airplane business, advised President Hoover on all things aeronautical and was awarded the Congressional Gold Medal.

(In later years, Lindbergh would embody different attitudes. In 1932, when times were not so fine but he was doing famously, his baby was kidnapped for ransom and murdered. During the war, his comments about the supremacy of the white race and the risks of diluting it with inferior bloodlines had many, including President Roosevelt himself, convinced that Lindbergh was a Nazi.)

And then, shortly after Lindbergh's famous flight, Mr Bentley Sr received a curious telegram from none other than Albert Einstein himself.

It seemed that Mr Einstein needed to borrow something from Mr Bentley Sr for a short time to use at some conference in Belgium.

Me.

PART IV

1927
MR EINSTEIN'S
SECRETARY

Einstein! Stop telling God what to do!

– Niels Bohr, physicist and friend of Einstein's

BELGIUM

1927

THE SOLVAY CONFERENCE THAT took place in Brussels, Belgium, in October of 1927 has gone down in history as one of the greatest meetings of minds of all time.

It was the fifth conference of that name, but it has become the most famous because of its incredible list of participants—fifteen of whom would eventually win Nobel Prizes—a list that included Einstein, Bohr, Curie, Schrödinger, Compton, Dirac, Planck and, controversially, Werner Heisenberg.

Einstein already had a secretary, of course, to manage his everyday requirements, but for Solvay he felt he needed an extra assistant with an understanding of physics to take notes for him during the lectures and meetings at which advanced topics would be discussed by the scientific titans there.

When Einstein telegrammed Mr Bentley asking if he could borrow me to be his assistant at the conference, Mr Bentley had happily obliged, thrilled to be able to brag once again that he had loaned out his secretary to the great Einstein.

Mr Bentley was also one of the few people in New York who was aware of my capabilities at physics and he was pleased to send me into the midst of the scientific maestros who would be present in Brussels.

And so in October, 1927, I sailed to the port of Antwerp in Belgium to be Mr Albert Einstein's secretary for the second time.

When I docked in Antwerp I was surprised to see a young man in a black suit waiting for me with a sign with my name on it.

Einstein wasn't there.

He was already at the conference venue in Leopold Park in Brussels, about thirty minutes to the south.

I had been told that the founder of the Solvay Conferences, the wealthy industrialist and philanthropist, Ernest Solvay, was known for lavishing his honoured guests with only the finest accommodations, gifts and travel arrangements.

Evidently, that largesse extended to the *assistants* of those honoured guests and I happily slid into the Renault limousine's luxurious leather back seat and glided south to Brussels in outrageous comfort.

----------→

1945.

The citizens of Antwerp live under near-constant bombardment from Germany's V-2 rockets.

Thousands of Wernher von Braun's deadly missiles strike the port city over a six-month period.

The targets are indiscriminate: cinemas, hospitals, apartment buildings.

In March 1945, Time *magazine will call Antwerp 'The City of Sudden Death'.*

←----------

The Belgian countryside was like something from a fairy tale: colour-ful hamlets nestled beside rivers; churches and castles sat on the high ground overlooking verdant valleys; and of course there were the gorgeous canals.

Arriving on the outskirts of Brussels in my luxurious limousine, I passed something far less whimsical.

Fort Breendonk was a grim grey concrete monstrosity that sat on the landscape like a troll.

It was a fortress, but a very odd one, at the same time both mod-ern and antiquated.

It was built around the beginning of the first war with modern materials—mainly reinforced concrete—but in design it was hope-lessly old, essentially a castle, with thick sturdy walls and a broad moat. Mechanised military technology would make it obsolete before the Great War even ended.

Its design, however, would prove to be very successful for another purpose.

July 1944.

I ride in another limousine down that same rural road between Antwerp and Brussels.

This car is bigger and considerably more luxurious than that Renault from 1927.

It is a Mercedes. Long, large and fast.

Only the most senior Nazis get Mercedes cars. Hitler loves them because they are wholly German and genuinely outstanding.

I sit in silence beside Speer as he reads a report about what's been going on at Fort Breendonk, now a concentration camp.

It has become a problem.

At the huge concrete fortress, I walk behind Speer and some senior SS officers as they discuss the evacuation of the camp.

In a vast system of unspeakably cruel concentration camps, Breendonk's reputation for cruelty stands unmatched except perhaps for Mauthausen.

And with the recent Allied landings in northern France, the Nazis are concerned that Breendonk will be used to unfairly malign the Third Reich's image.

Hence, Speer's visit.

The commandant, Schmitt, was known to set his dogs on prisoners. Worse was his wife, who was known to order arbitrary punishments herself.

The place smells of human excrement. I glimpse some prisoners, peering fearfully out from the shadows of the barracks. They are skeletons with eyes. Barely human anymore.

I feel ill. I have seen this too many times.

I have also seen the secret reports of what happened at Normandy. The Allied landings on the beaches there shocked the Nazis. They were of a scale and a level of daring that none of the German military elite had anticipated.

The Allies are not the dandies Hitler thought they were.

They are on European soil and now they are charging across France, heading for Belgium and Holland.

'I think we can have the whole place cleared by September,' Schmitt says to Speer. 'The guards here are very efficient. They're locals. Belgian SS. They'll get it done.'

Efficient, he says.

This is the kind of bureaucrat-speak that has become common in Nazi Germany's anodyne treatment of genocide.

'Efficient' means that at one of the cruellest camps in Europe, the guards—themselves Belgians—will execute all the inmates.

Speer gives them the go-ahead and we return to our Mercedes limousine and leave.

A short time later, my little Renault limousine arrived at the Institut International de Physique Solvay in Leopold Park, Brussels.

Einstein was standing there waiting for me, his arms wide, his smile even wider.

'My dear Hanna!' he exclaimed.

He was 48 then. His wild hair was already greying, but his natural exuberance was still high.

'Oh, my goodness, it is so wonderful to see you! Wonderful! Come, come!'

He guided me inside.

'Mark my words. *Nothing* can prepare you for what you will see and hear at this event.'

The participants at the 1927 Solvay Conference
1. Max Planck, 2. Marie Curie, 3. Paul Dirac, 4. Albert Einstein,
5. Erwin Schrödinger, 6. Arthur Compton, 7. Werner Heisenberg,
8. Niels Bohr.

THE MAIN TOPIC FOR discussion at the Solvay Conference of 1927 was the new atomic science.

To the common man it seemed like sorcery: that out of the smallest particles of matter could come unfathomable amounts of energy.

And these men—and one woman, the formidable and gruff Marie Curie—were the sorcerers.

They spoke in their own exotic language: waves and photons, neutrons and protons, isotopes and atoms; they even debated robustly about 'uncertainty' as a concept.

And what an odd band of sorcerers they were.

Skinny or fat, usually bespectacled, many of Jewish origin; they were variously British, German, French and Scandinavian.

Among this already incredible gathering of minds, two figures stood out.

First, Einstein, because of his sheer stature in the field.

The other was Werner Heisenberg.

For one thing he was young, visibly younger than the other participants. He was only 26 then, lean and handsome.

And brilliant.

He was the *Wunderkind*, the prodigy who had already made a mark by penning his uncertainty principle.

Unfortunately, he was also an arrogant ass. He often seemed enthralled by his own brilliance, to the point where it grated on his fellow geniuses.

Einstein was not yet on board with the uncertainty principle and Heisenberg, ever the confident young upstart, verged on rudeness as he batted away Einstein's queries with what could only be described as disdain.

I accompanied Einstein to all of the conference's speaking sessions and meetings.

And just as I accompanied him, so too was each of the other great scientists joined by a student or junior professor as their assistant.

Even the *assistants* were accomplished. A conference featuring them alone would have been something.

The American, Arthur Compton, whom I had met with Einstein at Princeton a few years earlier, brought a doctoral student from Yale named Ernest Lawrence.

Bohr brought a young and very gifted physics student named Alexei Zilberman from St Petersburg in Russia.

Heisenberg brought *two* assistants.

The first was a typically stiff male German doctoral student from the University of Göttingen named Kurt. Heisenberg's second assistant, however—typical of the debonair Heisenberg—was a beautiful blonde woman named Brigitte Weber.

Brigitte was a doctoral candidate in the department of physics at the University of Leipzig, where Heisenberg was about to begin his appointment as the head of the department.

She cut a glamorous figure at what was otherwise a very unglamourous conference.

Her shiny blonde hair was cut short and curled at the tips.

She wore a perfectly fitted maroon leather belted coat that accentuated her slim figure.

She coloured her lips with a vivid red lipstick that made many of the bookish scientists and their equally awkward assistants stammer in her presence, an effect that she clearly enjoyed.

And she wore the most delightfully erotic perfume I had ever smelled in my life. It lingered after she passed you, literally arousing your senses.

(For the record, I still wore my Californian Poppy perfume, in memory of my mother. While I still considered it joyful and vivacious, compared to Brigitte's scent, it seemed very conservative.)

In short, Brigitte was the most confident woman I had ever seen in my life and she was a *second* assistant.

For most of the time, she quietly took notes or whispered in Heisenberg's ear, but it must be said that on those occasions when she did ask a question about atomic science or the uncertainty principle, she spoke with a clear knowledge of the field.

Much has been written about the Solvay Conference of 1927 and the discussions and debates that were had there.

What has not been written about was a secret meeting late on the second-to-last evening of the conference that was hosted by the British physicist, Paul Dirac, in his private rooms.

It was attended by a select few of those august scientists, Einstein among them.

And since Einstein went, I went, too.

'So? Can it be done?' Einstein asked.

It was night, after supper. A fire crackled in Dirac's fireplace.

'Yes,' Dirac said. 'Fission of the atom is possible. As a power source, it would be incredible. This atom-based energy could—in theory—fuel humanity's energy requirements for centuries, millennia even.'

'What about as a weapon?' Einstein asked evenly.

'Yes,' Dirac said.

A silence fell over the room.

It was, they all knew, the theoretical consequence of Einstein's equation: $E=mc^2$.

If one could split the atom, one could—in theory—unleash untold amounts of energy.

It would not just be a weapon. It would be a superweapon. The bomb of bombs.

Einstein scowled.

Marie Curie frowned.

Niels Bohr stood up from his chair and pinched his nose in thought.

Arthur Compton said nothing.

Only Heisenberg seemed unperturbed. He slouched lazily in his armchair by the fireplace, sipping cognac. His two assistants, the German lad and the beauty, Brigitte, sat silently behind him.

'I don't see the issue,' he said. 'Don't see it at all. First, to do this, you'd need a whole new element or at least some isotope of uranium, which would be rare to the point of non-existence. Second, you'd need a lot of it. I mean, tons of the stuff. It'd take a thousand years to get the requisite material. And third, even if you did, how would you deliver this atomic bomb to your enemy? It'd be heavier than a small building. You'd have to put it on a cargo ship and sail it into your enemy's harbour, which means it could be torpedoed easily on the way. No. It's impossible.'

Einstein turned to Madame Curie. 'Marie? Your thoughts? You have more experience with uranium than any of us.'

She had won her first Nobel Prize for her work studying uranium rays.

Curie nodded. 'With the new equipment, yes, we are seeing more possibilities for the uranium atom. This development does not surprise me.'

Dirac said, 'Enrico says it can be done.'

Enrico was Enrico Fermi, an Italian physicist and pioneer in the new atomic science. A few years earlier, at the age of 20, Fermi had been one of the first to identify the 'dreadful amounts' of potential energy that Einstein's equation implied.

Heisenberg retorted, 'Fermi also said it wasn't possible in the near future, by which he meant the next century.'

Bohr said, 'The Russians have recently stepped up their mining of uranium. Isn't that right, Alexei?'

Bohr's assistant stepped forward. He was perhaps 25, gawky, thin as a rake, with wide horn-rimmed glasses.

Bohr said, 'Alexei is a remarkable young physicist from St Petersburg. He has studied under me in Copenhagen for the last six months.'

Alexei said, 'Back in 1905, a Russian geologist named Vladimir Vernadsky urged the tsarist government of Russia to start mining uranium in large quantities, but the royal regime ignored him.

'This new regime, these Soviets, while brutal, are smarter. They value science far more than the tsar did. And they read all of your scientific papers. Recognising that uranium might have more value than even Vernadsky thought, the communist regime in Russia now has a dedicated team of scientists based in St Petersburg acquiring uranium and examining its properties.'

Heisenberg shrugged. 'This is still just speculation.'

'That's why it's called *theoretical* physics, Werner,' Bohr said.

Dirac said, 'Have we opened a Pandora's Box with this science?'

Einstein chewed slowly on his pipe.

This was precisely what he was thinking.

Arthur Compton said, 'It also raises a further question: if a nation developed an atom bomb, so to speak, how would they deliver it? If not by Werner's cargo ship, could it be dropped from a plane?'

'That, or a rocket,' Dirac said. 'Fritz von Opel has said outright that he wants to transform his rocket-propelled cars into planes that will one day fly into space.'

'Space!' Heisenberg snorted. 'Rockets?'

He stood up. 'Gentlemen. Madame Curie. Since our conversation has now entered the realm of science fiction, I am going to bed. Good night to you all. Kurt, Brigitte. Come.'

He left, his two assistants hurrying after him.

Einstein turned to Bohr. 'What have you heard about these rocket-vehicles of Opel's?'

He was referring to the vehicles that had been built recently by the German automobile manufacturer.

Opel had staged several public demonstrations of his new technology, launching rocket-mounted automobiles down rails at incredible speeds.

They had been a sensation and the public had loved them. This, however, was the first time I had heard anyone say that Opel wanted to turn his rocket rail-vehicles into rocket-propelled flying aeroplanes.

Bohr said, 'I spoke with one of Opel's partners, Max Valier, and he says the physics are feasible. A rocket today might only be able to fly from Brussels to Antwerp, but in the future, he said, they could fly from Berlin to Paris, or even New York, or, yes, theoretically into space.'

'So the science is still nascent,' Marie Curie said gruffly.

'But then only a few years ago, so was ours, Marie,' Einstein said gently. 'We should keep an eye on Opel's work. Perish the thought that one day a rocket could carry an atomic weapon from one side of the world to the other.'

At eleven, the meeting wound down.

Most of the participants retired, leaving only Einstein, Dirac, Compton and Bohr, plus their assistants, which included the Russian lad, Alexei Zilberman, and me.

'There remains one final matter,' Arthur Compton said. 'We need to get Alexei out of Europe, to America, and we need to do it before this conference ends in two days.'

I looked up, shocked, but Einstein showed no similar alarm. He'd been aware this was going to be discussed.

Bohr saw my reaction.

'Alexei's is a brilliant mind, Hanna. He is a human calculator, capable of solving complex equations at a speed I have never seen before. Although the world doesn't know it yet, this new Soviet regime in Russia is openly hostile to Jews and there have been several horrific pogroms in which the entire Jewish populations of towns have been killed. We can neither let the Soviets take his life because of his faith nor let them harness his abilities in this new atomic science, so we are going to spirit him to America.'

Compton went to the door and said to someone outside, 'Come in now.'

Compton returned, guiding a new young gentleman into the fire-lit room.

I started, because I knew this man.

It was Dan Kessler.

DAN SHOOK HANDS WITH Einstein and the assembled nuclear sorcerers.

'This is Daniel Kessler,' Compton said, 'from the Office of Strategic Services. The O.S.S. will be handling Alexei's extraction from Europe and his relocation to the United States.'

'We call it defection,' Dan said as he shook Alexei's hand familiarly. 'Hello again, Alexei.'

'Dan,' Alexei said his name with visible relief. The young man was, I now understood, extremely nervous about his coming defection.

And suddenly I realised that everyone in that room had been waiting for this moment: Dirac the Briton; Compton the American; Bohr the Dane who had employed Alexei as his assistant and brought him to Belgium for precisely this reason; and Einstein, too.

Dan arrived in front of me and took my hand with a knowing nod.

'Hanna Fischer,' he said. 'Look at you. Professor Einstein's secretary.'

'*Assistant*, if you please, young man,' Einstein said. 'You know this gentleman, Hanna?'

'Yes, Herr Einstein. I do. We met in New York a few years ago. He was battling gangsters back then but now it looks like he has graduated to more worldly matters. This was why you went to Washington, Dan?'

'It was. Nice to see you. I'm glad to see you doing well.'

He turned to the group, his tone becoming professional. 'On Sunday morning, Alexei will leave Brussels on the dawn train to Antwerp. I will be waiting for him at the port there, as will a ship that is scheduled to sail to New York.'

He handed Alexei a train ticket.

Then, to my surprise, he handed one to me, too.

'What is this?' I looked from the ticket to Dan to Einstein.

Dan said, 'We need to be able to explain to anyone who asks why Alexei is leaving the conference early. That reason is going to be you. If anyone asks, you have been unexpectedly recalled to New York by your employer, Mr Bentley, but a fair maiden like you couldn't possibly be expected to travel alone at such an hour, so Alexei—at Professor Einstein's insistence—is accompanying you on the train ride to Antwerp to ensure you reach the ship safely.'

I turned to Einstein and he nodded. 'The boy needs our help, Hanna. We need to get him and his remarkable mind to a safe land.'

Dan smiled at me, that winning smile. 'We got you your own cabin on the boat. You'll be sailing back to New York first class, paid for by Uncle Sam.'

'All right,' I said.

Life is not easy for any of us. But what of
that? We must have perseverance and above
all confidence in ourselves. We must believe
that we are gifted for something and this thing
must be attained.

– Marie Curie

ON MY FINAL FULL day at the Solvay Conference—before my dawn
departure the next morning—I was sitting alone in the park eating
lunch when someone arrived beside me.

It was Marie Curie.

'May I join you?' she asked.

'Why, of course.' I stood quickly, brushing away the crumbs
from my sandwich.

'Oh, sit, sit,' she said. 'Albert told me this morning that you are
the daughter of Sandy Martin.'

I was surprised that the great Curie should know of my mother.

'I . . . I am, yes.'

'I met her once, during a visit to Berlin. She was an exceptional
physicist,' Curie said. 'I am so sorry for your loss and at such a
young age. It was very saddening to me, too.'

'Thank you.'

She leaned closer. 'Albert tells me you are also quite the student
of physics. Gifted, even.'

'He is very kind.'

'He rarely says it of anyone, so I thought I should come and
make your acquaintance. And give you some advice.'

'Advice?'

In the male-dominated world of modern science, Madame Curie had won two Nobel Prizes while raising two children on her own after the death of her husband. If she was going to offer me advice, I was going to listen.

'My advice is this,' she said. '*Get your formal qualifications*. In particular, a doctorate. The world of academic science is a world run by men and all men are peacocks who need to flaunt their status. Look at that ass, Heisenberg, with his two assistants. He brought them only to show off.

'But the only true sign of status in the world of science, young lady, is having the title "Doctor" before your name. That is how you get taken seriously. Your mother knew this and it gave her status. Acquire that title and you will go far.'

And with those words, she was done and she left.

Curie was known for being stern and short, aloof, but only because she didn't want to waste her time.

Her words—so plainly and directly delivered—left a profound mark on me.

I would have been embarrassed to tell the great Madame Curie that I had not even formally graduated high school. The only school I had actually matriculated from was secretary school in New York.

I determined then and there that when I returned to the United States, I would rectify this situation and get my qualifications.

A short time later, I stood to go and as I made my way back to the main hall, I passed Heisenberg's beautiful assistant, Brigitte.

As we crossed, she gave me a nod.

'I love your perfume,' she said.

'Thank you—'

'Is it Californian Poppy? By J. & E. Atkinson of London?'

I blinked. 'Why, yes. Yes, it is.'

'A beautiful fragrance. It suits you.'

She began to move off. Flattered by her attention, I wanted to keep conversing with her, about anything.

So I called after her, 'I very much like your perfume, too. May I ask, what is it called?'

She smiled with her ruby lips. 'It's called Shalimar by Jacques Guerlain.'

'It is a very bold and striking scent,' I said.

'My dear, it's better than that. It's animalistic. Sensual. Designed to awaken desire. Shalimar means "garden of love" and Guerlain himself declared that he wanted it to smell like his mistress.'

I gasped a little.

Brigitte winked. 'I can confirm its effect. This perfume drives men wild.'

She sauntered off down the path.

ON SUNDAY MORNING, SHORTLY before dawn, I arrived with Alexei at the northern train station of Brussels.

The horizon glowed pink. The city lay silent. The canals were as flat as millponds.

Aware of my companion's value to both America and Soviet Russia, I scanned the railway platform for anyone watching or observing us, but saw no-one suspicious.

For a secret mission, it was all rather plain, really.

Nothing like the novels I had read. There were no spies in black hats and dark overcoats leaning against lampposts, smoking cigarettes. No excitement at all.

Alexei and I took our seats in the third carriage and the train pulled out.

I relaxed.

We were on our way. We had made it.

I sat in the aisle seat while Alexei leaned his head against the window and fell asleep.

About twenty minutes later, as I saw the skyline of Antwerp come into view in the distance—it was a classic medieval European city dominated by the lone soaring tower of the Cathedral of

Our Lady—I left Alexei to use the toilet in the rear of the carriage.

When I returned shortly after, Alexei still lay with his head pressed against the window.

As the train crossed the bridge over the River Scheldt, bringing us into the city, I nudged him.

'Come on, sleepyhead, time to go.'

He didn't wake.

Didn't move.

I looked more closely as I shoved him again—

—and glimpsed the blood under his tweed coat.

I tentatively pulled Alexei's coat open and gaped in horror as I saw that his shirt was now stained with an expanding circle of blood.

In the short time I'd been gone, someone had stabbed the boy through the heart.

Murdered him.

My blood froze. I spun, fearful and alert, looking around for—

She was staring right at me.

She sat in a rear-facing seat across the aisle a few rows ahead of mine and she was gazing at me.

Her blonde hair, as usual, was perfectly coifed and she was wearing her narrow-waisted maroon leather belted coat.

Brigitte.

Her eyes never left mine.

They never blinked.

It was the ultimate warning: You didn't see anything. You don't know anything.

I found myself gazing dumbly at her blonde hair and suddenly I realised: it had always been perfect whenever I'd seen her and always the same. A wig.

With a squeal, the train pulled into the terminus at Antwerp and lurched to a stop.

I grabbed my armrest and threw a look at the dead Alexei.

My heart pounding, I whirled and stood up to find Brigitte standing right up close to me, nose to nose.

I didn't know what to do.

I'd never met an assassin before.

'I really do like your perfume,' she said in a Russian accent before sliding past me and stepping off the train, joining all the other passengers outside.

Peering out the window, I saw her walking at the rear of the crowd, where she quickly yanked off both her short blonde wig and her striking maroon jacket and tossed them both in a trash can.

Her hair beneath the wig was dark and her new clothes ordinary.

And then she was gone.

I released the breath I'd been holding.

Then my wits returned and I grabbed my things and scurried off the train. I didn't want to be there when Alexei was discovered by some conductor and have to explain things.

I left the poor boy in his seat, dead and alone, leaning against the window, his eyes closed, his body still.

I arrived at the dock thirty minutes later.

When Dan Kessler saw me coming on my own, he ran to meet me.

'What happened?'

I told him.

Dan scowled. 'Damn it. Of course the Soviets had an agent at that conference. They must've found out about Alexei's plan to defect.'

'I'm sorry, Dan,' I said, bowing my head.

'Oh, Hanna, no. This wasn't your fault. Not at all. You weren't there to protect Alexei. Hell, I'm sorry for putting you in danger. Brigitte—or whatever her real name is—could have killed you, too.'

He guided me toward the ship.

'Hanna, you did a great service to the United States today. It won't be forgotten. I have to head back to our station in Paris and write a very long report about all this.' He sighed. 'Till we meet again, *Fräulein*. Thank you.'

He waited at the bottom of the gangway as I walked up it.

I saw that he waited in that same spot for another forty minutes until the boat pushed away from the dock.

It only occurred to me later that he had done so not out of some kind of wistful fondness for me but rather to make sure no more Soviet agents like Brigitte boarded the boat to kill me.

I SPENT MOST OF the journey back to New York digesting everything I had experienced in Belgium.

The Solvay Conference, its titanic participants, the mental stimulation of the debates and discussions there.

The secret meeting at which I learned that a bomb of unimaginable power could, in theory, be derived from splitting an atom.

Marie Curie's advice.

The surprise reappearance of Dan Kessler in my life and my up-close encounter with a Soviet assassin known only as Brigitte.

I have to say that when my ship docked back in New York City, I was actually a little relieved . . .

. . . until I returned to work at the Woolworth Building where I learned that Mr Clay Bentley Sr was no longer my boss.

In fact, Mr Bentley Sr was no longer at the company that bore his name, having been rolled in a boardroom coup during my short absence.

I figured that, as his secretary I, too, would be out of a job, but that was not to be.

I was now, I was told, going to work for the *new* chairman of

Bentley & Sons Trucking and Shipping, the man who had orchestrated the boardroom coup.

Mr Clay Bentley Jr.

PART V

1927
MR BENTLEY JR'S
SECRETARY

You may have holes in your shoes, but don't let the people out front know it. Shine the tops.

– Earl 'Fatha' Hines, jazz legend

'HERE SHE IS!' CLAY Bentley Jr exclaimed as I entered his office, the same office that his father had occupied when I'd left for Brussels.

Junior had already changed the furniture: his desk, chair and couch were all far more modern than his father's had been.

I waited in the doorway, gripping my notepad uncertainly.

'Come in, come in, Hanna.' Junior ushered me to the couch. 'Sit, sit.'

I sat on the edge of the couch.

I felt tense and must have looked it, because he said, 'Relax. Please. A few things have changed around here, but nothing that affects you.'

That was an understatement.

Over the course of the following week, I learned what had happened.

Clay Jr had convinced the board that Clay Sr's strategies, in this gold rush time, were stale, old and out of date. The company could and should be doing better, and Clay Jr—his finger on the pulse of this new age—had the answers that would make all the shareholders rich.

He staged his coup at an emergency board meeting and in the

space of an hour, Clay Sr had cleaned out his desk and been marched out of the building by security.

I couldn't imagine what it must have been like for my old boss.

Stern as he could be, he was also kind and sensitive.

The humiliation of leaving the offices of the company that bore his name with the contents of his desk in a box must have been awful.

When I finally had a spare moment one Sunday afternoon, I took the train to his home on Long Island and paid him a visit.

Clay Bentley Sr's eyes lit up when he opened his front door and saw me standing there.

'Hanna! How delightful to see you!'

We sat on the back patio and drank lemonade as we watched the sun go down over Long Island Sound.

As was his way, before he would discuss what had happened at the company, Clay Sr insisted on hearing all about my time at the Solvay Conference.

I told him everything, except about Alexei Zilberman and his fate. He didn't need to know about that.

Our conversation turned to the company.

He shook his head.

'My own son. As a businessman, I can actually accept what happened with the board. Business is business. And shareholders will always want better returns and in times like these when every man and his dog seems to be making money easily, I can see why they would warm to Clayton's more modern plans and "company direction". But as a parent, oh Hanna, I just kick myself. How did I raise such a boy?'

I said nothing.

I wondered just how much he knew about his son beyond his callous moves to take over the family business: his womanising, cheating and his gambling with the likes of Baby Face Mancino.

'How are you faring?' I asked gently.

He shrugged. 'As soon as they dumped me, I called my broker and told him to sell all my shares in the company. I didn't do it out of spite. I just don't agree with Clayton's ideas. It's not my company anymore, so I have to let it go.'

'I didn't mean it that way. I meant, how are you feeling? Are you all right, sir?'

To my surprise, his face brightened.

'You know, it's early, but I have to say I'm actually enjoying this leisure time. After selling my stocks, I have more than enough money to live out my days in comfort. I golf and I lunch with old friends. I play bridge. Honestly, part of me wishes I'd retired and done this ten years ago. Oh, and I have been spending more time with—'

At that moment, I heard the front door open inside the house and a woman's voice called, 'Clay? Clay, darling, are you there?'

Mrs Henrietta Henderson appeared in the patio's doorway, wearing a bright dress and holding a bag of groceries.

'Why, Hanna!' she exclaimed. 'Hello!'

Clay Sr cleared his throat, finishing what he'd been saying: 'And I've been spending more time with Henrietta, who I am pleased to say is now my fiancée.'

I leapt out of my chair and embraced them both. I was so happy for them.

He might have lost his company, but Clay Bentley Sr was doing just fine.

WORKING AS CLAY BENTLEY Jr's secretary was not at all like working for his father.

It was, put simply, chaotic.

Junior was unstructured and impulsive, always changing meeting times and dates at the last moment, which invariably resulted in me telephoning the secretaries of the heads of major corporations to apologise and reschedule those meetings.

In his restructuring of Bentley & Sons Trucking and Shipping, Junior had also employed a slick-suited fellow named Art Dunkley who called himself, in the new language of the time, an 'economist'.

Junior had met Dunkley at some society function. Dunkley had graduated from Harvard and was a devoted believer in all things finance.

'Economics is *science*, men!' I heard him say to a gathering of senior executives in Junior's office one morning. 'It's no different from gravity. You do x, you get y. It's mathematics, albeit sometimes complex mathematics outside the abilities of the regular man on the street. And the smart man uses that science to make his money work for him.'

This last part was his mantra.

Make your money work for you.

Selling 'naked put options', using leverage: these were the ways one multiplied one's profits without buying more trucks or booking more train carriages.

And it worked—in the months after Clay Jr took over, the company's profits soared.

I also caught up with Fanny.

Only this time, it wasn't at our usual café near the Woolworth Building, it was in Brooklyn.

She and her husband, Raymond, had moved there after Raymond had been elected to the city council.

'Honestly, my little Polack just loves his politics. Lives for it, he does. Raymey wants to run for the State Senate next year. If he wins, we'll have to move upstate to Albany. Goodness me, at this rate, he'll be president by 1940. Can you imagine the yard signs: RAYMOND WOZNIAK FOR PRESIDENT!'

Of course, Fanny was thrilled to hear about my time in Brussels.

I told her about atoms being the building blocks of all things. I even shared with her the remarkable idea of splitting an atom and potentially unleashing untold amounts of energy.

She listened attentively to all of it but she was most impressed by my encounter with Marie Curie.

'I can't believe you met Madame Curie!' she exclaimed. 'She's just grand! What an outstanding woman!'

'I've taken her advice,' I said. 'Just the other day I enrolled in night school, to complete my high school diploma.'

'Atta girl,' Fanny said. 'Atta girl.'

'What about you?' I'd been talking about myself for far too long. 'How's your job in the world of high finance?'

'Oh, I left that firm on Wall Street. They were a pack of arse-holes. I'm actually thinking of starting my own little investment company here in Brooklyn,' Fanny said. 'Nothing big, mind you, just a little shopfront.'

'That's fantastic, Fanny! Good for you!'

'Gonna be hard getting new clients, but I want to give it a shot.'

'I think you'll do famously!' I said.

I mentioned our bombastic new economist at the company and his declarations about economics being a science.

Fanny nodded. 'A lot of new books are saying that, but I don't know. Would we call poker a science? Good players always do well in a poker game, but never forget there's an element of luck involved. In economics, that's the human element.'

'What do you mean?' I asked.

'What I mean is: *never get between a man and his money*. Money makes people do strange things. All that physics stuff you heard discussed at your conference in Brussels, that's science. You do x, you always get y. Economics isn't like that. I would say it's more about human behaviour than scientific fact.'

I always enjoyed talking with Fanny.

I liked the way she put things.

That said, following the modern economic theories of Mr Art Dunkley, for the next two years the profits of Bentley & Sons Trucking and Shipping soared like never before.

The shareholders were thrilled and in the boardroom Clay Jr basked in their praise.

Mind you, that was when Clay Jr turned up for work at all.

More than anything, during that time my job entailed organising his social calendar.

Managing the upkeep of the new mansion he and Stella had bought in Southampton. Paying the mooring fees for the new yacht he kept on his private dock there. Arranging the staffing and the catering for the enormous society parties Clay Jr threw in the summer.

I paid his bills and essentially managed his life so that he could live without a care in the world.

He never stopped to pay for anything.

I would just pay for it later.

I never worked so hard in my life.

'They're a rotten crowd!' I shouted across the
lawn [to Gatsby]. 'You're worth the whole
damn bunch put together.'

– From: *The Great Gatsby*
by F. Scott Fitzgerald

GIVEN ALL THE SOCIETY aspects of this work, I often had to liaise
with Stella, who, to my surprise, by 1929, despite the company's
soaring success, was now more preoccupied with being a mother to
their seven-year-old son than being a society wife.

'Little Charlie has learning difficulties,' she told me over coffee
one afternoon at their Southampton mansion.

We sat on a patio overlooking the Atlantic Ocean.

Waves lapped the shore. Hundreds of tiny lights hung from
strings above the massive lawn that stretched all the way down to
the ocean. I could see Clay's private pier jutting out into the water
down there, seventy yards away.

Rows of white-clothed tables and folding chairs were set out on
the lawn below the starry array of lights. Stella and Clay Jr were
hosting a party that evening.

It was, quite simply, magnificent, but Stella didn't seem to care.

She said, 'Charlie's teacher says his reading levels are far below
average and he is quiet with the other boys, not making friends.
Clay Jr says he just has to toughen up, be a man in the schoolyard
and all that, but I think the boy is—I don't know—different. Gentle.
And maybe a little slow.'

I remembered the Stella I knew at secretarial school. Beautiful and brash, strong-willed and confident. The secretary who went out and stole Clay Jr from his first wife in order to live the life of a society queen.

And here she was, in that very life, only now she was talking about her quiet little boy and not caring at all for the glamourous party she was hosting that night.

As I listened to Stella talk about her son and his difficulties, I couldn't help but think about what I also knew about her husband.

Like the mistress he kept in the city, in an apartment above a speakeasy down by the fish markets, whom he visited three times a week after lunch and took out most evenings for drinks and gambling.

I recalled the words I'd overheard J.P. Morgan whisper at Stella's wedding to Clay Jr: 'Whenever a man marries his mistress, he leaves a vacancy.'

And so life went.

I worked nonstop keeping up with Clay Jr—shuttling back and forth from the city to the Hamptons—all while studying two nights a week.

And then in August 1929, in a quiet ceremony at my night school on the Lower West Side, I was awarded my high school diploma.

Fanny came into the city to celebrate with me at a little restaurant that served wine under the table.

'What's next for Hanna Fischer, then?' she asked as we surreptitiously toasted my success.

'Keep following Marie Curie's advice: get those qualifications,' I said. 'I'm going to inquire at some universities about studying physics.'

Fanny guffawed and stood up, addressing the other patrons in the restaurant.

'You hear that, losers! This girl here is gonna become an expert in the building blocks of the universe!'

The crowd was unimpressed but Fanny didn't care.

She gave me a great bear hug and whispered, 'I'm so proud of you, honey. You go get 'em.'

Which was exactly what I planned to do, until three months later, when it happened.

WALL ST. IN PANIC AS STOCKS CRASH

– Newspaper headline, October 24, 1929

IN OCTOBER OF 1929, after a decade of unprecedented prosperity, the New York stock market crashed.

Spectacularly.

It began with stutters earlier in the month, 'down days' that after the decade-long bull run, were nonchalantly cast off as minor errors.

And then on October 24: catastrophe.

After an initial panic, the powerful heads of the New York banks—including J.P. Morgan—got together, made gigantic stock orders, and restored confidence.

Five days later, on Tuesday October 29, 'Black Tuesday' as it became known, the market crashed completely and there was no sign of those powerful bankers.

It would be the worst day in the stock market's history.

In a single day, the Dow lost 11.7% of its value.

Over the next two weeks, it would lose almost 50%.

By the time the market collapse was over in mid-1932, it would have lost 89% and the entire country would be in the grip of a crushing Depression.

The boom of the 20s had brought both the wealthy and regular folk to speculating in stocks.

Rich doctors and dentists convinced their assistants to invest their life savings in the market.

And many of these people—no doubt thinking that the market had reached, as Irving Fisher famously proclaimed on October 16, 1929, eight days before the first panic, 'a permanently high plateau'—invested with borrowed funds.

This would prove to be calamitous.

For it compounded their losses.

Not only did they lose *their* money. They also lost the money they had borrowed. Margin loans were called in but there was no money left to pay them off.

Families both rich and poor were wiped out. Ruined. Bankrupted in a matter of days.

Despite one sensationalist report by a British tabloid newspaper that lower Broadway was clogged with the corpses of stockbrokers who had thrown themselves out of skyscraper windows in despair, there weren't that many who killed themselves in this way.

Having said that, I did see the body of one jumper on the pavement only a minute or two after he'd thrown himself off the roof of his building.

The impact on the sidewalk had made a terrible mess. His body had essentially exploded.

July 1943. Near Linz, Austria.

I see an emaciated prisoner sail down through the air and smack against the base of the quarry, his body exploding.

I am at the Mauthausen camp, where starving prisoners quarry the stone intended to build Speer's grand new supercities.

I stand behind Speer and the camp commandant.

Above us rise the so-called Stairs of Death, up which the prisoners must carry heavy blocks of stone.

At the top of the grim uneven stairway, the SS guards play terrible games with the wretched and exhausted prisoners, laughingly calling this cliff 'The Parachutists' Wall' as they push them off.

Beside me, Speer does not appear to notice or care.

He asks the commandant how much more stone will be quarried in the next month and how production of the new Messerschmitt jet planes inside the camp's caverns is coming along.

←——————————

The financial losses from the stock market crash were staggering.

And while the losses suffered by the regular folk who had borrowed money to invest were substantial, in the professional world of brokers and traders, it was said that the ones who were hit hardest of all were the ones who had sold uncovered or 'naked' put options.

People like Mr Clay Bentley Jr.

Clay Jr did not show up for work on October 30.

Nor did he show up the next day or the next.

In the chaos of that tumultuous week, Clay Bentley Jr had disappeared.

I was sent to find him.

I must admit that my first thought was to go to a hospital or the morgue, to see if his body had washed up under the Brooklyn Bridge or been found somewhere with a self-inflicted bullet wound to the head.

Instead, I took the long train ride out to his mansion in Southampton, where I found him.

He wasn't dead.

It was worse than that.

I RANG THE DOORBELL of Clay and Stella's mansion but no-one answered, so I ventured around the side of the house.

I heard their voices before I saw them.

Male voices with Bronx accents.

I turned the corner and beheld the mansion's vast rear lawn running all the way down to the shore of the Atlantic, where Clay had his private pier.

At the very end of that pier, near his sailboat, I saw Clay Jr standing beside the sobbing figure of Stella, who held young Charlie in her arms.

Ten burly men in dark overcoats and black fedoras surrounded them.

At the head of this gang of ruffians, standing right in front of Clay, wearing his signature white felt fedora, was Baby Face Mancino.

It turned out that Clay Jr had not only traded his high-risk options for himself, he had also done so on behalf of his underworld associates, among them Baby Face Mancino.

And he'd lost an enormous amount of Baby Face's money.

I peered out from beside the house to hear Baby Face saying, 'Thought you were so smart, didn't ya, rich boy. Playin' yer fancy stock market wit' my money.'

'Now listen, Mancino, I'll get your money back, I promise,' Clay stammered. 'I just need a little time.'

His hands were tied behind his back and two goons held him firmly. I couldn't be sure, but it also seemed like Clay Jr was standing in something, a small metal tub of some kind.

Mancino shook his head. 'No, no, rich boy. You see, I don't do business the way you do.'

It was then that I saw a second child on the dock, standing among the gangsters: a boy of perhaps ten.

Baby Face's son, Douglas Mancino Jr.

Near the kid sat three opened suitcases.

Rumpled clothing had been tossed out of them, revealing jewellery, gold candlesticks and many wads of cash.

And suddenly I understood.

Clay and Stella had been about to do a runner—on his yacht, with the cash and sellable treasures—when Mancino and his goons had turned up.

'Come on, Doug—' Clay Jr said placatingly.

'*Shut up!*' Baby Face shouted suddenly, volcanically.

Clay bowed his head instantly.

Stella sobbed.

Baby Face began to pace. 'Ya see, rich boy, in my line of work, in my business, if someone fails me as spectacularly as you have, I gotta set an example.'

He nodded at the two men holding Clay Jr. 'Is it set yet?'

'Ready to go, boss,' one of them confirmed.

My eyes went wide as I realised what was in the tub in which Clay Jr was standing.

Cement.

Stella lunged forward, gripping little Charlie and screaming, 'No!' but another goon yanked her back.

I couldn't believe what I was seeing.

Mancino was literally going to drop Clay Jr into the ocean with concrete shoes.

And right then, without thinking, I did something I couldn't quite believe I was capable of.

I stepped out from the side of the house and called, 'Hey! Wait just one minute!'

The group of gangsters on the pier spun as one.

Several whipped up their pistols.

The two boys whirled, startled.

Stella and Clay Jr also turned.

'Hanna! Run! Get out of here!' Stella shouted.

'Hanna! Call the police!' Clay Jr yelled.

But I didn't run or call the police.

Baby Face eyed me coolly.

As he took me in, his eyes narrowed. He held up his hand, indicating for his men to lower their weapons.

I strode down to the pier, more calmly than I thought I was capable of.

Indeed, I felt an odd sense of peace as I approached the circle of gangsters.

'I know you . . .' Baby Face said slowly, examining my face. 'We've met before.'

I stopped on the pier in front of him.

'We have,' I said. 'Six years ago. Luigi's restaurant. The night Lucky Luciano tried to kidnap your son.'

I jerked my chin at the boy.

Mancino stared at me. 'That's right. Hanna. Hanna Fischer. You were with that Treasury agent.'

'I saved your boy's life.'

'That you did.'

'I want to call in that favour now,' I said.

'As I recall, I told you that night that our ledger was squared.'

'I think I still have some credit,' I said. I nodded at Clay Jr, Stella and little Charlie. 'Spare them. For me. And then we're square.'

Stella gaped at me.

Clay Jr, his feet gripped in the cement, looked desperately from me to Mancino.

'Yeah, yeah—' he said.

'No,' Baby Face said. 'This snooty little grease-fuck lost half my money and then he was gonna run. I can't let that stand, not in front of my guys or my son. Gotta make an example outta him.'

I held Baby Face's stare for a moment, then glanced at Stella and little Charlie.

Her tear-filled eyes were wide with fear.

I turned back to Baby Face.

'All right, then,' I said evenly. 'Kill him but spare the wife and the kid.'

Clay Jr's eyes boggled. 'What!? Hanna!'

Mancino gazed at me hard, his eyes inscrutable.

'She won't talk, will she?' he said.

I threw Stella a questioning look.

Stella shook her head vigorously.

'She won't talk,' I said.

'Sure about that?'

'She won't,' I said firmly.

'You got balls of pure steel, Hanna Fischer,' Baby Face said. 'You got a deal. But now we're definitely square.'

He turned to the two men holding Clay Jr and gave them a quick nod.

The two goons immediately shoved Clay Jr off the pier and with a shout of terror, Clay Bentley Jr splashed into the water, his arms bound, his feet embedded in the concrete-filled tub, and he sank, disappearing into the waves.

He never resurfaced.

The little boy, Douglas Mancino Jr, stared at the spot where Clay Jr had vanished under the surface.

Stella closed her eyes, gripped her son to her chest.

Baby Face turned to me. 'You don't talk about this to anyone. She don't talk about this to anyone.'

'We understand,' I said.

Baby Face spun on his heel. 'See you round, Hanna Fischer. You're a piece of work.'

And with that, the gangsters left, with the small boy walking among them.

Standing there on the windswept pier with Stella and her son, I could only watch them go in silence.

STELLA LOST EVERYTHING.

Her husband. Her house. Her car. Her jewellery. Her money. Her friends. And her status.

It was a strange time in those months after the crash.

New York society discovered who'd really had money and who hadn't.

The older money of the established families, built on sturdier foundations, largely withstood the financial storm.

The newer money—whether it was built on debt or loans or was just a plain façade—blew away like houses of straw.

The only thing Stella didn't lose was her son, Charlie.

But she was starting again, from nothing, as a single mother.

Clay Jr's debts had been far more massive than anyone imagined. Bentley & Sons Shipping and Trucking was liquidated completely and when the repossessors came calling for his personal items, they took everything.

I let Stella and Charlie stay with me during that time and I watched as her society friends shunned her and left her to fend for herself.

Put simply, Stella needed to work again.

The woman who had schemed so hard to remove herself from the working class needed a job.

Of course, no-one in the city was hiring anybody and even if they had been, Stella's resumé wasn't exactly current.

But I convinced someone to hire her.

'Hanna, you owe me big time for this,' Fanny said as Stella got settled in the outer office of Fanny's little operation in Brooklyn. '*Big time*.'

Fanny and her new business had survived the crash largely unscathed, chiefly because Fanny had sold almost all of her holdings a month earlier when she had received a tip from a doorman. ('This market is just out of control,' she'd told me at the time. 'Every idiot is making paper profits, so they think they're an expert. When doormen are giving you stock tips, it's time to get out.')

'You're a good person, Fanny,' I said. 'She needs help.'

'You think Stella'd do the same for us?' Fanny asked.

'I don't know. But it's what we'll do.'

Fanny groaned. 'All right, fine. Let's see if she remembers how to type.'

As for me, after the crash I lost my job as well.

When the company was liquidated, we were all let go.

When I received my severance papers, however, accompanying them was a note from Mr Clay Bentley Sr requesting me to call on him.

And so I went to his home on Long Island for afternoon tea again.

'Are you all right, sir?' I asked as I sipped my tea. 'I mean, after what happened to Clay Jr?'

He shook his head sadly. 'Clay Jr and I hadn't spoken for a while. He was a different man to me and, well, he chose his path . . .' His voice trailed off.

'Has the crash been hard on you?' I asked.

'Oh, no, not at all,' Clay Sr said, brightening. 'Turned out, getting kicked out of my own company was the best thing for me. As I said, I sold all my stock back then, so it didn't affect us.'

Henrietta sat beside him, smiling kindly.

Clay Sr leaned forward. 'But none of that is why I invited you here, Hanna. Now, I understand that with the dissolving of the company, you're out of a job, am I right?'

'That's right, sir,' I said.

'I figured as much, so I took the liberty of telegraphing an old acquaintance and asking if he had a position you could fill. He wrote back almost immediately and said he would love to employ you.'

I sat up. 'Why, Mr Bentley, that is most kind of you. Who is this gentleman?'

'Why, who else?' Clay Sr said. 'Albert Einstein.'

FROM THE SECOND
INTERROGATION
BERLIN, GERMANY, 1942

INTERROGATOR (OBERGRUPPENFÜHRER HEYDRICH):
Miss Fischer, you spent ten years or so living in America,
correct?

FISCHER: That is correct.

INTERROGATOR: When did you return to Germany?

FISCHER: Sometime around 1930, not long after the crash.

INTERROGATOR: Why did you come back?

FISCHER: I got a job working for Professor Einstein as his
research assistant.

INTERROGATOR: We would like to know about your time
with Einstein, including his connections with Niels Bohr
and Enrico Fermi. Be careful to tell us the truth now, young
miss, as we may know more than you think.

> To all the millions of discontented, Hitler in a whirlwind campaign offered what seemed to them, in their misery, some measure of hope. He would make Germany strong again, refuse to pay reparations, repudiate the Versailles Treaty, stamp out corruption, bring the money barons to heel (especially if they were Jews) and see to it that every German had a job and bread.
>
> – From: William L. Shirer, *The Rise and Fall of the Third Reich*

BERLIN
1930

I BEGAN WORKING FOR Einstein in Berlin in March of 1930.

By then he had employed Helen Dukas as his principal secretary. She managed his life and calendar and general correspondence. She was, I have to say, simply superb.

What he needed, however, was an assistant with scientific knowledge who could assess and prioritise the many research papers that were sent to him for review and endorsement.

Einstein was well aware that an endorsement from him could make a young physicist's career, so he had to be selective in those he chose. This was where I came in.

It was, put simply, marvellous.

All the while I worked for him, Einstein encouraged me to study in my free time and in this way, slowly, part-time, I began to study my beloved physics at a university level.

Germany, however, was not marvellous.

The Depression hit it hard. Millions were jobless, penniless and homeless.

Anger and resentment were everywhere and both were constantly stoked by Hitler and his rising National Socialist Party.

Hitler's genius was simple: he gave Germans someone to blame.

Jews. Marxists. Communists. The traitors who had signed the Treaty of Versailles. International bankers who were keeping Germany from its rightful place at the top of the global order.

Honest Germans had done nothing wrong. This had been done to them.

For almost its entire existence, the Nazi Party had been a fringe party of rabblerousers, garnering a tiny percentage of the vote in their best years.

In the national elections in September 1930 the Nazis won nearly 20% of the vote, becoming the second-largest political party in the country.

Two years later, on a platform of *ending democracy in Germany*, the Nazis won an astonishing 37% of the vote, giving it the largest number of members in the Reichstag but not yet full control.

Germany was in darkness and Hitler, with his promises of prosperity and national glory, offered a new source of light.

I settled into a new routine with Einstein.

Over the course of a year, he would work from three locations: his office at the University of Berlin; in America during the winter; and in the summer at his second home on the shores of Lake Schwielow in Caputh, about an hour from Berlin.

Einstein loved his cottage in Caputh more than any other place in the world.

Built on the edge of a pine forest overlooking the lake, it gave him the one thing he needed above all else: silence in which to think.

He famously loved sailing and it was at Caputh that he did it, often alone.

As is well known now, for his fiftieth birthday, three of his wealthy friends gave him a sailing boat worth 15,000 marks.

What few people know, however, is that this was actually a replacement boat.

Einstein—the brilliant Einstein, the unmatched genius, humanity's greatest living mind—had sunk his first boat in seven feet of water within metres of the dock.

That had been a much smaller boat, and as he had been about to get under way on a solo voyage out on the lake, Einstein—standing up to raise the sail—had overbalanced, causing the little boat to heave over too far and take on water, and before he could do anything to stop it, the boat flooded, tipped over completely and went under.

Einstein—who could not swim well—leapt for his life and managed to clutch on to one of the dock's wooden posts.

When he returned to the house—his clothes dripping wet, his wild mane of hair pressed flat, his moustache drooping—Elsa had laughed uproariously. She never let him forget it.

I would often go for walks down to that jetty.

From the shore, I could just make out the old boat's tilted white mast under the waves a few metres out from the dock. Einstein eventually tied a little red flag to the mast, so he wouldn't hit the submerged boat with his much nicer new one.

★ ★ ★

I should also mention one other important thing about Einstein's house in Caputh.

It was here that he kept his most important research documents and private correspondence—including correspondence with the likes of Bohr about atomic science and its theoretical military uses.

Concerned about people breaking into his office at the university to steal such papers—or just to steal souvenirs, which had happened twice—Einstein didn't keep any important documents there.

He kept them in a safe hidden under a loose floor tile near the coke oven in the cellar of his cottage in Caputh.

I had no idea my head was worth all that.

– Albert Einstein, regarding the bounty
put on his head by the Nazis

THE CALIFORNIA INSTITUTE OF TECHNOLOGY, LOS ANGELES, CALIFORNIA
1933

THE GREATEST TREAT THAT came from working for Einstein was accompanying him on his trips to America in the winter months.

Einstein's reasons for his American sojourns were threefold: rest, mental stimulation and the weather.

In Germany, Einstein was instantly recognisable but in California—with its busy Americans, always hustling—he could walk down a street completely unbothered.

At the same time, at the California Institute of Technology—one of the epicentres of atomic study—he could avail himself of conversations with some of the most brilliant minds in America.

And finally, the weather.

Honestly, winter in southern California is like summer anywhere else. Sunshine, sunsets, outdoor lunches and dinners. It is simply sublime.

On that last trip to Caltech in early 1933, I was present during a private meeting Einstein had with Niels Bohr who was also visiting.

I didn't know just how pivotal this meeting would turn out to be—not only to me, but to the world.

It took place in Einstein's office at Caltech, overlooking a lawn bathed in California sunshine.

I loved Niels Bohr.

Modest, quietly spoken and courteous to all he met, in the years since Solvay he had become a leading figure in atomic science.

Einstein asked him for an update on the topic they had first discussed at their secret meeting at the Solvay Conference in 1927: the weaponisation of atoms.

'Fermi says it is definitely possible,' Bohr said. 'He showed me his calculations. The numbers work. It then becomes a question of turning those calculations into reality.'

'And how feasible is that?' Einstein asked.

Bohr said, 'It would be colossally expensive. I mean *colossally*. But if you had the support of a national government and a small army of the field's finest scientists, it is technically achievable.'

It was shortly after that meeting—when Einstein and I stopped at Princeton on our way back to Europe—that I had saved Einstein from two Nazi kidnapper–assassins.

That was when I ended up inside the Ewing Township County Jail and endured my first prolonged interrogation.

After Kessler and Einstein burst in and rescued me—'She is my secretary!'—I went with them to a nearby Army base.

After making sure we were secure, Dan sat down in front of us and handed us each a small business card.

The card had a list of addresses and phone numbers on it for various cities: New York, Los Angeles, London, Paris, Berlin, even Moscow.

Dan said, 'Professor Einstein. Hanna. This is a very special card and we only give it to very special people. This is a list of safehouses in each of these cities. If you ever find yourself in trouble in any of these places, you can call the applicable telephone number or go to one of these addresses at any time. Any time, you understand.'

'Thank you, Agent Kessler,' Einstein said.

'Yes, thank you,' I said. 'Thank you very much.'

Truth be told, that attempt on Einstein's life had been a clumsy attack by an immature organisation not yet used to pulling the levers of power of an entire country. Once they became the government of Germany, the Nazis would get better at assassinations.

Exhausted from the whole incident, Einstein went off to bed.

Dan and I talked late into the night as we debriefed each other on the courses of our lives since Solvay.

As an agent of the O.S.S. who spoke fluent German, stationed in Washington, D.C., Dan had observed the Nazi Party's ascension to power as it had happened.

I told him about my life: including Clay Bentley Jr's demise at the hands of Baby Face Mancino in the days after the stock market crash in 1929 and my subsequent employment by Albert Einstein.

It was wonderful to see him again and I was so happy he was doing well.

I wished I could have stayed longer but a few days later, I departed for Berlin, travelling ahead of Einstein and Elsa, who would follow in a few weeks.

But as it turned out, Einstein didn't follow me back to Germany.

He would never return to Germany again.

I dare not enter Germany because of Hitler.

– Albert Einstein in a letter
to Margarete Lenbach, February 1933

ON JANUARY 30, 1933, Adolf Hitler was appointed Chancellor of Germany but it was in March of that year that the Nazis really exerted their newfound power.

For that was when they passed the *Enabling Act*, an amendment to the constitution that allowed Hitler and his cabinet to pass laws without the consent of the Reichstag.

The Nazis could now rule by decree.

They quickly eliminated rival parties and flooded Germany with racist and anti-Semitic propaganda.

At Dachau, they established their first *Konzentrationslager*, or 'concentration camp', to hold political prisoners.

The extraordinary thing is how openly they did all this. They were doing exactly what they had promised: dismantling democracy.

Einstein dared to speak out against the Nazi regime, resigning from the Prussian Academy of Sciences and renouncing his German citizenship.

The Nazis' response was swift.

Einstein was attacked relentlessly in the Nazis' newspaper, the *Völkischer Beobachter*, and his works were burned.

And a new, even larger, bounty was put on his head.

When Einstein's associate, the philosopher Theodor Lessing, was assassinated in Czechoslovakia as the result of a similar bounty— and his killers feted as heroes in Germany shortly after—the situation took on a whole new level of menace.

When I returned to Berlin in February of that year, the original plan had been for Einstein and Elsa to follow me a month later after making stops in England and Belgium.

But then came the burning of the Reichstag and the vicious attacks on Einstein in the press.

It was now far too dangerous for Einstein to return to Germany. He and Elsa stopped in England as planned but there they stayed.

And so suddenly I was in Berlin, at Einstein's office, alone, in the terrifying early days of Nazi Germany.

Which was when something very alarming happened.

The Nazis came calling.

It was officially called the 'Law to Remedy the Distress of the People and the Reich' but it became better known as the Enabling Act.

Through its passage, Germany essentially voted to alter itself from a democracy to a dictatorship.

– From: *A Modern History of Germany*, Samuel Spinello

BERLIN, NAZI GERMANY
1933

I WAS ATTENDING TO Einstein's academic and scientific business in his office at the University of Berlin when they came.

Returning to Germany from California had been like returning to hell from heaven.

Rain fell. Black clouds hung over Berlin.

Rallies were now being held almost weekly and they were frightening. Crowds of over 200,000 people shouted and yelled furiously.

The book burnings at the universities literally gave the night-time air a hellish aspect.

And then there were the gangs of Nazi thugs in their brown uniforms—the *Braunhemden*, the brownshirts or 'stormtroopers' as they called themselves—who could now roam the streets with impunity.

German society had been turned on its head.

Hysteria ruled. Knowledge, learning and expertise were deemed dangerous.

And the inmates were now not just running the asylum, they were prowling the streets with the open approval of the new government, beating anyone they chose, sometimes just for wearing glasses.

It is distressing to imagine just how close Einstein got to returning to Germany and being detained by the new regime.

But I was there.

The day the Nazis came, I was in his office filing the latest batch of scientific papers that had been sent to Einstein for endorsement.

As befitted a figure of his stature, Einstein had a small suite of offices at the university. He occupied an inner office while Helen and I did our work in the outer one. Branching off his inner office was a reading room and a filing room, its shelves packed with hundreds of papers and journals.

I should add that Einstein was also the recipient of many gifts from princes, presidents, nations and universities.

I had returned to Berlin to find many gifts waiting for Einstein inside the filing room.

A didgeridoo from the Australian government.

A Roman bust from Italy.

And, quite impressively, a five-foot-tall terracotta warrior from the government of China. (When the gifts came from the representatives of admiring nations, they usually took the form of an item that signified that country's culture.) Inconveniently for me, the terracotta warrior lay inside a long wooden crate in a bedding of straw in the centre of the filing room, so I constantly had to step around it to reach the shelves.

In any case, I was cataloguing some articles in the filing room when I heard footsteps and voices coming from the outer office.

'—have you heard about the Jewish professors? They're all going to be removed.'

'If they haven't fled the country already,' a second voice said.

I knew that second voice.

It was the voice of Werner Heisenberg.

The first voice was younger and male. One of Heisenberg's assistants, I guessed. 'Julius told me about Dachau. They turned the barracks there into a camp. Barbed wire, guards, dogs, the lot. For Jews and political types—'

Heavy boot-steps silenced them as someone else arrived.

This man's voice was deeper, stronger.

'I want everything he's got on the subject, Professor Heisenberg. Correspondence with Bohr. Any articles Bohr sent him. Calculations. Modelling. Everything.'

Heisenberg said, 'I'm telling you, Herr Heydrich, Bohr and his disciples are mistaken. It cannot be done.'

'We have to be sure,' Reinhard Heydrich's voice replied. 'Make sure.'

Heydrich's calm and measured tone sent a chill up my spine.

I held out hope that they didn't know about the cottage at Caputh with the loose tile in the cellar in front of the coke oven.

Then Heisenberg said, 'Einstein also has a summer house in Caputh by the lake. He might have documents or letters there as well.'

Heydrich said, 'I'll leave a squad of stormtroopers for you to use as you see fit. Go to Caputh when you're finished here. Like I said, I want everything. Tear the place apart if you have to. Heil Hitler.'

'Heil Hitler,' Heisenberg replied.

A door slammed. Heydrich left but his squad of stormtroopers evidently remained.

Heisenberg raised his voice. 'Men! You heard the Obergruppenführer. Find everything you can.'

My eyes boggled.

They were going to ransack Einstein's office *now*.

And I was trapped inside the filing room.

My eyes flashing, I searched for an escape, saw a lone small window high up by one of the shelves. It was too far away to get to.

Seconds later, the door to the filing room flew open and into it stepped Heisenberg and two armed stormtroopers.

To be met by a normal, empty filing room.

They saw nothing out of the ordinary.

Just shelves packed with files and journals and a long wooden crate with the lid half-closed.

Heisenberg threw off the lid and snorted at the priceless ter-racotta warrior lying inside it. 'Another gift. From the Chinese. Einstein is never coming back. Maybe I can put it in my garden.'

They moved on, grabbing files and boxes from the shelves, searching for correspondence or notes on the science of the atom.

I dared not breathe.

I lay as still as I could inside the wooden crate, *within* its bedding of straw, pressed up against the underside of the Chinese terracotta warrior.

I stayed there for an hour until finally they left the filing room and turned their attentions to the rest of Einstein's suite of offices.

It was dark by then, about six o'clock.

Careful not to make a sound, I slipped out through the high

window in the corner of the filing room and fled into the night, heading for the nearest railway station and a train to get me to Caputh before Heisenberg and the Nazis got there.

CAPUTH

1933

THE TRAIN HAD BARELY pulled to a halt at Caputh station when I ran out of it at full speed.

An old road led through the pine forest to Einstein's house by the lake, but I didn't want to take that.

If Heisenberg and the stormtroopers were going to the house, that was the route they'd take and I didn't want to be caught in the glare of their headlights racing to the same destination.

So I ran through the forest instead.

Fortunately, I knew the trails and with the moon rising overhead, I made good time.

After dashing through the darkened woods, I emerged on open ground and beheld Einstein's cottage overlooking the lake.

I breathed a sigh of relief and risked a smile—

—just as I heard the roar of truck engines and saw several pairs of headlights flashing through the tree trunks.

Heisenberg and the Nazis were arriving.

I sprinted across the wide lawn between the forest and the house— totally exposed—before disappearing behind the side of the cottage just as two troop trucks and a black Mercedes saloon car rumbled out of the forest onto the wide gravel turnaround in front of the house.

I entered the cottage via the back door, crept silently through its dark rooms.

I saw them through the front windows.

Heisenberg stepped out of the Mercedes and gazed at the house. A dozen stormtroopers jumped out of the trucks behind him.

I didn't have much time.

I raced into the kitchen and headed downstairs into the cellar.

It was cold and musty, unused since October.

I hurried to the coke oven.

It powered the house's central heating system but right now it lay dormant. A manufacturer's plate on its small cast iron door read: J.A. TOPF & SÖHNE.

I dropped to my knees and lifted the loose tile from the floor in front of the oven, revealing a small safe beneath it, sunk into the foundations.

I dialled the combination and yanked open the safe's door.

Three folders stuffed full of documents lay before me.

Albert Einstein's most private thoughts: correspondence with the greatest minds of the age, his own private research and notes, and perhaps most important of all, his correspondence about theoretical atomic weapons.

I snatched all three folders and dashed up the stairs, arriving in the kitchen just as someone kicked in the main front door.

Flashlight beams sabred through the entrance hall as storm-troopers rushed inside.

Peering out from the kitchen windows, I saw more Nazis fanning out across the lawn over which I had come, machine guns in their hands, forming a perimeter.

I couldn't leave that way.

My gaze shifted left, landing on the lake . . .

. . . and Einstein's gorgeous sailing boat parked at the end of it, bobbing gently in the water, all its windows and hatches battened down for the winter.

I had about ten seconds till the perimeter troops came fully around the cottage and blocked off that escape route, too.

I didn't have a choice.

I bolted out the kitchen door, running for all I was worth across the rear lawn, heading for the lake.

The last thing I heard was Heisenberg entering the house, calling, 'Tear it apart!'

If my method of concealment at Einstein's office—hiding under the straw inside the crate containing the Chinese terracotta warrior—had been somewhat strange, then the one I used at his Caputh house was outrageous.

The Nazi guards swept around the house, guns up, surrounding it, searching for anyone who might be nearby.

But they found no-one.

Not under the jetty, nor inside Einstein's new boat, which they ransacked completely.

I was not in that boat.

I was hiding inside Einstein's other boat, his old boat, the one he had sunk a few metres from the dock, whose tilted mast he had marked with a little red flag.

I bobbed in a pocket of air inside the sunken sailboat, underwater, unseen by the Nazis.

In the tight space, my breaths sounded as loud as cannon fire, but they evidently couldn't hear me, because they never found me.

I waited as long as I dared.

A few hours later, I silently emerged to see the house deserted, gripping my boss's three priceless—if now sopping wet—folders in my hands.

The Nazis had finished their raid of Einstein's home and gone on their way, unaware of the folders or their contents.

I would only discover later just how important this would turn out to be.

———————————⟶

Auschwitz, 1942.

Nine years after that night in Caputh, I see the same manu-facturer's plate on another iron oven door:

J.A. TOPF & SÖHNE

This time the plate isn't mounted on a small furnace that powers a home heating system.

This plate is on not one but three oven doors that are obscenely large.

Speer assesses the three doors with the cool eye of an architect. 'What's the capacity again? How many will it be able to dispose of per day?'

'One thousand,' the Topf company engineer replies.

Speer frowns. 'We need to ramp up our cremation capabilities. We have over 100,000 Soviet prisoners in custody right now and mil-lions more on the way. That's before we even mention the Jews . . .'

I stand silently behind Speer with my pencil poised over my note-pad, my mind overwhelmed with horror at what I am seeing and hearing.

Speer's voice trails off as it often does when calculations take over his busy mind.

He bows his head in thought as if he's solving a math problem and not murder on an industrial scale.

The Topf man says, 'These'll be much quicker than the original ovens. You'll be able to shove the bodies in more easily. Plus, you won't be using coffins like they do at regular crematoriums.'

I almost vomit.

The landscape around us is stark and barren. It is a sickly yellow, as if made of sulphur. Nothing grows here.

It is a fitting venue for hell on Earth.

I took a long, circuitous route back to Berlin.

It was late, two in the morning, when I arrived at a nondescript brick house a few blocks west of the Tiergarten.

I looked again at the address on the soggy card, the business card Dan Kessler had given to me after the incident at Princeton, the one with the list of safehouses and telephone numbers on it for use in the event of an emergency.

I knocked on the door.

A light came on and moments later I saw a shadow cover the other side of the peephole: someone checking to see who could possibly be knocking at that hour.

The door flew open.

Standing there, his eyes wide, was Special Agent Dan Kessler.

WHEN HE SAW ME standing in the doorway of his safehouse in Berlin that night, Dan swept me inside.

'What are you doing in Berlin?' I asked.

'The United States Government is very worried about the Nazis. I was ordered to Berlin just a few days ago to manage the O.S.S.'s operations here: watch the Nazis and report back to D.C. Jesus. This whole country has lost its collective mind.'

'You can say that again,' I said.

I then told him how I came to be at his safehouse: my experience at Einstein's office at the university and my dash to Caputh.

I handed Dan the damp files. 'For what it's worth, here are his documents from the cottage. Maybe you can get them back to him sometime in the future, after they dry out.

'And now,' I concluded, 'well, I can't go back to Einstein's office. And while the Nazis are in charge, Einstein isn't coming back. I'm out of a job and out of options in the middle of the worst Depression in modern history. I have no work, no family and practically no money.'

Dan looked at me, his eyes narrowing.

'You know,' he said. 'I might be able to get you a job. In fact, if you're up for it, I might be able to get you two jobs.'

THE NEXT DAY, DAN brought me into his office and handed me a dossier.

Paperclipped to its cover was a photo of a handsome young man with a long face and penetrating eyes. He had a curious asymmetrical hairline: it receded higher on the right side of his forehead than it did on the left.

'This is Albert Speer,' Dan said. 'He's an architect—young, only 27—and by all accounts, quite a good one. He's the protégé of Paul Troost, Hitler's favourite architect. Speer's well educated and comes from wealth, which is unusual in the Nazi Party.'

This was more than unusual.

The Nazis despised intellectuals and the wealthy with equal fervour. They prided themselves on being the party of the common man.

Dan went on. 'Speer joined the Nazi Party in '31, which is curious. From everything we've discovered about him, he's not a fanatic. And yet he joined the party well before its big recent election win.'

'How do you explain it?'

'In a word, *ambition*,' Dan said. 'He's smart—really smart—but he's also on a mission. We think Speer joined the Party because he saw what was coming and made a calculated bet. He knew that if he was already a member of the Party when the Nazis came to power, he'd be well placed in their regime. He was right. The Nazis honour early members much more than the Johnny-come-latelies who only joined up after they were in charge.'

'So how does this affect me?' I asked.

'Through my cover job running a steel importing company, I've met Speer at several business lunches. His boss, Troost, is very close with Hitler and Speer says that Hitler has grand plans for Germany: monumentalist architecture, triumphal arches, squares and boulevards.

'Troost's star is rising and, with it, Speer's. Speer told me just last week that Hitler himself praised some of his own designs. The guy was beaming, practically glowing with pride.'

I was still wondering where this was going.

Dan said, 'Now, through certain sources, I've discovered that Paul Troost is sick. Very sick. He may even be dying. If Troost dies, Speer will, in all likelihood, take over as Hitler's preferred architect.'

'And my place in this?'

'Speer told me last week that he and Troost are busier than ever, trying to keep up with all of Hitler's demands. Speer said he's so busy that he needs a second secretary.'

Dan let that last sentence hang in the air.

'Wait. You want me to be this young architect's secretary?'

Dan nodded. 'The United States Government would like to know as much as it can about Adolf Hitler. His movements, his moods and his plans for the future.

'This Speer is smart, educated, *cultured*, but don't be fooled. He's also shrewd. The way I see it, if he keeps rising the way he's been rising and Troost dies within the next few years, I think Speer's gonna be a player in the new regime, somebody who is very close to Hitler.

'I said I might be able to get you two jobs: you work for Speer as his secretary and at the same time, you work for me—reporting on what you see and hear during his meetings with Hitler and the Nazi leadership.'

I frowned. 'What about the Nazis? If this Speer becomes important, won't they find out who I am? The half-American daughter of a traitor of Versailles?'

'I can fix that. I mean, *Fischer* is one of the most common surnames in Germany. My office can create fake papers for you: birth certificate, genealogy, address history. The Nazis didn't exactly help themselves when they burned down the Reichstag: a whole lot of government documents were destroyed. That helps us a lot.'

I must have looked doubtful because Dan quickly leaned forward, adding, 'I mean, hey, nothing might come of it and if that's the case, you can quit and I can find you a new job somewhere else—'

I held up my hand and he cut himself off.

'Just so I'm clear. You want me to be a spy? For America? Against the Nazis?'

Dan swallowed. 'Well, I mean . . . I thought, given what happened to your father and to Einstein, you might, I mean . . . but only if you wanted—'

I held up my hand again, silencing him.

'It's okay,' I said. 'I'll do it.'

FROM THE SECOND INTERROGATION
BERLIN, GERMANY, 1942

INTERROGATOR (OBERGRUPPENFÜHRER HEYDRICH):
Miss Fischer, you are currently the principal private
secretary to Albert Speer are you not?

FISCHER: I am.

INTERROGATOR: And this work brings you into regular
close contact with the Führer does it not?

FISCHER: It does, yes.

INTERROGATOR: How did you come to work for Speer?

FISCHER: It was sometime in '33, as I recall. Speer
needed a second secretary so a mutual friend arranged an
introduction. I interviewed with Speer twice and got the job.

PART VI

1933
MR SPEER'S
SECRETARY

I, too, was intoxicated by the idea of using drawings, money, and construction firms to create stone witnesses to history, and thus affirm our claim that our works would survive for a thousand years.

– From: Albert Speer, *Inside the Third Reich: Memoirs*

The man who enjoys marching in line and file to the strains of music falls below my contempt.

– Albert Einstein

BERLIN
1933

ALBERT SPEER WAS A study in contradictions.

As I began working for him and got to know him better, I realised that Dan Kessler's dossier on him only went so far.

For instance, Speer didn't just hail from wealth. He hailed from great wealth.

His childhood and youth had been easy, free of any kind of want. As a young man he had gone on sailing holidays.

And he wasn't just *quite* brilliant.

He was an intellectual's intellectual, so well read in philosophy, science and history that he could quote Kant, Nietzsche and Schopenhauer at will.

And yet he worked for a group of boorish thugs.

About a year after I started working for Speer, it happened.

Speer's boss and mentor, Paul Troost, died.

And so, at the age of 28, Albert Speer became Adolf Hitler's chief architect and a member of the Führer's inner circle.

Hitler met with Speer every day, often during a morning walk or at dinner. The Führer was obsessed with architecture and loved talking with Speer about it.

At first, I was not present for these meetings.

That was the duty of Speer's primary secretary, an older lady named Mrs Liesel Veight, who would be waiting in the garden with her notepad at the end of their walks to scribble down all the things Speer had been commanded to build, accomplish or do by the all-powerful Führer.

I would linger in the background or on the periphery, receiving those notes back at our office or making sure the orders in them were carried out.

But then as winter came on, Mrs Veight took ill and could no longer tolerate standing outside in the cold. Soon she retired from work altogether and I became Mr Speer's principal secretary.

And with my elevation came proximity to the Führer.

The world would see Hitler from afar—in films and newsreels and in newspaper photos, waving from balconies, riding in limousines and giving incendiary speeches.

As a lowly secretary, lingering in the background, I would see him up close.

Dan Kessler could not have wished for more.

> I am beginning to comprehend some of the
> reasons for Hitler's astounding success . . . he
> is restoring pageantry and color and mysticism
> to the drab lives of 20th century Germans.
>
> – William L. Shirer, diary entry

HITLER.

What is there to say that is not already known?

If Speer was an enigma then Hitler was that, too, but multiplied a thousandfold.

To Germans, he presented himself as a humble man of the people, a pure patriot who hailed from lowly roots.

In private, however, he considered himself a sophisticate, a man of elegant and informed tastes.

And after taking power in 1933, he saw himself as something even more than that. He saw himself as a figure of great historical significance and so he comported himself accordingly.

This grand self-image created an ever-growing distance between the Führer and his original Nazi brothers, the brutes who had tried to seize power with him during his 'days of struggle' and the failed Beer Hall Putsch of 1923.

By 1933, they had all acquired mansions and high ranks, but they were, to Hitler, still the same brawlers from the previous decade.

Hitler deplored their tastelessness. They were not just uneducated and lacking in sophistication, they were *embarrassing*.

For he was a statesman now. His former comrades, he said openly, were philistines.

Hitler was also, it must be said, intuitively cunning, the most naturally cunning individual I have ever met.

He could read people—foreign politicians and ambassadors; his own Nazi associates scheming for influence with him; whole crowds in stadiums—like no other.

It was as if he had an innate understanding of a given person's motivations, their incentives, and he could manipulate such people as easily as he breathed.

Not even Goebbels was that good.

Joseph Goebbels only had one gear: full throttle. Hitler had about ten. He could play almost any man like a fiddle.

And yet he was vain.

Extraordinarily vain.

While all the other Nazis wore regular party badges, he alone wore a special badge: his was made of gold and, uniquely, featured an eagle with a swastika gripped in its talons.

His vanity also applied to his lodgings and offices.

Appalled by the ageing state of the presidential residences and offices he had inherited upon attaining the Chancellorship, he redesigned and refurnished all of their interiors.

He could not possibly host international visitors in such shabby rooms, he said.

His offices needed to represent the might and primacy of the German Reich.

As for the exteriors of his government's buildings, well, he had far grander plans for them.

For his was to be a thousand-year Reich.

And this was where Speer came in.

Die Juden sind unser Unglück

(The Jews are our Misfortune)

– Banner at a Nazi rally

NUREMBERG, NAZI GERMANY
1934

SPEER'S FIRST TRIUMPH FOR Hitler came at the Nuremberg rallies of September 1934.

Speer turned the Zeppelin Field at Nuremberg into a colossal shrine to Nazism.

A gigantic steel eagle with a hundred-foot wingspan towered above an elevated stage. Dozens of floodlights sent vertical shafts of light shooting into the night sky above 160,000 uniformed Nazis, arranged in innumerable perfect rows. Red, black and white swastika banners billowed in unison, too many to count.

The famous director Leni Riefenstahl would film these rallies and images of them—and the might of the new Germany—shot around the world.

Just as Hitler wanted.

It was the ultimate piece of propaganda and it was a wild success.

Throughout all this time, fuelled by ambition, Speer worked tirelessly, which meant I worked tirelessly, too.

Every two or three months, I would meet with Dan Kessler by a goose pond in the Tiergarten and inform him of the plans, schemes and machinations within the Nazi elite.

After Speer's triumph at Nuremberg, Speer slept for three days.

I was exhausted, too, and would have done the same were it not for some unexpected news that found its way to me via a secretary I knew in the department of births and deaths.

It was about my sister, Ooma.

Inside a prison at Brandenburg, she had died.

And in her will she had left everything she owned to me.

SINCE SPEER WAS TAKING a few days off, I took the opportunity to travel to Brandenburg.

Ooma had died in a *prison*.

I recalled our past—and her appropriation of my life—and wondered what other trouble she must have got into in order to land there.

I arrived at the prison in the old town of Brandenburg.

I stepped up to the reception counter, introduced myself, presented the record of Ooma's death, and said I was there to collect her personal effects.

The director of the prison came out to greet me.

He flipped through a sheaf of records. After my years in America, I'd forgotten how fanatically attentive to record-keeping Germans were.

'Ah, yes,' he said. 'Norma Fischer. She was actually a patient here when it was a sanatorium for lunatics and schizophrenics, before it was converted into a criminal prison. She was selected for sterilisation.'

The sterilisation law.

Or more formally: *The Law for the Prevention of Progeny with Hereditary Diseases*.

It was passed by the Nazis almost immediately after they came to power so that the mentally ill could not have children and thus weaken the German bloodline.

------------------------→

1940.

I am at the same jail, standing in the same reception area with Speer, only now the facility is called the Brandenburg Euthanasia Centre.

It is a place of horror and screams.

The Nazis have progressed from sterilisation to extermination.

Now they execute the disabled and the mentally ill, for such 'subhumans' dilute the purity of the Aryan race.

←------------------------

'She was *sterilised*?' I asked.

'It appears so, yes,' the prison director said, verifying it in the file. He said it so blithely, so casually.

Jesus, I thought. *They sterilised her.*

'We're just a regular prison now,' he said. 'You know, thieves, rapists, murderers, political undesirables, communists and the like.'

I frowned. 'What was Ooma—Norma—doing here? She wasn't a criminal.'

He flicked some more pages.

'Says here she assaulted her nurses several times. She was a biter. After she bit one nurse in the face, she was charged with assault and convicted. That was around the time the camp became a prison, so she was just kept here.'

With the thieves and rapists and murderers, I thought. *Oh, Lord.*

He opened a door for me. 'Come inside. Her things are in here and as the next of kin, you'll have to let us know what to do with the body.'

After walking down a long hallway, I entered a morgue-like room where a body lay on a steel tray table, covered by a sheet.

So, this is what became of Ooma, I thought.

The director handed me a small bag filled with Ooma's worldly possessions: a purse, a couple of dresses, reading glasses.

I paused.

Ooma had never worn reading glasses.

The director swept back the sheet and I saw the body lying on the steel tray.

It wasn't Ooma.

THE PRISON DIRECTOR NO doubt thought my involuntary gasp of shock was the natural reaction of a family member seeing the corpse of their loved one.

But my horror was of an entirely different kind.

I saw instantly what had happened.

At some point during her time at the concentration camp for the mentally deranged—maybe during its transformation from camp to prison—Ooma had switched identities with some other inmate.

I weighed up whether or not I should inform the director of the error and decided not to. After hearing his nonchalant description of forced sterilisation, I disliked him.

But the fact remained.

Living under some other identity, Ooma—my sister, my calculating sister—was out there, somewhere, in this bizarre country known as Nazi Germany.

Most [of the Nazi leadership] had never been outside Germany; if one of them had taken a pleasure trip to Italy ... the person in question was considered a foreign affairs expert ...

Of the fifty Reichsleiters [national leaders] and Gauleiters [regional governors], the elite of the leadership, only ten had completed a university education ... the majority had never gone beyond secondary school.

– Albert Speer

BERCHTESGADEN, BAVARIA
1935–1936

SPEER BECAME INCREASINGLY CLOSE with Hitler and, after a time, he was considered—along with Goebbels, Himmler and Bormann— part of the Führer's trusted inner circle.

Speer dined with Hitler almost daily: at the Führer's apartments in the Chancellery in Berlin, and at his mountain retreat at Berchtesgaden or, as some called it, Obersalzburg.

Of course, such proximity to the Führer gave Speer enormous power in the Party.

He and I became so well known to Hitler's bodyguards that they soon waved us through the increasingly secure barricades protecting the Führer's various domiciles.

But after a year or more of these dinners, Speer revealed in a rare private outburst to me that he was growing weary of his master.

'Good God,' he exclaimed one morning after yet another dinner with Hitler. 'The man just repeats himself over and over, saying the same things at every single meal. He is like a broken phonograph. And no-one dares say to him, "Sir, we have heard this tale." Lord, if I hear about his time as a courier in the trenches during the war one more time, I swear I shall have a fit.'

In addition to being dully repetitive, Speer said, Hitler was unworldly, humourless, not nearly as cultured or intelligent as he considered himself to be, and racist.

These observations were, of course, coloured by Speer's own arrogance: for, by any objective comparison, he *was* far more cultured and educated than Hitler was.

Speer had equally derogatory opinions of his fellow senior Nazis.

Himmler was obsessed with pseudosciences and pseudohistories that advanced his bizarre theories of a great Germanic race.

Heydrich, the head of the Gestapo, was a psychopath. 'A born killer,' Speer said.

Bormann was a sycophant, ever praising of Hitler, albeit a cunning one. He went wherever Hitler went and soon became Hitler's personal private secretary, managing everything from his calendar to his royalties from *Mein Kampf*.

Bormann was the ultimate Nazi true believer. His wife would ultimately produce ten children for the Reich.

'The man is a pig,' Speer said one day. 'For all his pontificating about the purity of Christian–Nazi dogma, after lunch he goes into a back room off his office and fucks his secretary, Gertrude Schneider.'

Goebbels was a maniac. But he was also slippery. Speer said he should be watched at all times.

Rudolph Hess was just bizarre. When he insisted on bringing his own 'organic' foods to Hitler's dinners, Hitler stopped inviting him altogether.

More important for me—and for my occasional debriefing sessions with Dan Kessler by the goose pond in the Tiergarten—were Hitler's views about the world and rival nations.

Britain was to be respected.

It had a long history of fending off attacks from various European empires and, as Hitler had seen for himself during the first war, its men had fought in the muddy trenches with bravery and resolve.

Japan was a nation that could be considered a legitimate world power, although when Hitler allied Germany to Japan a few years later, it was reluctantly, as it was difficult for him to accord his blue-eyed blonde-haired views of an Aryan master race with an alliance with 'yellow-skinned men'.

Italy was unreliable and Mussolini a useful fool.

And then there was America.

'The Führer thinks America is soft,' I informed Dan one day by the pond in the Tiergarten.

'Soft?' Dan said.

'Because it has never been truly tested. America hardly participated in the war, Hitler says, not until the very end, in 1918. I have heard him say this myself. Hitler dismisses America as a bastard nation that could not be more different from the purity of Germany: a street dog born out of multiple inferior immigrant breeds. He is planning for the upcoming Olympic Games in Berlin to exemplify this.'

The staging of the 1936 Summer Games in Nazi Germany was a very controversial issue at that time.

The Games had been awarded to Berlin by the International Olympic Committee *before* the Nazis had taken power, but now that they were in charge, many countries, fearful that Hitler and his Nazi regime would use the Olympics to advance their racist ideologies, demanded that the Games be stripped from the Germans. The IOC refused.

'That's exactly what Hitler intends to do,' I said. 'He said as much to Speer a week ago.'

'How are their plans progressing?'

'Speer is loving it. Hitler has given him an unlimited budget and Speer enjoys nothing more than a vast canvas. Three days ago, we did a rehearsal for the light show that he has concocted for the closing ceremony. It's simply colossal. It'll make the "Cathedral of Light" that he put on at Nuremberg look quaint.'

Dan nodded.

Then he looked at me closely.

It turned out that his bosses also had an ulterior purpose for the 1936 Olympic Games.

Dan said, 'On the Soviet Olympic team are two brothers—Igor and Anatoly Kurtzov. They are both officers in the Red Army and champion pistol shooters who are expected to win medals. They are also high-level mechanical engineers in the field of liquid-fuelled ballistic rockets who want to defect to the United States.'

'Okay . . .'

'America would very much like to accommodate the Kurtzov brothers. As you can imagine, we'd love to know what the Soviets have been up to in this field, to discover where they're at and maybe learn a few new things.'

'I'm sure,' I said.

'Then you'll also understand that spiriting high-level rocket scientists out of the Soviet Union is not exactly easy. But for two weeks in August of this year, these two Soviet rocket scientists will be in Berlin, among hundreds of athletes and thousands of spectators. We're going to use the cover of the Games to carry out the defection of the Kurtzov brothers to the United States.'

'I see.'

'Has Speer ever mentioned anything about rocketry and the Nazis?'

'A few times. They have a team working on it at the Wehrmacht base in Kummersdorf. It's all being run by some whiz-kid genius.'

'What about atomic science?' Dan asked.

'There is a unit of scientists working on that at the Kaiser Wilhelm Institute. Speer said once that Hitler doesn't think much of atomic science. He considers it Jewish science. Of far more interest to the Führer is the rocket work coming out of Kummersdorf.'

Dan said, 'Is there any way you can find out more?'

'In a few days, I'll know a lot more,' I said. 'Speer and the senior leadership group have been commanded to attend a briefing with the Führer next Monday to report on the status of both the rocket-science and atomic-science projects. I'll get back to you after that meeting.'

THE REICH CHANCELLERY
1936

THE FOLLOWING MONDAY I walked across the pretty little garden
nestled in the courtyard of the Reich Chancellery building, heading
for that meeting.

———————————————————▶

1945.

Russian artillery shells boom as I run headlong through the
Chancellery's garden with Bormann.

It is now a foul mix of dirt, rubble, blood and human body parts.

We race past Hitler's charred corpse lying in a bomb crater beside
Eva Braun's as we flee into the night, trying to outrun the Red Army
now only blocks away.

◀———————————————————

From the garden, I entered the Chancellery and headed upstairs to
the main meeting room.

There I took up my position by the wall with the other secretaries behind Speer, Hitler and the assembled Nazi leadership.

Moments later, the room's enormous door opened and in walked the two scientists in charge of the programs to be discussed.

The man responsible for the rocket program at Kummersdorf was astonishingly young, but his reputation as a genius in the field of rocketry preceded him.

His name: Wernher von Braun.

The man in charge of the atomic science program at the Kaiser Wilhelm Institute, however, was someone I had met before, at the Solvay Conference back in 1927.

Werner Heisenberg.

Heisenberg's star had risen greatly over the last decade, although it must be said that without any Jewish physicists to compete against, the road had been somewhat cleared for him.

I was concerned that he might recognise me from the Solvay Conference and link me to Einstein.

I needn't have worried.

When Heisenberg entered that room with its long table packed with the most senior Nazis in Germany, he did not so much as glance in my direction.

But I remembered him.

Especially how he had led the twin raids on Einstein's office and cottage three years earlier.

Heisenberg was still good-looking, with his swept-back hair and aquiline nose. It also quickly became apparent that he still had an incredibly high opinion of his own intellect.

'Gentlemen,' he began, 'our laboratories here in Germany are the finest in the world. We are, I can confidently say, years ahead of all other nations in our studies of the powers and properties of the atom.'

At the head of the giant table, Hitler listened in unblinking silence.

Bormann feigned interest, glancing thoughtfully at Hitler every few seconds. Behind him, his secretary and mistress, Gertrude Schneider, took rapid notes.

Heisenberg said, 'This *atomic energy*, as we call it, will, in the near future, be a boundless source of power for German cities, factories, even submarines—'

'Get to the point,' Bormann cut in coarsely. 'Can it be used for a weapon? We are told that this science—much of it Jewish in origin, deriving from the work of Einstein—could be used as the source of some kind of *super*weapon, as it were. That is what the Führer wishes to know.'

Heisenberg nodded. 'Right. Well. Theoretically, yes, this is true, but not in the current state of the science—'

'Theoretically?' Speer said, leaning forward.

Heisenberg hesitated. 'I say that because of two things. First, breaking or "fissioning" a nucleus is still just a concept. It has never actually been done. And second, such a theoretical weapon would require an exotic element—in fact, an isotope of that exotic element—known as uranium and, well, sirs, it would take *decades* to amass the requisite amount of uranium for the core of such a weapon—'

'So, it cannot be done,' Hitler said softly and the vast room fell instantly silent.

'No, *mein* Führer,' Heisenberg said.

'Then you are dismissed,' Hitler said.

Heisenberg hesitated again, unused to Hitler's abruptness, before packing up his notes and folders and leaving the room like an admonished schoolboy.

The room's attention turned to the other scientist, von Braun.

His presentation concerned the new science of rocketry and his first photograph—displayed on an easel—brought audible gasps from the assembled Nazis.

Hitler himself leaned forward.

I was shocked by the image.

The photo depicted a rocket that must have been eight storeys tall.

Von Braun said, 'Gentlemen. Our early tests with the Aggregat series of rockets have been exceptionally promising. We have achieved thrust levels in excess of 3,000 pounds and with gyroscopic stabilisation, we expect to achieve stable supersonic flight within a year.'

'What do you mean?' Bormann asked. Science wasn't Bormann's strong suit.

Hitler answered. 'Dr von Braun is talking about a missile that could be launched from Germany and strike London. Am I right, Herr Doktor?'

Von Braun nodded and pointed at his photo of the giant rocket.

'*Mein* Führer, you are indeed correct. However, I think we can do even better than that. I will build you a rocket that can be launched from Germany and strike New York City.'

It was a brilliant chess move by von Braun.

From that moment on, Hitler became obsessed with the rocket program. If it needed extra funds, men or munitions, it got them.

It would have galled Heisenberg to know that von Braun—to Heisenberg, the rocketeers were little better than automobile mechanics—had outplayed him in that room that day.

Heisenberg had been far too theoretical.

Von Braun, on the other hand, had gauged his audience perfectly, and his audience had not been the Nazis assembled around that table.

It had been Hitler.

And Hitler didn't care for lectures about theoretical physics, exotic elements or isotopes. He'd seen war up close, seen men turned into meat by grenades and explosives.

A rocket flying all the way from Germany to an American city: he could picture that.

After von Braun left, Hitler turned to his leadership group. 'Gentlemen? Do you have anything to add to what we have heard?'

Heydrich pushed up his spectacles. '*Mein* Führer, if I may? My agents in Moscow inform me that the Soviets are making significant strides in rocketry. And just as we could fire missiles at America, it would be a terrible thing if, in a year or two, the Soviets could fire missiles from Moscow at Berlin. Two of the Russians' key rocket scientists, a pair of brothers by the name of Kurtzov, will actually be coming to Berlin in a few months to participate in the Olympic Games.'

'What are you suggesting?' Speer asked.

'Rocket science is the future of warfare and we cannot allow the Soviets to advance in it,' Heydrich said. 'I suggest that at the end of the Games, at the conclusion of the closing ceremony when they are briefly separated from their Soviet minders, we abduct the Kurtzov brothers and kill them.'

I had to let Dan know about this.

I managed to meet with him, very briefly, just before the Games began and I told him of the Nazis' plan to assassinate the Kurtzov brothers.

'Damn,' Dan said. 'Do you know how they intend to do it?'

'No. All I know is that Heydrich conceived the plan himself and that he'll have Gestapo agents on the infield dressed as German athletes.'

'They'll have agents on the field? Shit,' Dan said. 'How can we compete with that?'

I said, 'I may have a solution. I was thinking about something I noticed during the rehearsal for the closing ceremony and Speer's light show. There might be an opportunity there, a very slim one, but an opportunity nonetheless.'

'Go on.'

'We grab the Kurtzov brothers *during* the closing ceremony . . .'

I told Dan my idea.

When I was done, he nodded.

'Not much margin for error, but it's not like we have a choice. If it doesn't work, the Nazis'll nab those two Russian boys and they're as good as dead. Let's do it.'

BERLIN
1936

THE BERLIN OLYMPIC GAMES of 1936 were a spectacle on a scale the world had never seen.

This, I reflected—as I watched the opening ceremony from the opulent 'leadership stand' of the new *Olympiastadion* with 100,000 roaring German spectators below me—was what happened when you gave a major international event to an authoritarian regime obsessed with its own self-aggrandisement.

Nazi flags ringed the stadium at perfect intervals. Like soldiers marching in time, they even fluttered in symmetry, a sea of swastikas: red, black and white.

It turned out that Hitler's plan to use the Games to promote the Nazi Party and its racist and anti-Semitic worldviews was far more elaborate than anyone, even Dan, had contemplated.

For these would be the first Olympic Games broadcast on radio and via newsreels and Hitler was a master manipulator of these new forms of media.

Just as he had done at the Nuremberg rallies, he employed Leni Riefenstahl to make a film of the Games, a film created solely to document the superiority of the Nazi ideology.

For these Games, Hitler insisted, would be the perfect vehicle to display what he termed the 'aristocratic principle of Nature', namely, the superiority of the white Aryan race.

Unfortunately for him, a black athlete from America, Jesse Owens, had other ideas.

Owens quickly became the unrivalled star of the Games, winning four gold medals.

'It's as if fate sent Owens to spite Hitler,' I said to Dan Kessler as we stood together in a long queue leading to a food stand amid the bustle of spectators at the *Olympiastadion*.

The atmosphere at the *Olympiastadion*, as it had been at all the other Olympic venues, was like that of a grand carnival.

It was the final day of the Games.

The closing ceremony was only hours away and Dan and I had planned to meet in this queue: just two spectators chatting in the long line as they waited their turn.

The Games, like all Olympics, had created heroes and controversies.

An unfancied American rowing team had defeated the very Aryan German team that everyone had assumed would win gold.

The German equestrian team won every single gold medal in that discipline, a mathematically dubious achievement that raised eyebrows among international journalists. (The local German journalists did not dare question any German achievement, as it could result in their arrest.)

The Kurtzov brothers from the Soviet Union placed fourth and fifth in the pistol-shooting, narrowly missing out on medals.

'It was as if they had other things on their mind,' I said to Dan as we shuffled forward in the queue.

'All right,' Dan said quietly. 'Everything is in place. We're gonna do it during your little window in the closing ceremony, the only time the Kurtzov brothers are out of sight of their Russian minders.'

For the duration of the Games, the Soviet team's members had been watched and escorted by stone-faced chaperones from their homeland.

Hitler, Heydrich, Speer and Dan Kessler were all well aware that these 'chaperones' were officers from the N.K.V.D., the U.S.S.R.'s Commissariat of Internal Affairs, its secret police, making sure that none of the Soviet team took the opportunity to flee during the Games.

That said, Berlin was abuzz.

The citizens of the city delighted in the Games—filling every stadium, cheering every medallist, packing into bars and singing in the streets as they walked home after a given day's events.

And then, when it was all done, the closing ceremony began.

It was night, and the *Olympiastadion* was illuminated by many floodlights. Speer was the master of night-time illumination and he had outdone himself here.

The stadium was full, packed to the brim with spectators.

The infield and the track were covered in athletes from all over the world. They smiled and embraced each other, their races run. Dressed in their national outfits, some wore medals around their necks, others waved flags. All wore smiles.

The atmosphere was actually rather wonderful, despite the Nazi banners looming above it all.

And then the key moment arrived: the extinguishing of the Olympic flame.

And suddenly, right on cue—just as Speer had planned and just as I had seen during the rehearsal—*all the mighty floodlights went out.*

The stadium was plunged into darkness, save for the Olympic flame mounted high up at one end of it.

A hush fell over the *Olympiastadion* as the 100,000 spectators in the stands and the hundreds of athletes on the field all turned as one to face the flickering flame.

Which was when Dan sprang into action.

'When the floodlights go out, that's your chance,' I'd said as I outlined my plan to Dan a week earlier. 'I don't know how you get yourself onto the field—dress up as a security guard or some-thing—but you do. When the stadium goes dark, you whisk Igor and Anatoly Kurtzov from the stadium via an athletes' tunnel to the underground parking garage where I'll be waiting to guide them to a maintenance passageway that leads to the U-Bahn on the west side of the *Olympiastadion*.

'In the U-Bahn tunnel is a manhole to a sewer pipe that runs all the way to the river, where you have a truck waiting. Throw the Kurtzov brothers into the truck and take them to the airport and they'll be out of the country before the stadium is empty.'

The floodlights went out.

The stadium went dark and Dan—positioned on the infield in the uniform of a security guard—made his move toward the Kurtzov brothers—

—when suddenly the two Russian scientist-athletes were grabbed by four men in *German* team uniforms and shoved off the field toward the athletes' tunnel that led to the parking garage.

It was our plan . . . only the Nazis were doing it.

They'd had the same idea.

I was waiting in the garage.

It was filled with the limousines of the Nazi elite, including Hitler's bulletproof Mercedes-Benz. Their drivers were all out by the field, watching the once-in-a-lifetime spectacle. I could hear the muffled cheers of the massive crowd above me.

As Speer's secretary, it was perfectly acceptable for me to be stationed beside his limousine—waiting for my master—and the four tracksuit-wearing Gestapo men registered my presence and ignored me as they appeared at a run with the Kurtzov brothers gripped between them.

My surprise at seeing the group of kidnapper–assassins was genuine and I leapt out of their way as the agents thrust Igor and Anatoly Kurtzov down the very same maintenance passageway leading to the U-Bahn tunnel that I had intended for Dan and me to use.

I peered down the maintenance passageway after them and watched as their six shadows got smaller until they reached a door at the far end—

Flashes of light burst out from that distant end of the passageway.

Machine-gun fire.

The six shadows convulsed and dropped. One Gestapo agent drew his gun and fired it at some unseen attacker.

At the same time as the gunfire erupted, a gigantic roar came from the crowd above me, drowning out the sound of the machine guns.

I just stared at the scene in horror.

The Gestapo team had run into a trap, an ambush.

Someone else was down there.

Someone who had been *waiting for them*.

My mind reeled.

If it had been Dan and me in that passageway with the two Russians, we'd have been shot to ribbons and killed.

I was still staring in shock at the scene when one of the Gestapo agents came staggering out of the passageway, pushing Anatoly Kurtzov ahead of him.

Both men were covered in blood. Bullet wounds covered the Gestapo man's chest, but he was gamely trying to escape with the Russian.

Kurtzov was also wounded, shot in the leg, and he limped painfully as he came to my end of the passageway.

Then a gunshot rang out and his head exploded. An instant later, the Gestapo man was shot through the back and his chest erupted with a geyser of blood.

They both fell.

A voice came echoing from the depths of the dark passageway.

'*You really thought you could get away with this?!*'

The voice spoke in German, but its accent was Russian.

A woman's voice.

My horror became complete when I realised that I had heard this voice before.

It was a voice I had heard nine years earlier at the Solvay Conference.

I scurried away from the entrance to the passageway and dived into the only hiding place available to me: the back seat of Speer's limousine.

I peered out fearfully from the car.

Anatoly Kurtzov was dead but the Gestapo agent with him was not. He lay on the concrete floor, moaning.

It was then that *she* emerged.

From the passageway, walking at an unhurried pace, gripping a Soviet-made machine gun in her right hand.

The woman I knew in Brussels as 'Brigitte'.

She stood over the two men and fired two quick shots into Kurtzov's heart to make sure he was dead.

Then she came to the wounded Gestapo man on the ground and aimed her gun at his face.

'You Nazis. So stupid. You really thought you could kidnap our scientists?'

She shot the Gestapo man between the eyes.

She spun to go . . .

. . . but then she paused.

And raised her nose, as if smelling something.

Then she cast her gaze searchingly around the parking garage.

I froze.

Then the woman I knew as Brigitte blinked out of her trance, turned and slipped into the darkness of the maintenance passageway and just as quickly as she had arrived, she was gone.

I could only stare after her.

Two days later, I regrouped with Dan and he told me what had happened.

'Her real name is Svetlana Sarkovsky,' Dan said. 'She's one of the best assassins in Russia. Over the last six years, she's taken out four of our spies in London and Paris, and turned one consulate official. She's the ultimate honey trap: gets a guy into bed and blackmails him until he's no more use to her. Then she kills him.'

'I actually met her in Brussels back in '27,' I said. 'She was the one who killed Alexei Zilberman on the train to Antwerp.'

Dan frowned. 'This is worse than just a hit: *the Soviets have an agent inside the Nazi leadership*. They knew everything about the Nazis' kidnap plan, including the exit strategy through that maintenance passageway.'

I nodded. 'The Soviets also knew the Kurtzovs were going to defect. They may be a more dangerous enemy than the Nazis. Who's to say they weren't aware of our plan?'

Dan looked at me hard. 'That's a worry, but in the end, I don't think they knew about our plan.'

'How do you know that?' I asked.

'Because, if they did, you and I would be dead right now, killed by Svetlana Sarkovsky.'

NAZI GERMANY

Nuclear program and rocket program sites plus key camps

> The mind-staggering network of camps—
> housing, handling, immiserating, exploiting,
> and killing millions of innocent, martially
> and physically unthreatening people—was
> the largest institutional creation of Germany
> during its Nazi period.
>
> – From: Daniel Jonah Goldhagen,
> *Hitler's Willing Executioners*

AFTER THE 1936 OLYMPICS, while the world continued to grapple with the Depression, Germany went into industrial overdrive, most of it overseen by Albert Speer.

Autobahns, airports, bridges, infrastructure.

And more covertly—in defiance of the Treaty of Versailles— weapons of war.

Tanks, planes, warships, U-boats, heavy artillery, and of course, rockets.

I toured these facilities on a weekly basis with Speer.

When we returned to Berlin from these tours, Speer would report to Hitler while I would secretly visit Dan Kessler and share with him what I had seen and learned.

I lived in a state of constant fear that I would be found out, discovered. The Gestapo were known to storm into an office during the day or into someone's home during the night and take them away, never to be seen again.

Sleeping alone in my little apartment, I would often spring awake at some ungodly hour, woken by a loud banging sound, thinking it was the secret police kicking in my door.

But it never was.

At Peenemünde, Speer and I saw Wernher von Braun's progress with his liquid-propellant rockets. Von Braun's star continued to rise.

We also visited Heisenberg at his facilities at the Kaiser Wilhelm Institute in Berlin and at his home in Hechingen.

His progress was *not* good.

The German atomic program had not advanced in any worthwhile way, meaning—Heisenberg reported to Speer—that Heisenberg could see no practical way of utilising the new science as a weapon of war.

'Herr Hitler may prefer his physics to be Aryan,' Heisenberg said to Speer, 'but physics doesn't care for race and the Jewish scientists we chased out of Germany took with them an enormous amount of knowledge. I'm doing the best I can but I'm working with many second-rate physicists here.'

While Speer and I crisscrossed Germany on our tours, Speer also made a point to visit a new horrific feature of the German landscape.

The camps.

After opening their first *Konzentrationslager* at Dachau in 1933 right after taking power, the Nazis went on a spree of camp-building.

There was a camp for every type of state enemy: criminals, degenerates, perverts, but also communists, writers of banned works, the sick, the infirm and the mentally unstable. In other words, anyone who questioned the Aryan ideal or who might dilute the strength of the German bloodline.

Often were the times I marvelled at the German people's acceptance of such horrors.

Germans, it has to be said, are obedient people, compliant, and utterly zealous rule-followers. The speed with which they acknowledged and accepted the camp system as just a new part of daily life was astounding.

And then in 1938, soon after the Anschluss, a new camp was opened in Austria, one that held particular interest for Speer.

It was located just outside Linz, at a place called Mauthausen.

'The granite is of extremely high quality, Herr Speer, and there is a lot of it,' the too-eager-to-please commandant said as we took our first tour through the new camp in late 1938.

'Excellent,' Speer said. 'Excellent.'

He needed vast amounts of granite to build Hitler's new Berlin, the capital of the thousand-year Reich.

This new Berlin would feature gargantuan structures, including a triumphal arch that would dwarf the one in Paris, towering government buildings, vast plazas, glorious boulevards, and a colossal domed central building called the Great Hall.

While this Berlin was Hitler's dream, it was Speer who designed it, so it became his, too.

Speer held a sample of granite in his gloved hand, turned it over, examining it.

'Yes. Yes, this will do nicely.'

The commandant said, 'There is also a collection of caverns and tunnels within the mountain that the Reichsminister may wish to see with a view to potential uses.'

We toured the caverns.

They were breathtaking in size.

Speer gazed at them with knowing eyes.

The commandant said, 'The caverns are connected by a series of natural passageways. The innermost ones are not exactly stable, but they go all the way through. If you wanted to devote a few hundred inmates to the cause, you could fashion those passages into clean tunnels that emerge on the other side of the mountain.'

As we drove away from Mauthausen an hour later, Speer said to me, 'Hanna, take a note, please. "Wehrmacht engineering corps. Prepare caverns of Mauthausen for high-value munitions and weapons construction." Also, contact the president of Messerschmitt and tell him I have found the location for him to build his new jet fighters in safety. That mountain is strong, its roots deep. Its caverns are the perfect site to build and protect our secret weapons.'

May 1945.

American forces liberate Mauthausen.

The stories they hear from the inmates are sickening.

The worst atrocities, they are told, were reserved for the Soviet prisoners.

One particular incident from early 1945 is mentioned many times.

The Hare Hunt.

On the night of 1–2 February, a group of 500 Soviet prisoners effected a mass breakout.

Using wet blankets, they scaled the electrified fences and escaped into the surrounding countryside.

Their freedom was short-lived.

They were so starved and malnourished that they were easily chased down by the camp's SS guards.

Indeed, the Nazis were so amused by the pathetic escape attempt that they assembled members of nearby towns to join them on horseback in a 'hunt' for the escapees, likening it to an old-fashioned fox hunt.

The guards and the townsfolk treated the whole thing as a lark—gleefully hunting down and executing the escapees: variously shooting, hanging or beating them to death.

Of the 500 prisoners who escaped, only 11 survived.

← ———————————

Speer and I returned to Berlin, where we made our last stop on that tour.

Speer had been tasked by Hitler to debrief a Russian spy who had been captured while trying to steal documents from the rocket facility at Peenemünde.

This spy, we were told, had blackmailed a German scientist on von Braun's team into handing over a folio full of research documents. But both had been caught by the Gestapo at their rendezvous point and been taken to the Gestapo's prison:

Spandau.

AFTER THE WAR, SPANDAU Prison would become one of the most famous prisons in the world.

Before and during the war, however, it was essentially the private fiefdom of the Gestapo.

As the Nazis' camp system grew, the Gestapo used Spandau as a kind of waystation for problematic or unique prisoners, holding them there until it could be determined where best to send them.

Spandau basically looked like a medieval castle, with high brick walls and crenellated battlements.

Its grim main gate was flanked by two brick towers that looked like they should have been manned by archers.

Speer and I arrived at the main gate in his limousine and headed inside.

July 1947.

It is after the war and I walk inside the main gate of Spandau, alone.

It's a different place now, run by the Allies, the victors of the war.

Amazingly, the prison's grim medieval gate survived the bombing that destroyed much of the rest of Berlin.

It houses only seven inmates: Nazi war criminals who were all tried and convicted at Nuremberg.

My O.S.S. pass gets me through the reception area with barely a pause and I am guided by two British guards to a cell marked:

PRISONER NO. 5

SPEER, ALBERT

One of the guards opens the door and I gaze inside the cell.

Speer is pale, thin, gaunt. His hair is grey and thinning. His cheap prison clothes hang off his frame. He has aged a lot in the years since we visited Spandau together.

Only now he is not a visitor.

Twenty years, they gave him.

◄───────────────

Speer and I sat in an interrogation room with four Gestapo officers, all wearing belted leather jackets and blank stares.

Most Nazi officials who met with Speer bowed and scraped obsequiously.

Not the Gestapo.

Of course, they knew who he was, but they barely acknowledged him. After all, he might be one of their guests in the near future.

We would meet with the German first, the hapless scientist who had been blackmailed into giving up his secrets.

He was a pathetic little man named Dr Ernst Rennicker.

'Please! Please, you must understand! She seduced me!' he said.

'She wanted me to give her actual components of the rocket system, but I didn't do that, oh no. I just let her look at some plans, that's all.'

Dr Rennicker possessed advanced degrees from three of Germany's most esteemed institutions of higher learning but for all that he wasn't smart enough to know that the Gestapo was incapable of sympathy.

After Speer was done with him Dr Ernst Rennicker was taken out the back and shot, his brilliant brain left dripping down a wall.

Speer said, 'Bring in the Russian. Hanna, could you please step outside for this.'

I nodded and left the interrogation room. I waited a short way down the corridor.

A few minutes later, the Russian spy was brought in.

Even though she was dressed in prison garb, she sauntered down the prison corridor like she owned it. With her shapely figure, she even made her prison clothes look fashionable. She never saw me as she turned into the interrogation room and vanished from my view.

But I saw her.

And I gasped in shock.

That the Soviet spy was a woman was not at all surprising.

The Nazi leadership group—especially the pants men like Bormann and Göring—had been warned many times that the best Russian spies were beautiful women who'd been trained to lure them into compromising situations.

What was surprising was that I had met this Soviet spy before.

Twice.

At the 1927 Solvay Conference and at the 1936 Olympics.

The woman who strode into that interrogation room was Svetlana Sarkovsky.

SPEER AND THE GESTAPO men spent the next three hours with Svetlana.

I took that time to wander the brick-walled halls and courtyards of Spandau.

It was sparsely populated at that time, since most of its few prisoner groups—communists, dissidents, Jews—had been moved to specialised camps.

As I turned a corner, I heard a commotion and beheld a grim infirmary where a woman sat in a dentist's chair, struggling fiercely.

She was bound to the chair by leather buckles. Four nurses and a doctor gripping a syringe grappled with her, trying to keep her down.

The woman's head was shaved and she was thrashing with all her might to stop the medical staff from injecting her with the syringe.

I froze.

Even with her shaved head, I recognised her.

I didn't know how they'd found her or what she had done to be captured and brought to Spandau, but it seemed that her period of freedom from the prison in Brandenburg hadn't lasted long.

It was my sister.

It was Ooma.

The nurses eventually restrained Ooma long enough for the doctor to inject her.

Ooma's struggling ceased almost instantly, her body sagging, and the medical staff left the room.

They shoved past me as I stood there in the doorway dumbly watching Ooma on the bed.

I was stunned.

I hadn't seen her since that day in Berlin back in 1924 when Einstein and I had questioned her in front of Lukas about stealing my life and Einstein had revealed her true identity by showing the two scars on her left wrist. Then she had fled through a window in the ladies' room, leaving my life in Berlin in ruins.

As I stood there watching her, Ooma rolled onto her side and in that moment her glazed eyes found mine and they sprang wide in recognition.

She tried to sit up, fighting the soporific drugs in her bloodstream.

'Hanna . . .?'

I honestly didn't know what to do or say.

I stepped forward tentatively.

'Ooma, is that really you?'

'Oh, sister, sister. Come here. It's been . . . so long and I want . . . to tell you something . . .' Her voice was groggy.

'Yes?'

'I really . . . enjoyed . . . your life.'

Then the drugs won and she fell asleep.

I was thrown—confused and hurt and downright angry—but

then Speer emerged from the interrogation room and called for me and I hurried off to join him and we left Spandau.

As we drove away in his limousine, I regathered myself and asked, 'What will become of that Russian spy? For a captured foreign agent, she seemed awfully sure of herself.'

Speer gazed out the window, lost in thought. 'Because she knew we'd send her back to Moscow unharmed.'

'Why?'

'Six months ago, the Soviets caught two of our best spies in Stalingrad. She knew she'd be traded. It's what happens in the spy business.'

A week later, I returned to Spandau with six armed guards and the paperwork that would see Svetlana Sarkovsky returned to Russia.

I deliberately stayed out of her line of sight as she was taken down a long underground corridor to a loading bay where a truck was waiting to take her to wherever the trading point was.

As she reached the doorway at the far end of the corridor, however, Svetlana stopped suddenly and raised her nose higher.

She did not turn around as she called in English:

'I know you're here, Poppy! I can smell you! Like I smelled you in that parking garage during the Games! You turn up in the most peculiar places. Solvay, the Games, now here. Perhaps you are not as sweet as you appear. I shall have to keep an eye out for you, sweet poppy!'

Then she stepped through the door and vanished from my view.

It took me a few minutes to compose myself, but I did.

For I was staying behind in Spandau that day for my own reasons.

'WELL, LOOK AT YOU,' Ooma said. 'Don't you clean up nice.'

'Hello, Ooma,' I replied.

We sat in the same interrogation room Speer had used to debrief Rennicker and Svetlana, in chairs that were bolted to the floor, on opposite sides of a steel table also affixed to the floor.

I can't imagine how we must have looked.

Me, in my conservative woollen dress suit, my short hair neatly combed.

And her, my twin, in her grey prison rags with her head shaved to the scalp.

'Did I apologise for stealing your life all those years ago?' she asked. 'Sorry about that.'

'I was told you died at Brandenburg Prison.'

'I was really saddened to hear about my death, too,' Ooma said with a smirk.

'I saw the body. I knew you'd escaped. I figured you stole another inmate's identity like you stole mine.'

'Let me give you some advice, sister,' Ooma said. 'Should you ever get imprisoned—unlikely as that is, in your case—whether it's in an asylum, a sanitorium, a camp or a jail, escape within the first three days. That was my mistake here. I didn't do it early enough. After three days, you're done. You need energy to escape and they don't feed you, so you lose the energy you need to flee.'

'What did you do to get sent here?'

'Bit of bad luck, really.' She shrugged. 'I was fucking this Nazi governor from Poland when his wife walked in on us. She was one of those Party freaks who believes all this Aryan Christian bullshit. Bitch turned me in. She didn't turn him in, though, because she liked the high life of a governor's wife. What about you, Little Miss Perfect? What does a prim and proper girl like you do in this new Germany?'

'I'm a secretary,' I said.

There was no way I was going to tell her who I worked for.

'Can't just be any old secretary,' Ooma said, leaning forward. 'No ordinary secretary could waltz into Spandau and get to talk with me in an interrogation room all by herself.'

I stood up. 'I'm leaving. Goodbye—'

'You know, I've been thinking about making a wig,' Ooma said suddenly.

'A wig?' I grabbed the doorknob.

'Yeah.' She stroked the stubble on her head. 'Make me look pretty again. So guys'll fuck me, hard and fast, like your sweet Lukas used to.'

I opened the door.

'Don't go!' she said, trying to stand, but the handcuffs chaining her to her chair wouldn't let her.

Her voice became a shriek. 'Don't go, Hanna! I'm sorry! Don't leave me here! Come back!'

Her screaming voice followed me down the corridors as I hurried out of there.

A single bomb of this type, carried by boat and
exploded in a port, might very well destroy
the whole port together with some of the
surrounding territory.

– From: Albert Einstein's letter to
President Franklin D. Roosevelt
August 2, 1939

IN 1938, WHILE GERMANY—exhorted by Hitler's ferocious speeches and organised by Speer—built ever more rockets, U-boats, tanks and planes, a key theory in atomic science became a reality.

Nuclear fission was achieved.

The atom had been split.

News of the incredible achievement quickly spread throughout the academic world.

Joliot in France and Szilard in America quickly expanded on this concept, deducing that if you could split one atom into fragments, then those fragments could split *other* atoms, creating an exponential chain of fissions.

This 'chain reaction' could, in theory, produce *vast* amounts of energy, energy that could be channelled via nuclear reactors into electricity generation or—ominously—unbelievably powerful bombs that could destroy entire cities.

And so in August of 1939 the most famous letter in history was written.

Szilard persuaded Einstein to add his name to a letter to President Franklin Delano Roosevelt warning of the dangers of the Nazis acquiring such a bomb.

In that letter, Einstein made only one error.

Thinking that such a powerful 'atomic' bomb would have to be quite large and cumbersome, Einstein warned of such a bomb being delivered to a port city by ship and how the subsequent explosion would destroy the entire port and much of the surrounding landscape.

Brilliant as he was, Einstein hadn't considered that such a bomb might end up being smaller than this and thus deliverable by airplane or—if the atomic warhead could be reduced even further in size—by the parallel science of ballistic rocketry.

The letter was sent and it had its desired effect: the creation of the Manhattan Project, the greatest and most expensive scientific project ever conceived.

Bohr had said such an undertaking would be colossally expensive, the inference being that no government could ever actually spend the massive amount of money required to do it. Yet America was doing just that.

A month after Einstein sent his letter to Roosevelt, the Nazis invaded Poland, catapulting me into the middle of the most terrible conflict in history.

> By September 1941, the international situation
> looked quite bleak for the world but quite
> positive for Germany . . . Most of Europe
> was under Nazi occupation, German panzer
> divisions were plunging into Soviet Russia and
> the United States was still officially neutral.
>
> – From: David C. Cassidy, *Physics Today*

MUCH HAS BEEN WRITTEN about the European theatre of the Second World War, so it is not necessary that I dwell on all its many battles here.

That said, it is easy to forget that the greatest conflagration in history lasted only six years.

Year by year, it went roughly like this:

1939: Germany invaded Poland.

1940: Germany took France, Belgium, Holland, Denmark and Norway. Germany attacked Britain with many air raids but the British people held out and a German invasion of Britain was delayed.

1941: Germany invaded Russia, almost reaching Moscow.

1942: At Stalingrad, in a battle fought street by street, the invading German army was surrounded and defeated.

Thus the tide turned.

1943: Now Germany retreated as Russia—with vastly superior manpower—pressed forward.

1944: In the west, the Allies invaded occupied France at the beaches of Normandy and began to push forward on that front.

1945: By April, squeezed from both sides, Nazi Germany faced a humiliating defeat.

The first two years of the war—where Germany gained victory after victory—only reinforced the Nazis' high opinion of themselves.

They were the master race. They ruled Europe. Only Britain remained free and it would eventually fall.

Many have rightly wondered what might have happened to history if Hitler had stopped there.

But he didn't stop.

In the summer of 1941, in search of the 'living space' that he believed to be the birthright of the German people, Hitler ordered his armies to commence the single largest military operation of all time: the invasion of the Soviet Union.

Operation Barbarossa.

Barbarossa would change the course of the war.

By instigating it, Hitler instigated his own eventual downfall.

Barbarossa would consume so many soldiers and so many resources that Nazi Germany would not be able to fight the other war against the Allies taking place on its western front.

Also, the unspeakable atrocities committed by German soldiers during their charge *into* the Soviet Union would come back to haunt Germany when the momentum shifted at Stalingrad and the far larger Soviet Red Army began its march *back* toward Berlin.

The Red Army would give Germany a lesson in atrocities.

Of course, much was happening elsewhere in the world—in the Pacific, north Africa and Italy—but my war was in Germany.

By 1942, as the Soviet Union's gigantic forces began to push back, Hitler proclaimed to the German people that

Wunderwaffen—'wonder weapons'—were being developed at secret locations and that these would bring about a triumphant German victory.

The reality was much starker.

As the Nazi armies suffered losses on the battlefield, they began to experience severe shortages in munitions, weapons and fuel.

Hitler needed a master organiser to marshal the nation's resources and ensure the production of his wonder weapons.

To that end, in early 1942, Hitler made Albert Speer Minister for Armaments.

A week after Speer's appointment, the Gestapo came bursting into our suite of offices. All the secretaries working at their typewriters around me whirled, startled and frightened.

'What is the meaning of this!' Speer demanded, emerging from his office.

The head of the Gestapo team gave him a sly grin. 'Forgive us, Herr Reichsminister, but we have reason to believe that someone working in these offices is passing secret information to the enemy. Someone here is a spy!'

His searching gaze found me.

'You. Come with us. Right now.'

He pointed at Gertrude Schneider. 'You, too.'

FROM THE SECOND
INTERROGATION
GESTAPO HEADQUARTERS
BERLIN, GERMANY, 1942

INTERROGATOR (OBERGRUPPENFÜHRER HEYDRICH):
Miss Fischer, my sincere apologies. You are free to go.

FISCHER: What . . . what's happened?

INTERROGATOR: It turns out that you're not the spy we
were searching for. Miss Schneider was. She has admitted
everything.

FISCHER: Gertrude was a spy?

INTERROGATOR: She was. Sometime in the last year she
was seduced by a Russian agent.

FISCHER: Have you arrested him, too?

INTERROGATOR: No, the Russian agent was a woman. A
woman who engaged with Gertrude Schneider in unnatural
sexual acts. While they engaged in their trysts, a second

Soviet agent took photos of them. The Russians then blackmailed Miss Schneider into revealing information she acquired while working for Reichsleiter Bormann.

FISCHER: Goodness. Gertrude. I would never have guessed.

INTERROGATOR: Our apologies again, Fräulein. Thank you for your time. Heil Hitler.

REICH MAIN SECURITY OFFICE
PRINZ-ALBRECHT-STRASSE
1942

I EMERGED FROM GESTAPO headquarters three days later, ragged, sleep-deprived and utterly, utterly relieved.

When they'd burst into our offices, I'd thought I was done for. They'd finally uncovered me. They knew who I was.

But they didn't know.

They'd been after somebody else.

I was also shocked at what I'd learned about Gertrude. Turned out, it wasn't just men who could be seduced by alluring female Soviet spies.

Usually in cases like this the boss of the traitor in question would also be interrogated—and, in all likelihood, executed—but Martin Bormann was no ordinary official.

He was one of the few Nazis who could overcome a scandal like this.

For one thing, he was a recipient of the *Blutorden*, the Order of the Blood, which was given only to veterans of Hitler's original 1923 putsch and those who had served jail time for the Party. He and the Führer went way back.

He was also a Reichsleiter.

Only a select few Nazis would ever hold this rank. It meant

'Reich Leader' and was one rank below 'Führer' itself.

Bormann would emerge from the affair unscathed.

Reinhard Heydrich, to the relief of many, would be dead within a few months when his limousine was ambushed by Czech assassins early one morning in Prague. During the attack, Heydrich was wounded by the blast of a grenade thrown at his open-topped car.

He was taken to hospital where he writhed in pain for a week before dying of sepsis.

For my part, I went home, took a long bath, and then slept for twenty-four hours straight.

THE WAR TOURS

ONCE HE BECAME ARMAMENTS Minister, Speer's inspection tours around Germany and the German-held territories increased fivefold.

I accompanied him on all of them.

This meant constant travel, by train, car and airplane.

We called on Heisenberg at the Kaiser Wilhelm Institute in Berlin. He maintained that the idea of using the atom as a weapon was fanciful.

(After this visit, Dan Kessler asked me specifically about Heisenberg and his atomic research. When I relayed to him what Heisenberg had said, Dan nodded sagely, saying, 'Good. This is good.')

In occupied France, Speer and I visited the bases in the north of the country from which Wernher von Braun's rockets were being launched across the Channel at England.

The bases were excellently placed, but this also made them targets for Allied bombing attacks.

Speer wanted a more fortified facility to protect Germany's most prized superweapons from such attacks.

He designed a facility never before seen in the world.

It would be constructed in Helfaut in northern France and

everything about it would be gigantic: a protective concrete dome weighing one million tons and so sturdy it would be able to withstand any RAF bombing, plus giant concrete-walled hangars for the storage and fuelling of the rockets, complete with supersized doors that would be seven storeys tall.

It would be the bunker of bunkers.

It was classic Speer: bigger and more audacious than anything ever conceived.

When I returned to Berlin after that trip, I met with Dan and told him the exact location of this planned facility in Helfaut.

--------->

July 1944.

One month after the Allied landings at Normandy on D-Day.

After two years of construction, the colossal German V-2 rocket facility in Helfaut, France, is almost complete and ready for use.

On the night of July 17, a squadron of Royal Air Force bombers attack it, dropping dozens of six-ton Tallboy bombs with uncanny accuracy.

Amazingly, the superbunker's mighty dome withstands the ferocious bombardment.

But the surrounding hillside and the entryways leading into it do not.

They are catastrophically damaged.

Speer's superbunker at Helfaut never fires a single rocket.

It is as if the Allies knew it was there.

<---------

Unnerving as that tour was, more unsettling was the trip I took with Speer in 1942 to a former military base outside the town of Oświęcim in Poland.

It was called Auschwitz.

It stood on a barren, lifeless plain in the countryside, which suited it, for it would become a temple to death.

Auschwitz had originally been built in 1940 as a standard concentration camp to house Poles arrested or detained during the initial invasion of their country.

But as the war turned against Nazi Germany, Hitler accelerated his 'Final Solution' to the Jewish Problem and certain concentration camps were reconfigured as 'death camps'.

Auschwitz, located in almost the exact geographical centre of Germany's annexed lands, would become the largest and most feared of these extermination camps.

Nuremberg, 1946.

Standing in the witness box in his prison clothes, Speer is cross-examined about his knowledge of the Nazi plan to exterminate all European Jewry, their Final Solution.

'I knew nothing of this plan. Nothing. Indeed, I was shocked when I learned of it—and the extent of it—after the war.'

He is asked if he was at the Wannsee Conference, the notorious meeting held on January 20, 1942, convened by Reinhard Heydrich to outline exactly how the Nazis would murder the 11 million Jews in greater Europe.

'I was not at Wannsee,' he says.

This is true.

'I did not know what was discussed there.'
This is a lie.

There were actually several subcamps at Auschwitz.

The biggest was Birkenau and it was here that the majority of the killings took place.

Guided by an SS-Sturmbannführer, Speer and I walked through a bathhouse.

'It's really quite ingenious, the way we do it,' the SS man said. 'We bring the prisoners straight off the cattle wagons and in here, telling them we have to wash them. They strip off and enter willingly, only instead of water, gas comes out of the showerheads. It is very efficient.'

That word again: *efficient.*

I couldn't believe what I was hearing but Speer just nodded sagely.

'And getting rid of the bodies?' he asked.

We were guided into the crematory, where an engineer from an oven company waited to guide us.

It was here that I beheld the ovens, with the nameplates of their makers proudly stamped on them:

J.A. TOPF & SÖHNE

'What's the capacity again? How many will it be able to dispose of per day?' Speer asked.

'One thousand,' the Topf company engineer said.

'We need to ramp up our cremation capabilities. We have over

100,000 Soviet prisoners in custody right now and millions more on the way. And all must disappear. That's before we even mention the Jews . . .'

I stood behind Speer, taking notes in a state of disbelief.

The Topf man said, 'These'll be much quicker than the original ovens. You'll be able to shove the bodies in more easily. Plus, you won't be using coffins like they do at regular crematoriums.'

'The Wannsee Protocol is clear,' Speer said. 'The numbers will be large.'

I did not know what this 'Wannsee Protocol' was. I would later discover that it was the name for the minutes of the Wannsee Conference.

Hitler, famously, did not attend that meeting.

Standing there at Birkenau, Speer said, 'Make the ovens as big as you can.' Then he walked away.

That afternoon, we were recalled to Berlin at the order of Hitler himself.

We were to return immediately which meant travelling by plane.

At that time, if a senior minister or military official needed to get to Berlin urgently, landings could be made on an emergency landing strip in the Tiergarten.

Essentially, Charlottenstrasse, the east–west avenue that ran down the length of the gardens, became a landing strip for small planes like the Fieseler Fi 156 Storch or 'Stork'. The avenue would be used for such missions right up to the end of the war, including the famous 'final flight out of Berlin' by the German ace, Hanna Reitsch.

The urgent meeting had been triggered by the battle going on in

Stalingrad. Winter was falling and the fighting there was bogging down.

'Hitler wants an update on his *Wunderwaffen*,' Speer said. 'The longer our forces get stuck in Stalingrad, the longer the Russians have to gather more men to fight. And the one thing they have more of than we do is men. The only way we can counter such a man-power disadvantage is with better and more destructive weapons.'

We arrived back in Berlin, landing in the middle of the Tiergarten, and headed directly to the Reich Chancellery.

Emergency airstrip at the Tiergarten

ALREADY WAITING FOR US were the Führer, Himmler, Goebbels and Bormann.

Hitler wanted reports on the progress of the V-2 rockets coming out of Peenemünde and on the *Uranverein*, Germany's atomic fission project.

To that end, Wernher von Braun and Werner Heisenberg had also been summoned to the Chancellery and they were waiting, too.

Von Braun appeared first in front of that intimidating group of senior Nazis.

He came dressed in his full SS uniform and he stood ramrod straight as he gave his report in clinical, clipped sentences. He was only 30 years old.

As Bormann's (new) principal secretary took notes, von Braun spoke about his achievements in his short military style.

Those achievements were formidable.

His rockets, he said, would soon be able to fly with greater accuracy, for longer distances and with greater destructive power.

Hitler was dazzled. He nodded enthusiastically.

'This is marvellous news, just marvellous,' he said.

'What do you need from us?' Bormann asked.

Von Braun said immediately, 'I need more productive capability. More workers and a larger facility to build the bigger rockets, the V-2s.'

'Speer,' Hitler said. 'Assign as much slave labour as Dr von Braun needs. And find a larger location for his plant. His rockets will win this war for us.'

Von Braun was thanked for his service and departed.

Heisenberg came in next.

He cut a vastly different figure to von Braun.

He wore civilian clothes. His tie was lazily knotted. I noticed he had put on weight.

Unlike von Braun, he spoke in long rambling sentences filled with jargon.

'Our research into cyclotrons and heavy water is well ahead of the rest of the world,' he said.

Hitler was growing impatient and Bormann saw it.

'Can the science be used for a weapon?' Bormann cut in. 'A superweapon? That is what the Führer wishes to know.'

Heisenberg nodded. 'Well, theoretically, yes, but—'

'But what?' Bormann said.

'Well, it would take *decades* to build such a weapon, even if you requisitioned every scientist in Germany to the cause. According to my calculations, and as I have said before, it would take at least twenty years to amass the requisite amount of the key element that would form the core of such a bomb.'

Hitler said nothing. But his face showed his disappointment.

Bormann stood. 'Then that is all we need to know—'

Then Himmler cut in, 'I have a question for Professor Heisenberg.'

Bormann sat down again to listen.

Himmler said, 'Back in September of 1941, you travelled to Copenhagen to meet with the Jewish physicist, Niels Bohr.'

Heisenberg swallowed, clearly unnerved that Himmler might know of that trip.

'Bohr . . . Bohr is a Christian, sir,' Heisenberg said. 'I know this for a fact—'

'And I know for a fact that his mother was Jewish,' Himmler said in the eerie tone for which he was famous. 'And Jewishness is passed down through the mother. Bohr has long been one of the leading minds in the world of atomic science. Tell us, what did you and Professor Bohr discuss in Copenhagen?'

Heisenberg fidgeted nervously.

Himmler—as he so often did—had neutralised Heisenberg's arrogance with his knowledge of Heisenberg's travels.

Heisenberg regathered himself, raising his chin a little as he answered the Reichsführer-SS.

'I asked him about the Allies' attempts to weaponise the atom. I had long maintained to Bohr that such weapons could not be built and, I am pleased to inform you that, in Copenhagen, Bohr finally conceded that I was right. Bohr told me that the Allies' attempts to build a so-called "atomic bomb" in America were failing miserably. Our meeting in Copenhagen ended with me telling Bohr that Germany was far ahead of everyone else in this field and that any further efforts on their part would be a waste of time.'

Himmler nodded and turned to Hitler.

'This accords with our own intelligence coming out of America, *mein* Führer. The Americans have hit countless dead ends in their effort to produce a bomb. Our agent in Washington reports they are saying that a viable bomb is fifteen years away.'

Hitler stood, so everyone else stood, too.

'Thank you, people. This is all I need to know.'

He left and the meeting concluded.

Later that night, I found myself in a bar a few blocks from the Brandenburg Gate, not far from the Chancellery.

It was called Mueller's Bar and the atmosphere was vibrant, bright even. Germany was still winning the war.

Music played. Toasts were made. SS men danced with pretty girls in lipstick and swirling dresses.

I was sitting at the bar with a glass of wine when a handsome officer in the black uniform of a Gestapo Sturmbannführer sat down beside me.

'Good evening, *Fräulein*,' Dan Kessler said.

'Sturmbannführer.'

After the Tiergarten's main avenue had been converted into an emergency landing strip, we had shifted our meetings from the goose pond to this bar.

Dan had also taken to wearing a Gestapo uniform: it had the brilliant effect of keeping people away from him.

'Bohr was great in Copenhagen,' I said. 'Heisenberg believed every word of it. He thinks the Allies have wasted their time trying to make the bomb.'

'Excellent,' Dan said. 'Who was there?'

'Hitler, Speer, Himmler, Goebbels and Bormann,' I said. 'They're all now also of the opinion that your atomic program is useless.

The information you fed to their spy in D.C. has made it all the way back here to the highest ranks of the leadership.'

Dan stood to leave. 'Outstanding work, Hanna. Be careful, now. I probably won't see you for a while. Gotta leave the country to get orders. I'll be in touch when I get back.'

He touched my shoulder and smiled.

In the middle of that terrible war, that horrible time, I liked it when Special Agent Dan Kessler smiled.

FROM THE THIRD
INTERROGATION
SOVIET COMMAND POST
BERLIN, MAY 1945

INTERROGATOR: By 1943, what was the Nazi leadership's view of the state of the war?

FISCHER: Hitler held on to delusions that secret miracle weapons would be built and change the course of the war.

INTERROGATOR: The V-2 rockets?

FISCHER: Yes. And the new jet fighters being built by Messerschmitt.

INTERROGATOR: We captured the rocket-building facility at Peenemünde but found nothing there. Where did the rocket program go?

FISCHER: In the middle of '43, because of all the Allied bombing raids on Peenemünde, the rocket program was moved to the centre of the country, to a massive underground factory called Mittelwerk. It was staffed by prisoners from the nearby concentration camp, Mittelbau-Dora, a subcamp of Buchenwald.

INTERROGATOR: Slave labour?

FISCHER: Yes.

INTERROGATOR: Captured Russians?

FISCHER: Yes.

INTERROGATOR: How many?

FISCHER: Perhaps 60,000.

INTERROGATOR: And how many survived?

FISCHER: Maybe half.

> In a lonely valley in the Harz Mountains . . .
> I inspected the extensive underground
> installation where the V-2 was to be
> produced. In enormous long halls prisoners
> were busy setting up machinery and shifting
> plumbing. Expressionlessly, they looked right
> through me . . .
>
> – From: Albert Speer, *Inside the*
> *Third Reich: Memoirs*

MITTELWERK UNDERGROUND ROCKET FACTORY CENTRAL GERMANY
1944

GUIDED BY WERNHER VON Braun himself, Speer and I took a tour of the Mittelwerk facility.

If Speer's rocket-launching bunker in northern France was colossal, this was an order of magnitude larger.

It was the largest interior space I'd ever seen: a giant tunnel bored into the heart of the mountain.

We passed thousands of prisoners—emaciated, starving, many of them Russian troops captured during the first half of the war—working on an assembly-line system that was producing hundreds of V-2 rockets each week.

Von Braun said, 'I need more slaves, Reichsminister. These ones are weak, useless. They drop dead at their fucking stations. I hear there are plenty at Mauthausen-Gusen. Send us some of theirs.'

'I'll have more brought in,' Speer said. 'Hanna, make a note.'

HAIGERLOCH CASTLE
SOUTHWESTERN GERMANY
1944

Guided by Werner Heisenberg himself, Speer and I were led into the medieval bowels of Haigerloch Castle.

Because of the Allies' constant bombing raids on Berlin, Heisenberg's atomic research team was moved from the Kaiser Wilhelm Institute to the historic town of Haigerloch in the deep southwest of Germany, not far from Heisenberg's home in Hechingen.

'It's down here,' Heisenberg said as he ushered us through a disguised door in the old castle's church and then down some stone stairs into a secret cellar.

And there it was.

Heisenberg's atomic reactor.

It was a curious-looking thing.

Strings knotted with dozens of chalky-black cubes—uranium cubes—dangled above a round tank of heavy water.

'The science is complex,' Heisenberg said in his typically supercilious way, 'but a larger version of this reactor could power this entire region of Germany for years.'

I marvelled at the thing.

It was about twenty feet tall. That so much power could come from something so small was truly incredible.

I knew the science, but I didn't let Heisenberg or Speer know that.

The heavy water and graphite were used as moderators in the nuclear reaction: they slowed neutrons, allowing the reaction to be sustained.

The uranium cubes were also of great interest to me. They were the beating heart of any atomic device.

'The Führer once again wants to know—' Speer began.

'No,' Heisenberg cut him off. 'It cannot be used as a weapon.'

'Hanna, make a note.'

We left the secret cellar underneath Haigerloch Castle's church.

MAUTHAUSEN-GUSEN CAMP
UPPER AUSTRIA
1944

Our next stop on that tour was the vast Mauthausen-Gusen camp complex in Austria.

Of all the camps in the Nazi system, only Mauthausen-Gusen was a 'Category III' camp: the most brutal kind. It was made up of a network of 49 subcamps and had acquired a reputation for unparalleled barbarity.

We had been here before, a year earlier, when I had seen the prisoner fall to his death.

It had grown markedly since then.

As at Mittelwerk, to keep the work areas safe from Allied bombing raids, the main factories at Mauthausen-Gusen were now located inside the vast underground tunnels and halls that had been hewn by prisoner-slaves.

I gazed in awe at the place.

Thousands of slaves went about their work in the gargantuan caverns.

They were all starving.

Most, we were told, were Soviet infantrymen and officers

captured in the early days of Barbarossa.

Speer's goal on this visit was to check on the production of the Messerschmitt company's Me 262 fighter jets. These were reputedly 100 miles per hour faster than even the best American fighter, the P-51D Mustang. A true wonder weapon.

The camp's commandant, Franz Ziereis said proudly, 'Reichsminister, we are producing over 1,200 planes a month! Mauthausen-Gusen is the pride of the Reich!'

The pride of the Reich, I thought. *This place.*

Hollow-eyed Soviet prisoners glared at us as we walked by. Beaten though they were, they still had fire in their eyes. Pride is never fully extinguished.

'Come,' the commandant said, 'let us adjourn for supper. My chef has prepared a divine sweet-onion soup and foie gras for us.'

We returned to Berlin the following day where I met up with Dan. He'd returned from some recent travels with surprising news.

'The Allies are already planning for what happens *after* the war,' he said as we sat together at Mueller's.

'But it's not over yet,' I said.

The Allies had stormed the beaches at Normandy in June but had not yet set foot in Germany.

'Oh, it's over,' Dan said. 'We've done the numbers. There's no way Nazi Germany wins this thing; their defeat is inevitable. So now the O.S.S. and the Army are setting up a new division called "ALSOS". When Germany eventually collapses and surrenders, America's gonna be in a race with the Soviets to find and grab Germany's best scientists and weapons-makers: guys like Heisenberg and von Braun, especially von Braun. It's ALSOS's job to get to them first.'

When I arrived at Speer's office at the Chancellery the next morning I was met with some surprising news from the German side of things.

Hitler's right-hand man, Martin Bormann, had been promoted and, having been assigned important new duties, he required an extra secretary and he wanted one with proven experience operating at the highest levels of the regime.

'Someone who already knows who is who and where everything is,' he said. 'I don't want to train some new idiotic girl.'

For that role he specifically requested me.

My experience obviously counted for a lot, but I could also feel his wandering eyes scanning my body as he made his demand.

Of course, Speer could do nothing about it. Bormann outranked him.

I would switch offices the next day. From that day on, I would be the secretary of Reichsleiter Martin Bormann.

PART VII

1945
MR BORMANN'S
SECRETARY

The Reich Chancellery

If what I have seen comes out, we will all be wading up to our knees in blood.

– A fitter for J.A. Topf & Sons who installed exhaust fans at Auschwitz

I know Bormann is coarse. But whatever
he takes on, he does it with both hands and
feet and I can absolutely trust that my orders
will be obeyed immediately, overcoming all
obstacles.

– Adolf Hitler

KAISERODA SALT MINE
MERKERS, CENTRAL GERMANY
JANUARY 1945

MARTIN BORMANN COULD NOT have been more unlike Albert Speer.

Speer was in thrall to Hitler and went along with the Nazis to make history, build monuments, leave a mark on the world, to be remembered. He was married and, so far as I knew, never strayed. He was also courteous and polite.

Bormann was completely different.

He cared for no-one but himself. Everything he did was in service of his own needs.

He was not an intellectual; indeed, he despised such folk. He was a creature of the street with a keen nose for strength, power and fear.

His sexual appetites were lusty and quite disgusting, even though he was married with many children. While I managed to fend off his advances, he had convinced many a secretary, cook or waitress to sleep with him in exchange for his promises.

I even knew of occasions when, while visiting a camp, he would point at some poor female prisoner and later that woman would be brought to his quarters for his gratification.

When I started working for him in early 1945 and it became apparent that a German defeat in the war was more and more likely, Bormann's instincts for self-preservation kicked in.

This became clear on my first inspection tour with him.

Our itinerary was very similar to my last tour with Speer yet also not.

For instance, my first stop with Bormann was the Kaiseroda salt mine in Merkers, about two hours from Mittelwerk, where Wernher von Braun continued to produce rockets in his enormous underground works.

Inside that salt mine in Merkers was gold—400 million Reichsmarks' worth of gold—plus priceless artworks stolen from every corner of Europe.

The amount of it was staggering.

Bormann spoke to the Nazi in charge. 'Have it all taken to Genoa. A U-boat will be waiting there. It will take it all to Buenos Aires. The project codename is *Eagle Flight*. Say that and you'll be waved through every checkpoint.'

I couldn't believe it.

The Nazis, for all their quasi-religious pretensions about master races and Aryan superiority—and their hateful extermination of 'races' they deemed inferior—were nothing but common thieves.

Germany was in ruins. The American armies had crossed into German territory in the west and the Russians were advancing from the east. Air raids in Berlin happened four times a week, often in broad daylight. Germany would fall, maybe within months.

And yet the rats who had led it into war were leaving the sinking ship.

And Bormann was hard at work planning that escape.

TEMPELHOF AIRFIELD
JANUARY 27, 1945

His next stop was in the south of Berlin.

As Allied bombs fell on the city creating distant booms, Bormann inspected an isolated hangar at Tempelhof.

Two airplanes were kept there, fully fuelled, but far from all the other hangars.

Each plane had two crews who were ordered to sleep in alternating shifts so that they would be ready around the clock.

'If Berlin should fall, these planes shall spirit away the leadership,' Bormann said to the men. 'This is of the utmost importance, you understand. Heil Hitler.'

'Heil Hitler!' they replied, thrusting their arms into the air.

To this day, I'm not sure if Hitler knew about those escape planes.

Even as the Soviet Army bore down on the German capital, he never acted as if he would flee from Berlin.

Bormann and I returned to our offices in the Chancellery around noon.

A message was waiting for me on my desk:

> *Sturmbannführer Kriegler of the Gestapo wishes to see you at your earliest convenience.*

BOMBS SCREAMED OVERHEAD AS I met Dan at Mueller's an hour later.

It was an unusually heavy day of bombing. Booms rang out close by.

'We're leaving,' Dan said simply as I sat down beside him.

'Leaving?'

'You and I have been ordered out of Berlin. It's already too dangerous here with all the raids and headquarters thinks the Russians will arrive within weeks. The 12th Army under General Bradley is coming at Berlin from the west but I don't think it'll get here in time; I spoke to their S-2, their intelligence officer. And the 6th Army is way down in the south of the country, heading for Munich and then Berchtesgaden. HQ wants us out. Now.'

I smiled with relief. This was the news we'd been waiting for. Our war was over. We were going back to America.

Dan said, 'I gotta meet a Red Army liaison here in an hour—to discuss plans for after the war—and then I have to destroy some documents and stuff back at the safehouse. I have a car ready to go and false papers to get us to the American lines in the south. We leave this evening, at seven p.m.'

'Seven p.m.,' I said.

'Go back to your office now, finish off the day just like any other. You just won't be turning up tomorrow.'

I went back to the office, secretly thrilled.

Bormann, as always, was hard at his next task for Hitler.

As the Soviets and the Americans entered Germany from both sides, Hitler had ordered Bormann to evacuate the camps and prisons in and around Berlin, and to dispatch their inmates to the death camps like Auschwitz-Birkenau, Mittelwerk and Mauthausen-Gusen.

My last task with Martin Bormann was to visit Spandau Prison in preparation for its evacuation.

SPANDAU PRISON, BERLIN

BORMANN AND I ARRIVED at Spandau around 4 p.m. to find activity everywhere.

Equipment was being packed up. Inmates were being marched onto trucks that departed for nearby railway stations.

I saw Nazi guards leaving with gold necklaces and jewellery dangling from their pockets: possessions of the inmates who would no longer need them.

'Mauthausen-Gusen!' one young Nazi guard holding a clipboard shouted at the top of his lungs. 'This lot to Mauthausen-Gusen!'

A gang of sorry-looking inmates were shoved up a plank into the truck beside him. They clearly had no idea of the hell they were going to.

A series of outdoor cages had been set up in a courtyard adjoining the loading docks. They looked like chicken coops only they were filled with people.

One cage was jammed with female inmates. They clutched whatever personal items they could carry: bags, shoes.

'Hanna!' a voice shouted. 'Hanna Fischer!'

I turned and saw her, squeezed in among the other women in the cage, pressed against the wire and yelling through a ghastly leather contraption strapped over her mouth.

My sister.

Ooma.

As Bormann went about his business—ever the meticulous German, he wanted a precise record of the exact numbers of inmates being sent to their doom—I stepped over to the cage.

Like all the other women, Ooma's head was shaved and she wore standard striped prison clothing.

The brown leather muzzle covering her nose and mouth had been stamped: BEISSER.

Biter.

'Hanna, please,' she said through the leather mask. 'You've got to get me out of here. Word is, we're being taken to Mauthausen for extermination. You have to help me.'

I stared at my sister, my errant sister, the woman who had stolen my life for a time and who had spent much of her own life in sanatoriums, camps and jails.

Did she deserve this fate?

That she had never been 'right in the head', I was certain. She was also still my sister. I recalled my mother's tearful exclamation the day Ooma had hugged her.

I turned to one of the guards beside her cage. 'When do these women ship out?'

'First thing tomorrow morning, ma'am,' the guard said.

'I'll see what I can do,' I said to Ooma. 'I'll try to get a transfer order signed back at the office.'

Bormann was leaving, finished with his work. 'Let's go,' he called.

'I'll be back later, I promise,' I said to Ooma before I departed with him.

On our drive back to the Chancellery, I saw an Allied bomb come shrieking out of the sky and obliterate a church.

One moment the church was there, the next it was a cloud of smoke and fragments.

In the few hours I had left, I typed up a transfer order for Ooma, assigning her to a female cleaning team at a civilian hospital in western Berlin. I handed it to Bormann amid a bunch of other forms for him to sign and he signed it without even looking.

Then I was out the door.

I had it all planned.

I would link up with Dan at Mueller's Bar near the Brandenburg Gate, we would get in our car and leave. On our way out of the city, I would drop in at Spandau and hand over Ooma's transfer order to the guards at the reception desk.

Once Ooma arrived at that hospital, she would essentially be free to escape. Whatever she did after that would be her concern. My family loyalty only went so far.

I hurried to the bar, through the gritty smoke of that bomb-filled day.

Then I turned a corner and beheld Mueller's . . .

. . . just as another Allied bomb came screaming out of the sky and blew it apart in a shower of bricks and fire.

THE EXPLOSION THREW ME off my feet.

Shattered bricks whizzed over my head, slamming into the shop-fronts around me.

After a moment, I stood up and saw the bar—our bar—or what was left of it.

Its roof looked like the lid of a peeled-open soup can, twisted upward at an extreme angle, leaving the wrecked interior of the place open to the elements.

Luckily, it hadn't been a direct hit.

The bomb had actually landed on the building next door. It had been obliterated. It was just *gone*.

Flames billowed from Mueller's.

Its brick chimney toppled with a loud crash.

Everything was charred black.

I heard the sirens of fire trucks in the distance, but who knew if they were coming here or going to some other bomb site.

I raced toward the wreckage, searching for Dan.

I leapt into the ruins, hurdling the smashed-open front windows, calling, 'Dan! Dan!'

The bodies of the bar's regulars—civilians and military men

alike—lay covered in blood and scorch marks, dead.

'Dan! No—'

'Hanna . . .' a hoarse voice said from the back alley behind the bar.

I raced that way and found him, in his Gestapo uniform, his face covered in blood and a pile of broken bricks concealing his legs.

A woman's body lay beside him, her face and torso covered by the same brick pile.

'Dan!' I started heaving the bricks off his legs. 'Are you all right?'

He winced painfully. 'Not . . . really . . .'

As I removed some more bricks, I saw his left leg.

It was broken in several places. Exposed bone jutted out of the skin near the ankle.

Dan Kessler wasn't going to be leaving Berlin tonight, let alone traipsing across half of Germany. Dan wasn't going to be able to walk for some time.

'Hanna, get out of here,' he said. 'Take the car and go—ah!' He grimaced in pain.

I didn't know what to do. I wasn't going to leave him, that was for sure.

At that moment, the woman in the brick pile groaned. She was alive. I hurriedly yanked the broken and charred bricks off her face.

When the last brick came free, I froze.

It hadn't dawned on me that Dan's final meeting with a Russian Red Army liaison officer—a spy—would be with a woman, let alone *her*.

Lying there in front of me in that alley behind the ruined bar was Svetlana Sarkovsky.

I STARED AT THE Soviet spy as her eyes fluttered open.

She had black hair now, but her beautiful face was unmistakable.

She saw me but also didn't see me, still dazed by the blast.

But then she smelled me.

'Californian Poppy . . .' she said drowsily. 'How nice to see you again.'

Blood dripped from her temple. It matted the hair on one side of her head and slicked her whole neck.

She reached with bloodied fingers for her waist and suddenly I saw it. A twisted piece of metal stuck out from the left side of her stomach, leaking blood.

She touched it and screamed in agony.

I sprang into action.

First, I hauled Dan into our car. It was parked nearby, ready for our escape. Fortunately, it had not been too badly damaged by the bomb blast. Its windshield had been cracked by flying bricks and it had a few scratches, but otherwise it worked.

Then I went back and dragged Svetlana out of the rubble and slung her in the car, too.

Then I drove both of them to the nearest infirmary: an

underground field hospital that had been set up in the U-Bahn station in Potsdamerplatz not far from the Chancellery.

Dan's Gestapo uniform got him special treatment and he and Svetlana were whisked to a clean corner of the field hospital where some doctors attended to them immediately.

Three hours later, they both lay in clean beds in that converted U-Bahn station, bruised and bandaged but alive.

Svetlana was asleep, knocked out by morphine. Her stomach wound had been severe and required many stitches.

Dan was awake and as I sat on the edge of his bed, he just shook his head.

'Of all days, not today,' he said. 'Not today. Hanna, listen to me. You have to leave.'

'I'm not leaving Berlin without you, mister.' I nodded at his splinted left leg and ankle. 'By the look of that, you're not going anywhere soon. Get some rest. I'll figure something out. I've got to go and help my sister now. I'll be back in a few hours.'

I leaned forward and kissed him gently on the forehead.

'Rest now,' I said. 'I'll be back soon.'

Night had fallen fully by the time I arrived back at Spandau in the car and hurried through its twin-towered castle-like gate.

As the Reichsleiter's secretary, I was allowed in immediately.

When I asked to go to the holding cage containing the female inmates, the guards smirked.

They knew of Bormann's appetites, too, and his occasional request for a captive woman to be brought to his city apartment for 'questioning'.

'That one there,' I said, pointing at Ooma. 'Bring her to the interrogation room. I have some questions to ask her on behalf of Reichsleiter Bormann.'

The guards shoved Ooma into the bolted-down chair at the bolted-down table.

'You can take that off.' I nodded at her leather gag. 'You're not going to bite me, are you?'

She shook her head.

The guards unlocked the padlock at the back of the leather gag and left, slamming the iron door behind them.

We were alone.

Ooma removed the gag fully and I saw her face. It looked like mine, except for the shaved head and a hollowness in the cheeks from malnutrition.

She held her ragged little bag of possessions tightly in her lap.

'Oh, sister,' she said, her eyes shining. 'Look at you. Look how far you have risen in this world. Secretary to the Reichsleiter.'

'Ooma,' I said, taking the transfer order from my purse. 'Listen, I've got a transfer order for you—'

She moved as quick as a whip.

Her hand came lunging out of her ragged little bag and I glimpsed a cloth in her fist.

She reached across the table and jammed the cloth over my nose and I had enough time to detect a stinging chemical reek: chloroform. Where she'd got it from, I didn't know; she'd probably slipped it into her pocket during a visit to the infirmary.

I slumped in my chair, struggling to maintain consciousness.

My vision blurring, my muscle strength fading, I saw Ooma step around the table and casually pick up the transfer order.

She then extracted something from her bag, something shaggy or furry.

It took me a moment to figure out what it was.

A wig, a small wig that was the exact same colour and style as my own hair.

'Thank you so much for coming back, sister,' she said, her voice sounding distant.

Then she reached down and took my beloved silver bracelet off my wrist and casually slipped it onto her own.

'You were literally my only hope,' she said. 'I hate doing this to you *again*, I really do, but your lovely life is going to be mine once more. Worse, this time my life is going to be yours.'

Then I lost consciousness completely and everything went black.

I WOKE IN FREEZING darkness, lying on the wooden floor of a moving cattle car amid the shifting feet of twenty other female prisoners, with Ooma's leather mouth-gag strapped tightly over my face.

The floor on which I lay was covered in hay that was damp with human urine and stank of shit.

My head ached.

I picked myself up off the floor and touched my skull.

And felt stubble.

My hair was gone.

Ooma had shaved it off.

My left wrist was slicked with blood. I checked it and saw two brand new cuts, cuts that matched the ones Ooma had inflicted on herself as a teenager.

Oh God, no, I thought.

I gazed out through the gaps in the wall slats of the cattle car and saw fields lit by moonlight rushing past.

I was on a train racing south through the countryside. And I was there in Ooma's place, heading for the worst camp in the entire German camp system, Mauthausen.

MAUTHAUSEN-GUSEN CONCENTRATION CAMP
JANUARY 29, 1945

I ARRIVED AT MAUTHAUSEN late the next afternoon.

My initial shock at waking up in that cattle car had transformed to anger then outright fury at Ooma for doing such a thing to me, especially when I had gone back to Spandau to help *her*.

Snow fell.

A chill wind whistled.

Along with the other female prisoners, I was shoved out of the train and down a long path flanked by razor wire toward the camp complex nestled at the base of the mountain.

I alone wore an anti-biting mask.

As I passed through the gates of that awful place, my feelings of fury transformed again, this time into ones of dread.

I spent my first night in a barracks sleeping on a bare wooden floor positioned head to toe with the other women.

It was freezing and we pressed against each other for warmth. One of our number died of exposure that night. She was carried out in the morning by some male prisoners and dumped in a pit that was filled with stinking corpses.

We were put to work immediately.

A teenaged Nazi questioned each of us in turn, asking if we had any special skills.

Word had quickly spread through the women's barracks that working inside the caverns within the mountain was a guarantee of death.

I had other thoughts on my mind.

First, something Ooma had said:

'Let me give you some advice, sister. Should you ever get imprisoned, whether it's in an asylum, a sanitorium, a camp or a jail, escape within the first three days. After three days, you're done. You need energy to escape and they don't feed you, so you lose the energy you need to flee.'

And second, on one of my previous visits to Mauthausen with Speer, I recalled a Nazi engineer telling Speer that the tunnels inside the mountain went all the way through. They were unstable, sure, but they emerged on the other side.

When my turn came to be questioned by the Nazi teen, I said, 'I have worked in sheet-metal machining, sir.'

I was immediately assigned to the Messerschmitt plant inside the mountain, to work on the Me 262 jet fighter assembly line in there.

I went in that very day.

The rumours turned out to be true.

After I passed through the gigantic hangar-sized entrance to the mountain and entered the vast industrial works inside it, I didn't come out through that entrance again.

ONCE I STARTED WORKING at the fighter jet works inside the mountain, I slept inside the mountain.

By that time, the Nazis didn't bother giving prisoners cots or mats to sleep on or even food to eat. They just let us sleep on the cement floor and worked us till we died of exhaustion or starvation. From my time with Einstein back in the 30s reading about physics and atomic reactors, I knew some basics about fashioning metal, so I faked my way as best I could in the metalworks.

One night became two and as my energy faded, I kept thinking that Ooma's advice was right. I had to get out of here soon or I would never leave.

And then on my third night at Mauthausen, a commotion arose and some of the SS guards from the main camp came running inside the jet-works, calling to the guards.

Roused from my sleep, I heard the SS men exclaim, 'You won't believe it! A gaggle of stupid Russian inmates in Block 20 over at Mühlviertel have escaped! Five hundred of the fools! Come on! We're going to hunt the starving sons of bitches. It'll be grand!'

Mühlviertel was a subcamp of Mauthausen where Soviet prisoners were kept in preparation for execution.

For my young Nazi guards, this was the most exciting thing to happen at Mauthausen and they all hurried over to hear everything from their SS friends. Many raced out with them to see what was going on.

I didn't waste a second.

With their backs turned, I took off, running the other way, into the depths of the caverns.

Still wearing my mouth-gag, panting for breath, but energised by the barest hope of escape, I dashed into the maze of raw tunnels beyond the jet-works, hoping to get through to the other side.

In a war filled with vile atrocities, the 'Mühlviertel Hare Hunt' would go down as one of the worst.

The SS guards and the local German townsfolk gaily hunted those 500 Red Army escapees and took unbridled joy in killing the wretches.

It would last for three weeks.

IT TURNED OUT THAT the tunnels inside the mountain did extend all the way to the other side.

An industrial vice in the jet-works made short work of the padlock on the back of my mouth-gag. It opened with a crack and I yanked it off, sucking in air.

Then I grabbed a flashlight from a bench and ran for all I was worth into the tunnels.

I dashed through the first few passageways, zigging and zagging left and right. As I ventured deeper into the tunnel system, the walls became visibly rougher.

Then I rounded a rough stone corner and stopped suddenly.

Two figures were on the ground in front of me, engaged in vigorous sexual intercourse. A woman and a man.

The woman was a prisoner, the man a guard.

She sat astride him, naked, riding him like a bucking horse, while he lay on his back, moaning and grunting with pleasure. This was, I knew, a sad reality of every prison camp: no doubt she received special treatment for this. Extra food, blankets, maybe a promise of release when it was all over.

I froze—completely exposed and fearful that my escape would

be over almost before it had begun—but the way they were posi-tioned meant that he was facing *away* from me and she was looking directly at me.

Our eyes met.

She knew exactly what I was doing.

With a flick of her eyes, she nodded me onward as if to say, 'Go, keep going', never once pausing in her hip-rolling. The guard never saw me, never stopped his moaning.

I ran on, his grunts of delight echoing down the stone-walled tunnels behind me.

It took me seven hours to do it, bending and winding my way through raw caves and passages—some of them barely wide enough to squeeze through—but at last I emerged from a crevice on the other side of the mountain to behold the forests of Upper Austria.

Where to, now? I asked myself.

Germany was collapsing.

The Americans were coming from the west.

The Russians were descending on Berlin . . .

. . . where I had left Dan, his leg broken, in a field hospital inside the Potsdamerplatz U-Bahn station near the Chancellery, in a fake Gestapo uniform.

When the Russians took Berlin and found him, they would exe-cute him on the spot.

I had to save him.

I had to get back to Berlin before the Red Army got there.

And so I ran.

While the guards and townsfolk hunted down those poor Soviet prisoners-of-war on the other side of the mountain, I fled the other way.

★ ★ ★

Berlin was far to the north.

But getting there—let alone venturing into the centre of the war-ravaged city and escaping from it with Dan—was not something that would be easily accomplished.

I'd need help if I was going to do that.

And so for the next few weeks I weaved my way westward across the southern reaches of Germany, heading for the one group of people I knew could help me.

The American 6th Army.

The last few months of the war saw specialised
units of the US and Soviet armies charging into
Germany not for territory but for knowledge
in the form of German scientists.

America's search for German technical
specialists was organised by the ALSOS
mission—which after the war became
'Operation Paperclip'—while the Russians had
the 9th Chief Directorate of the NKVD . . .

– From: *1945 – The Last Days of World War II*
by William Hammonds

MY TRAVAILS ON THAT journey were many and are a tale for another
time: how I stole clothes from a bombed-out store in Enns, slept
in haylofts and abandoned farmhouses, avoided the main roads,
walked on abandoned railway tracks, dodged units of lost and starving German soldiers and ate whenever and whatever I could, until
almost four weeks later, I ran into the 6th Army outside Stuttgart.

'You there, halt!' an American scout yelled as I emerged from the
tree line with my hands raised.

'I mean you no harm!' I called in English as I walked toward
his team of men. 'I have been working for the Office of Strategic
Services! Please take me to your S-2! I have vital information for
your ALSOS people!'

They were the magic words and they worked.

No ordinary German could possibly know what the O.S.S. or an
S-2—an intelligence officer—was, let alone something as secret as
ALSOS.

I was taken to a mobile command post where two colonels met me, a smaller one named Beizer and a bigger one named Rosenberg.

The short one, Beizer, stared at me with amazed eyes.

'Okay, I'll bite. Who are you and what are you doing talking about ALSOS?'

'My name is Hanna Fischer. I've been working throughout the war in Berlin with O.S.S. agent Daniel Kessler reporting on German rocket and atomic capabilities.'

Colonel Beizer looked decidedly unimpressed.

'All right,' I said. 'Have you been through Haigerloch yet?'

'Yeah . . .'

'And you found the German atomic research labs there?'

'Yeah.'

'But did you find the reactor?'

He paused.

'No . . .'

'Do you still have people at the castle?'

'I'm not going to tell you that.'

'Radio them and tell them to look underneath the castle's chapel. There's a secret lab down there with a reactor array of uranium cubes in it.'

Beizer nodded to his colleague. 'Call the ALSOS guys at Haigerloch and tell 'em to look underneath the castle's chapel.'

Rosenberg went outside while Beizer and I waited in silence.

At length Rosenberg returned. 'Jesus Christ, she knows her shit. The team at Haigerloch just found the lab she was talkin' about. They also said that Daniel Kessler is legit. HQ wants to meet her, ASAP.'

Beizer said, 'Okay, Miss Hanna Fischer. You just earned yourself an all-expenses-paid flight to ALSOS headquarters.'

PARIS, FRANCE
MARCH 1, 1945

THEY DIDN'T TELL ME that ALSOS headquarters was in France, at l'Opera in the middle of Paris.

I was flown in a puddle-jumper directly from the front lines to Paris.

Once I was at l'Opera, my GI escorts handed me to a gaggle of four office secretaries who gave me a dress and some make-up to clean myself up. My hair didn't need brushing since it was still very short from its shaving four weeks earlier.

As one of them reached forward to help with my make-up, I said, 'Excuse me, miss, but if you have any food around, I'd really appreciate it. I've been foraging for almost a month and would love something to eat, anything you can find, really.'

'Absolutely, ma'am,' she said as she hurried out. She returned shortly after with a tray of baguettes and tarts. I wolfed them all down.

As they fussed around me, I noticed that the secretaries treated me with hushed reverence, as if I was some seasoned field operative with grand experience, which now that I think of it, I kind of was.

I heard two of them whispering, 'She's the one who revealed the location of that huge German rocket base in Helfaut. That probably saved thousands of lives in England . . .'

'I heard she knows about atomic science . . .' another one said.

I smiled to the secretary who had handed me the dress. It was daffodil yellow in colour.

'Excuse me, please,' I said, 'what's your name?'

'Dorothy, ma'am. Dorothy Summers.'

'Forgive me, Dorothy, but do you have something more like a suit? This is lovely, but where I'm going, I don't want to look lovely, I want to be taken seriously. Perhaps something darker and woollen?'

'Oh, yes, of course,' she said and scurried out.

She came back ten minutes later with a very stylish skirted suit.

'Nice,' I said.

'We're in Paris,' she replied with a smile, 'with no budgetary constraints and some great department stores close by.'

'You're a hell of a secretary, Dorothy,' I said.

'I went to the finest secretary school in America, ma'am. The Graham-Coulson Secretarial School,' she said.

My eyes sprang wide. 'I went there, too, many years ago! Rule Number One . . .'

She joined me as we said: '*Your job is to help your boss to do his job!*'

We laughed.

Once the other girls—several of whom were also graduates of the Graham-Coulson school—discovered that I was an alumnus of that august academy, they lavished me with extra attention.

For not only was I a secretary, I was one who had risen to become someone of significance, someone who was about to see their commander.

My skirt-suit went on. Make-up was applied by my newfound team of friends. I was even offered a fetching wig but this I declined.

I figured my ultrashort hair made a very clear statement about who I was and what I had been through.

I was then ushered into the offices of the commander of the ALSOS mission: Colonel Boris Pash.

'So this is Miss Fischer,' Colonel Pash said as I entered his office. 'I've seen many of your reports over the last few years.'

Pash wasn't your usual big-chested military commander. With his wire-framed spectacles and receding hairline, he looked more like a high school principal.

'Nice to meet you, Colonel.'

'Albert Einstein says you're quite the physicist. Hence your knowledge of uranium-cube matrices in labs hidden underneath churches.'

'When I saw that lab, I knew it was important,' I said.

'You were working for Speer for a long time, correct?'

'Yes.'

'But that stopped recently.'

'I was transferred to Martin Bormann and let's just say he has different interests from Speer.'

'What else can you tell us about the German weapons programs?'

'What do you want to know?'

'Werner Heisenberg. Where is he?'

'I can give you his home address in Hechingen.'

'The Messerschmitt factory?'

'Underground at Mauthausen. There's another one at Mittelwerk.'

Colonel Pash leaned forward. 'Von Braun and the V-2 program?'

'Also at Mittelwerk. Underground.'

He had many other questions. Some I could answer, others I could not.

When he was done, Pash said, 'Miss Fischer, you've done America a hell of a service during this war. I think you deserve a well-earned rest here in Paris.'

'That's very kind of you, Colonel,' I said. 'But given all I've done for the war effort, I'd like to ask you for something.'

'What?'

'I want you to get me back to Berlin.'

WHEN I TOLD PASH about Dan—an American agent in a Gestapo uniform holed up in a German field hospital in a U-Bahn station in central Berlin; one who had spent almost the entire war undercover and in extreme danger; and the agent who had enlisted me and aided me throughout my time there, too—he said, 'Are you serious? You wanna go back there, *now*, with the Russian army right on the doorstep?'

'Sir,' I said. 'Every decision comes down to a choice. This is the right choice.'

After I said that, Boris Pash did all he could to get me to Berlin.

But this, it turned out, was something even he, the commander of the ALSOS mission, couldn't order on his own authority.

Precious weeks ticked by. As they did, I listened to every report I could about what was happening in Berlin.

The Red Army were edging closer to it, well ahead of the U.S. 12th Army led by General Omar Bradley which was approaching the city from the west.

The Russians were going to get there first and they were going to tear Berlin apart.

Then in late April, Pash called for me.

General Bradley's army was less than fifty miles from Berlin and Bradley wanted to send a reconnaissance team into the city in a stolen Luftwaffe aircraft to determine the full extent of the Soviet advance.

'There's an extra seat on that plane,' Pash said. 'I called in some favours to get you on it. If you can get Kessler back to the plane by the time that recon team leaves, go for it. But they won't cover you or wait for you. Once you're in Berlin, you're on your own. Good enough?'

'Good enough.'

I was going back to Berlin, into the heart of that burning city, as the entire Russian Red Army bore down on it.

What I didn't know was that in the weeks I had been away, I had been living a parallel life there.

PART VIII

1945
MR BORMANN'S SECRETARY
– SECOND TIME: OOMA –

The Führerbunker

'It's no use going back to yesterday, because I was a different person then.'

– Alice in *Alice's Adventures in Wonderland*
by Lewis Carroll

BORMANN'S OFFICES
THE REICH CHANCELLERY
FEBRUARY–APRIL 1945

IT ONLY TOOK ME a few days to figure out Martin Bormann.

The man was a lech and I had met his type before.

It quickly became apparent that, so obsessed was Bormann with serving his precious Führer—a man who struck me as withered and feeble—that he barely knew Hanna or any of his other secretaries.

That things in Berlin were rapidly deteriorating into absolute chaos also helped me infiltrate Hanna's life.

Bormann and I spent most of our time racing back and forth between the Reich Chancellery and what became known as the 'Führerbunker', a lavish complex of heavily reinforced air-raid shelters that extended underneath the Chancellery's garden.

I could not have been happier.

The Führerbunker was, quite simply, the safest place in Berlin.

It was also abundantly stocked with food and water, even alcohol. And it was luxuriantly appointed with expensive furniture and artworks. Hanna's life, now mine, pleased me immensely.

Better still, Bormann was actively engaged in planning his escape from Germany to South America with a cohort of other Nazis. They intended to flee in a submarine that was to depart from the Italian port city of Genoa as soon as the order was given to evacuate Berlin.

I would get myself onto that U-boat.

Arranging my place on it turned out not to be difficult at all.

With a well-timed wink to Bormann, I soon had him fucking me from behind in his back office, gasping, 'I knew you wanted me, you little minx. I knew it!'

My access to the Führerbunker also gave me insights into the war.

It was a fucking disaster.

Standing in the back of briefings where senior staff told Hitler of the two enemy armies rampaging across Germany from the east and the west, I just stared, blank-faced, at the Nazi fools who had tricked an entire nation into letting them wage war in its name.

The Nazis, including Hitler, were deluded idiots.

The senior officers of the Wehrmacht, with their haughty bearings and names starting with 'von', were pompous aristocratic asses.

And Bormann was just a weasel, always praising Hitler and telling him how brilliant he was, ever ready to implement his every command.

The world was literally crashing down around them and they talked of wonder weapons and armies that didn't exist.

There was only one realistic one among them, the Reich Minister for Armaments and War Production, Albert Speer. He was shrewd, measured, articulate when the others were crass and vulgar. I could see that he chose his words very carefully, for to openly question the Führer's delusions could be fatal even to someone as senior as he.

But then at one crisis meeting in the Führerbunker, as someone else spoke, Speer suddenly appeared beside me and whispered, 'Hello, Hanna.'

I hesitated, till it came to me. At the time she'd first found me at Spandau—God, when was that; before the war, sometime in

'38 or '39—I hadn't known the powerful official for whom my sister had worked. So it was him.

'Herr Reichsminister,' I replied softly with a nod.

'You are well? Working for Bormann has not been too . . . difficult?'

He seemed concerned for me—or, rather, for the real Hanna.

'It has its moments,' I whispered back.

'If it gets . . . complicated . . . I mean, if he . . . wants you to perform any acts with which you are not comfortable, let me know,' he said awkwardly.

Clearly, Speer knew of Bormann's sexual predilections. His concern would have been sweet if he weren't entirely complicit in all the other wicked fucking things the Nazis had done. Monsters come in many shapes and sizes, no matter how cultured they appear.

Thankfully, he was called away and I didn't speak with him again.

On April 20, Russian forces entered the city limits.

Bormann wouldn't leave.

By April 27, the Russians were threatening the city centre.

Some of the Nazi leadership fled on planes that were taking off from an improvised runway in the Tiergarten. Still, Bormann wouldn't leave.

The secretaries in the Führerbunker who were virgins asked the younger military officers to fuck them now, gently, so that their first carnal encounters would not be with a line of twenty Russian infantrymen waiting their turn.

Hitler flew into wild rages, oscillating between declarations that the war was lost to exclamations that Wenck's XII Army would return to Berlin to hold off the Russian hordes.

But I knew from Bormann that no such rescue was coming.

I also knew that the German forces in Berlin would soon run out of ammunition entirely.

By April 29, Russian forces had entered the city centre and were engaged in pitched battles inside Gestapo headquarters and in the Reichstag.

On the morning of April 30, Hitler declared that he would fight to the very end alongside his fellow Germans.

That afternoon, he killed his wife and then himself.

With Hitler dead, Bormann was free to leave and he wasted no time.

He bolted.

I bolted with him.

TIERGARTEN EMERGENCY AIRSTRIP
CENTRAL BERLIN
APRIL 30, 1945, 11:30 P.M.

As DOZENS OF ALLIED bombers roared by overhead, our stolen German Storch plane swooped down toward Berlin, heading for the Tiergarten not far from the central government district.

The dark city below us was a web of shadows and fire. The park was simply a dark rectangle on this background.

There was no flak or anti-aircraft fire: the Germans had long since lost that capability. Indeed, the bombers above us were now dropping their ordnance only on very specific targets, so as not to hit the Russian forces in the city.

It was an audacious plan, this reconnaissance mission, and I was happy to tag along.

I sat in the back of the plane in black coveralls with a black beanie over my still-short hair, staring forward.

The three battle-hardened American troops with me threw odd glances my way, but knew not to speak to me. They had their own mission to accomplish anyway.

Our plane touched down in the Tiergarten and pulled to a halt near the Brandenburg Gate.

The American troopers rushed out of the plane and vanished into the burning city.

'We're out of here in thirty minutes, lady, on the tick of midnight!' the pilot called to me as I leapt out of the plane into the park. 'Not a second longer!'

It was going to be close.

It would take me about ten minutes to reach the U-Bahn station at Potsdamerplatz—at a sprint—and another ten to get back, assuming I encountered no obstacles or Russian troops and assuming Dan could even walk.

'I understand!' I called.

As earth-shaking impacts shuddered all around me, I ran off into the government quarter, heading for the Chancellery and Potsdamerplatz U-Bahn station.

Artillery shells boomed all around me as I dashed through the empty streets.

The air stank of carbide.

Black smoke hung over everything. Fires burned.

An entire building to my left exploded as I ran past it.

I glimpsed shadows crouch-running across alleyways and I heard the taunting howls of men: Russian soldiers stalking through the ruins, baying for blood.

Then I came to the Reich Chancellery and Potsdamerplatz station.

I hurried down the stairs into the station and beheld the field hospital where I'd left Dan months before—

It had been abandoned.

Every cabinet lay flung open. Any drugs that had been in them were gone, especially morphine.

Those patients who could walk had evidently departed with the medical personnel. Those who couldn't had simply been left here to their fate.

They still lay here—moaning, crying out in pain—in their beds, bereft of medical attention and morphine.

I didn't know how long it had been since the staff had fled, but I guessed maybe a day.

I didn't care.

I raced over to the corner of the hospital where I had left Dan and Svetlana Sarkovsky, rounding a set of toppled screens . . .

. . . to see that both their beds were empty.

'No,' I breathed. 'No, no . . .'

I CHECKED MY WATCH.

It'd been eleven minutes since I'd left the reconnaissance team's plane.

A groan from under one of the beds made me whirl and I saw Dan lying on the floor *under* a bed, hidden by a tent of sheets.

His left leg was still in its splint and while he was pale, he actually looked better than when I'd left him.

There was no sign of Svetlana.

'You came back?' Dan's voice was pained.

'I said I would, didn't I?' I heaved away the bed and kicked aside some other trash that was in the way.

'You said you'd be back in an hour or so.'

'I kinda got sidetracked.' I looped his arm over my shoulder.

As I did, our faces were close and he looked me right in the eye. 'But you came back now. Into all this? To get me?'

'I like you,' I said, risking a quick smile. 'I like you a lot. Always have, Dan Kessler.'

I lifted him to his feet, taking half his weight on my shoulder.

'Feeling's mutual, Hanna Fischer,' he said. 'You're one hell of a girl, you know that? We get out of this, I'd really like to take you to dinner again. Somewhere nice. No gangsters or el-trains this time.'

'I'd like that.'

'Hey, your hair's short. Did you cut it? Where *did* you go?'

'Shut up, we have to leave.' I heaved him toward the stairs. 'What happened to Svetlana?'

'I don't know. I woke up one morning and she was gone.'

'When did the medical staff flee?'

'A few hours ago. Someone came running in shouting that Hitler was dead, that he'd killed himself and abandoned them, leaving them all to face the Russians. How close are the Russians?'

'Real close. Come on.' I checked my watch again. 'We have about fifteen minutes to catch our ride out of here.'

We hurried up the stairs together.

On the way up, we stepped over the body of a dead German soldier. Wincing with pain, Dan grabbed the man's pistol.

No sooner were we outside than a volley of Russian artillery shells slammed down on the street.

Explosions boomed to our left and right and when the smoke cleared, both ends of the street were blocked.

'Damn, this'll slow us down,' I said. 'This way. We can cut through the garden behind the Chancellery.'

THE FÜHRERBUNKER
BEHIND THE REICH CHANCELLERY

WITH HITLER DEAD, IT became every man for himself in the Führerbunker.

Everybody fled.

Bormann stashed whatever important documents and papers he could carry into a satchel and ran for the door.

I took off after him, determined to stay close.

He was my ticket out of Europe, to a new life in South America. Once we got there, I could steal some gold from him and vanish, but till then I had to stay by his side.

We emerged from the Führerbunker, rising up into the crater-filled garden outside it.

The sky glowed fiery orange, the clouds reflecting the light of the burning city.

We passed the shallow crater containing the charred corpses of Hitler and Eva Braun. Hitler had ordered that his body be burned after his death, so it couldn't be paraded through the streets of Moscow.

So this was what became of Hitler. The man who had plunged Europe and the world into war. A burnt-out body in a ditch.

Bormann didn't so much as glance at his former boss.

Self-preservation was the only thing on his mind now.

As we raced away from the two bodies in the dirt crater, two figures emerged from the other side of the garden, coming from Voss Strasse.

A woman with a wounded man draped over her shoulder.

As they came closer, I stopped dead.

Seeing them, Bormann stopped, too, because—just as I had done—he'd recognised the woman and was suddenly confused, because she had my face.

It was Hanna.

Halfway across the garden behind the Chancellery building, with Dan hanging off my shoulder, I froze.

I'd seen the two figures burst out from the entrance to the Führerbunker and start running across the courtyard toward us, but it was only when they got close that I recognised them.

It was Martin Bormann and Ooma, dressed as me.

THE FOUR OF US stood there in that bombed-out garden, facing each other in stunned silence.

Dan shoved himself off my shoulder and stared open-mouthed at Ooma and then at me.

'What the hell—?'

I could see what he was thinking.

'Dan, wait . . .' I began.

Then Ooma shouted, 'Dan! Wait! That's Ooma! That's my sister, the one I told you about!'

Dan took a hobbled step away from me, gripping his pistol, staring at me with wary eyes.

I couldn't believe it.

I knew what he was seeing: me, with my shaved head and coveralls, and Ooma with a full head of hair cut in the style I had always used, dressed in the skirt-suit I had always worn, *and wearing my precious silver bracelet on her wrist.*

Bormann didn't know what to think either.

He turned to Ooma. 'Hanna? Who—what is this?'

'Hanna?' Dan blinked twice, trying to clear his head.

Then he raised his pistol . . .

. . . and aimed it *at me*.

Ooma saw her chance. 'Shoot her, Dan! She's come back to try and steal my life again! Shoot her, now!'

Dan's eyes flashed from me to her and back again.

Then his gaze fell to my left wrist and he saw the twin scars there.

'Dan, wait—' I said.

Ooma yelled, 'See the scars! It's her! Kill her!'

I stared into Dan's eyes over the barrel of his pistol.

Which was when he asked the question, a question I never expected.

'If I travelled for a thousand years at the speed of light, how long would I travel for?'

What the hell is he talking about? I thought, frowning.

Oh, Dan, you clever man, I thought as I saw Ooma's face go blank, revealing her complete lack of understanding of the question.

'A thousand and five years,' I said quickly.

Bang.

His pistol went off.

Ooma's chest blew out in a gout of blood.

The blank look of incomprehension remained on her face as she dropped to her knees and then fell face-first into the mud, dead.

Dan turned his gun on Bormann and pulled the trigger.

Click.

No more bullets.

Bormann—his first instinct, as always, being to save his own skin—seized the opportunity and fled from the garden, out of our sight, off into the flaming city.

Dan and I were left staring at Ooma's body lying face-down in the mud, unmoving.

Neither of us said anything for a moment.

I said, 'A thousand years at the speed of light, huh? A good question to ask in the circumstances.'

'I figured only the real you would know the answer,' Dan said. 'That was a memorable dinner even before the gangsters showed up.'

'I know but let's talk about that later. We can't stay here. We have to run.'

'Right,' Dan agreed.

We fled from the garden, but not before I scurried back and yanked my bracelet off Ooma's dead wrist. Then we were off.

And flee we did, back up Ebertstrasse to the Brandenburg Gate and into the Tiergarten.

Our encounter in the Chancellery's garden had slowed us and we needed to hurry if we were going to make it to the escape plane in time.

We emerged from the tree line at the spot where my plane had parked.

The plane was gone.

I looked down Charlottenstrasse and saw it lifting off into the sky, heading west.

We'd missed it by minutes.

'Damn . . .' I breathed.

'What do we do now?' Dan gasped.

'I have an idea,' I said. 'But we need to move fast. We have to catch up with Bormann.'

Forty minutes later, after a hair-raising dash across the city, we caught up with Martin Bormann at Tempelhof Airfield just as he was boarding one of his escape planes—and just as two squads of Russian paratroopers burst out onto the runway and stopped the plane.

The Russians took us away, along with Reichsleiter Martin Bormann.

SOVIET MOBILE COMMAND POST
BERLIN
MAY 4, 1945

A RED ARMY MOBILE command post in the ruins of Berlin is the site of my third interrogation.

Hitler is dead. Germany has surrendered.

Of course, as a senior Nazi, Bormann was on Russia's list of high-value captives, men who were to be taken alive, if possible. Since we were caught with him, we were taken alive as well.

Dan and I spent three days in a holding cage before we were brought to the interrogation cell.

It was only when we arrived there that we saw what the Russians did to captured senior Nazis.

Bormann was raped repeatedly before our eyes.

Yet for some reason, Dan and I were not touched.

As I watched Bormann get violated by the four dirty Russian soldiers, I can't say I felt sorry for him.

And then our interrogators arrived.

There were two of them.

Both were colonels and they wore uniforms covered in medals and decorations.

'Hello, Hanna,' the senior one said. 'My, my, you've been busy.'

'Hello, Svetlana,' I replied.

★ ★ ★

'Are you going to kill us?' I asked. I was beyond pleasantries now.

Svetlana Sarkovsky smiled. She cut a formidable figure in her full colonel's uniform.

'Hanna, you mistake me,' she said. 'When I heard that it was you and Agent Kessler who had been picked up with Bormann, I gave strict orders that you were both to be brought here, untouched. During my time in that U-Bahn hospital, Agent Kessler told me all about you, your whole story, from fleeing Germany to living in New York City, to working for Einstein and some capitalists, to saving the young son of a gangster. You are an impressive woman, Californian Poppy.'

She paused.

'I also owe you a personal debt. After I was wounded with Mr Kessler a couple of months ago, you dragged me to safety, to that field hospital. You saved my life.'

She gave me a nod, the curt nod of a professional.

'Tell me,' I said, 'was it you who seduced Gertrude in Bormann's office?'

'No, that was one of my girls.' She eyed me sideways. 'I'm too old for that now, although in my time I did introduce a few innocent young maidens to such delights.'

'That was how you knew about Bormann's escape planes at Tempelhof?'

'Yes.'

'So what now?' I asked.

Svetlana smiled again. 'The war is over. It's time for us all to go home. I shall hand you over myself to the Americans in exchange for two of ours that they have picked up.'

I jerked my chin at Bormann, whimpering in the corner, gripping his bleeding buttocks. 'What will happen to him?'

In reply, Svetlana drew her pistol and shot Bormann in the face. He flopped to the floor, dead.

'His body will be tossed into a street somewhere in Berlin for the rats to feed on,' she said.

Then she stood and left.

1945–1947

IN THE MONTHS AFTER the end of the war in Europe, things didn't move quickly.

Revelations of the extent of the Nazis' extermination camps shocked the world.

It was estimated that as many as six million Jews had been murdered plus countless Soviet prisoners-of-war and other minority groups.

Amid all that, a chill descended on American–Soviet relations and the former allies were suddenly not so friendly anymore.

After Dan and I were handed over to the American forces in Germany, we were airlifted to Paris where I was reunited with the ALSOS team at l'Opera.

Soon to be renamed 'Operation Paperclip', the next phase of their work was only just beginning.

It would be their job to find brilliant Nazi engineers and scientists like Wernher von Braun and Werner Heisenberg before the Russians did and spirit them to America.

Of course, I had a role to play in this and I remained in Paris for many months with Dan and Colonel Pash, answering questions and identifying many of the secret installations I had visited.

★ ★ ★

In late 1945, war crimes trials were held at Nuremberg.

Albert Speer was one of the defendants.

He claimed to have had no knowledge of the Holocaust. This was laughable, but his charm and contrition at his trial saved his life.

While most of the other Nazis were sentenced either to death or life imprisonment, Speer received a twenty-year sentence to be served at Spandau Prison.

SPANDAU PRISON
JULY 1947

In mid-1947, I visited him at Spandau.

Even in his drab prison clothes, he cut an aristocratic figure. He had, he told me, started writing his memoirs.

'So, you were reporting back to the Americans the whole time you were working for me?' he asked sullenly.

'The whole time,' I said.

He shook his head as he stared blankly at the floor. The look on his face was a mix of betrayal and, quite frankly, disbelief that a man as brilliant as he could be duped by a secretary.

'The atomic bombs the Americans dropped on Japan,' he said. 'The Americans figured out the science while our people— Heisenberg's team—could not?'

The dropping of the two atomic bombs on Hiroshima and Nagasaki two years earlier in August of 1945 had caused a world-wide sensation. That a single bomb—using the principles of Einsteinian physics—could obliterate an entire city was literally fantastical to the person on the street. The Nazis had blustered about building superweapons. America had built one.

'They sure did,' I said.

'You knew about the American program?'

'Yes.'

'When our spies were told that the Americans were *failing* miserably at atomic science, you knew that was false?'

'I did.'

He shook his head once again in disbelief.

I said, 'I have to ask, how could you do it? Build all those things for Hitler and the Nazis: the buildings, the camps, the ovens?'

Speer paused, raising his chin in thought. 'When does a man get to build history?'

I stared at him for a long moment.

Then, without another word, I left.

I never saw Albert Speer again.

And then one day in October of 1947 I was informed by Colonel Pash that I could go home.

Dan got the same orders.

Because of our long and distinguished service, we were to be granted VIP travel to wherever we wished to go.

The question was, where was home for me now?

ATLANTIC OCEAN
OCTOBER 1947

I SAT ON THE deck of the ocean liner, gazing out at the horizon, heading back to New York.

I was on a ship loaded with war heroes from the European theatre and we were sailing back to America in style.

Many of the heroic young men on that boat with me had suffered wounds during the fighting, thus delaying their return.

As I sat on the sundeck that day, I struck up a conversation with one of them, a young corporal from Iowa named Dawkins.

After he'd told me all about his time in Europe—he'd stormed the beaches on D-Day and drunk from Hitler's wine glasses at Berchtesgaden—he asked where I came from and what I'd done during the war.

I said I couldn't tell him about that, which he understood instantly. I didn't tell him that I, too, had drunk from those same wine glasses at Berchtesgaden.

But I did tell him about how I had come to America.

'My father was German but my mother was American. I grew up in Berlin but then moved to New York City in 1919. I lived down near the fish markets during the 20s.'

'The fish markets in New York, you say?' he said. 'Then you'd know all about Baby Face Mancino?'

'Of course. Gosh, I remember when he killed all those other gangsters at the warehouse by the fish docks. And the time Lucky Luciano tried to kidnap his son, Douglas Jr. I was actually there when that happened.'

'You were there?' Dawkins said.

Then he shouted to some of his friends. 'Yo, boys! Where's the dago? Where's Dougie?'

There was some shouting and calling and then a stout-chested dark-haired young man of perhaps 25 stepped out onto the deck.

He looked just like his father, except younger and trimmer, and his eyes weren't wild or crazy. They were narrow, perceptive, hardened by battle.

I gasped. 'Douglas Jr . . .'

'Do I know you?' he asked.

'You wouldn't remember it, but we met when you were about four. I rescued you at a restaurant when Lucky Luciano tried to kidnap you. I was with a federal agent named Dan Kessler.'

His eyes went wide. 'That was *you*? My mom and dad talked about that night all the time, about some woman who took me up onto the railway tracks to save me from Lucky's boys.'

I nodded. 'I also saw you when you were, I don't know, maybe nine or ten, when your father—well—when your father tossed Clay Bentley Jr off his dock in a pair of cement shoes.'

Now the young man's eyes boggled.

'Jesus, lady . . .' he whispered. 'That I do remember. Holy shit, I'll never forget it. That was you who stood up to my dad?'

'Sure was.'

'Geez, you made an impact on him that day. He often said, "That dame on the dock, man, she was the most cold-blooded, hard-eyed negotiator I ever met."'

'What happened to your father?' I asked.

'He died a few years ago. Went down the same way as Capone: for tax avoidance. Got sent to Sing Sing and while he was there, some asshole shanked him.'

Turned out, Doug Mancino Jr, son of an Italian gangster, had joined the Army in 1941 and served in Italy and Germany, earning himself two Purple Hearts and a Silver Star. He had saved his entire unit at Monte Cassino.

We chatted for the whole afternoon as our liner powered west across the Atlantic, toward the setting sun and home.

That evening, I stood on the bow of the ship, thinking.

Dan joined me. 'You know, I don't think I ever thanked you for saving my life back in Berlin. Flying back into that burning city, while the Russians were storming it, to rescue my ass.'

'You're welcome.' I smiled.

'What are you thinking about so hard?' he asked.

'The future. I've got nothing waiting for me in New York. Again. No job, no money, no prospects, no family, no life.'

Dan nodded silently.

Then he said, 'You know, *technically*, Hanna Fischer—secretary to Albert Speer and Martin Bormann—was shot and killed in Berlin on April 30th, 1945. A lot of records were lost during the war. If you wanted to start a new life in New York—a *whole* new life, a fresh start—you could, you know.'

'What do you mean?' I asked.

'I mean, look at what the American Government is doing for all those Nazi scientists, inventing new identities for them and all that. I could easily get my people to create a whole new identity for you. Hell, I think I could even arrange a funeral for your old self.'

'Let me think about it.'

'Sure. Oh, and Hanna. I'm not so sure you've got nothing waiting for you in New York.'

The next day we sailed into New York Harbor and docked at Staten Island.

As Dan and I strode down the gangplank, Dan touched my shoulder and pointed to the right.

I saw three people standing at the rail, smiling and waving at me.

Fanny and her husband, Raymond.

And Albert Einstein.

OF COURSE, DAN HAD sent a telegram and informed them of our impending arrival.

Einstein gave me a long embrace.

'My dear Hanna. I'm so sorry I sent you back to Germany ahead of me in 1933. If I hadn't done that, you would never have been stuck there.'

'Oh, sir, it wasn't your fault. It turned out for the best: I managed to keep your research away from the Nazis. I had to hide inside your sunken sailboat at Caputh.'

'Inside my boat?' he exclaimed. 'Well, that explains the state those documents were in when they were finally returned to me. Thank God you found them first. They contained my early calculations on an atomic device.'

I turned to Fanny as she leapt forward and enveloped me in an almighty hug of her own while her husband Raymond looked on.

It was only when Fanny released me that I noticed how lovely her clothes were. She was wearing a very expensive dress-suit, and Raymond's suit was nicely cut, too.

'My little investment business has been doing rather well on the stock market these last few years,' Fanny said, seeing my look. 'Got loads of clients. While Raymond here got himself elected to the state assembly, I made us a few million bucks, I did.'

I burst out in a huge grin. 'Oh, Fanny! Well done! I'm so proud of you! You've come a long way from reading those books in our dorm room at secretary school.'

'As have you, Hanna,' she said. 'Both in travels and in wealth.'

'Wealth? I don't understand.'

'Did you forget that you gave me some of your earnings way back in 1919 to invest in the market? You were my first client!'

I had indeed forgotten.

The look on my face must have shown it.

Fanny clapped me on the back. 'I've been investing it all this time and holding the profits in a trust account for you. You're worth 1.8 million dollars, young lady.'

I almost fainted.

PART IX

1948
NO-ONE'S
SECRETARY

It's never too late to be whoever you want to be.

– F. Scott Fitzgerald

PRINCETON CEMETERY
PRINCETON, NEW JERSEY
JANUARY 20, 1948

I AM AT MY own poorly attended funeral, watching it from the bell-tower of the church overlooking the cemetery. I run my fingers over my beloved silver bracelet as I look down over the scene.

Einstein begins his eulogy.

'I first met Hanna Fischer in Berlin when she was a little girl. She was a sweet thing and she showed signs of her brilliance at a very early age. We were next-door neighbours and I was friends with her father. To those of us who knew Hanna—'

Suddenly, a loud gaseous hiss cuts him off. A bus has arrived at the gate to the cemetery a short distance away. It wheezes to a halt.

Einstein looks up.

The bus is labelled: PRINCETON UNIVERSITY.

A second identical bus pulls in behind it, then a third.

They always had trouble starting them on really cold days.

To my surprise, people emerge from the three buses.

Lines of them.

Young physicists from the Institute of Advanced Study at Princeton University, most of them Einstein's students, many of them the offspring of the Jewish physicists who had fled Germany in the 30s.

Einstein has told them all about me and my exploits.

Some of the giants of atomic physics are there, too, including Niels Bohr and Arthur Compton, along with many of their students.

Stories about me have travelled via them as well.

Then a smaller bus arrives.

Out of it pours a line of young women: all dressed in fitted skirt-suits with kerchiefs around their necks; walking with great poise, their heads held high.

It is only when I see the tall, older woman emerge from the bus behind them that I realise where they come from.

Mrs Katherine Graham-Coulson.

Dark-haired and statuesque, even at her advanced age, the owner of the Graham-Coulson Secretarial School for Ladies still cuts a commanding figure.

I smile when I see her.

Behind the buses come cars, among them some limousines.

Out of one steps Mr Clay Bentley Sr, now in his eighties but that wide round face with its neatly parted white hair is unmistakable. Clutching his arm is his second wife, Mrs Henrietta Bentley, née Henderson. Their coffee date, arranged by me when I had control of his diary back in 1920, appears to have worked out well for them.

A striking blonde woman of maybe 50 arrives, her arm linked through that of a short bald gentleman perhaps a decade her senior. She is well dressed, perfectly groomed and beautiful. A young man in his twenties accompanies this couple; he is also blond and quite handsome. The woman touches Fanny's shoulder and gives her a warm smile in greeting. Fanny hugs her.

I realise who it is.

It's Stella.

She has aged but she is still gorgeous. Fanny has told me that

Stella worked for her for ten years until she married one of Fanny's employees, a diminutive accountant named Levi Hoffman. In her youth, Stella had wanted to be the wife of a high-society WASP. She ended up marrying a sweet little Jew.

The handsome twenty-something is Clay Bentley III, the quiet little boy I knew as Charlie, who I last saw on his father's dock in the Hamptons, the day Clay Jr was dropped into the ocean wearing concrete shoes. Charlie's learning difficulties passed as he grew and I am informed that he has become a fine young man.

Einstein restarts his eulogy, now addressing the enormous crowd gathered around my grave.

'Hanna Fischer had a brilliant mind. As a little girl she once told me with the utter earnestness of a child, that she would be the greatest physicist ever.

'There are many here—myself included—who boast doctorates and prizes awarded to us in honour of our so-called accomplishments. But there is no prize for what she accomplished.

'For instance, it is difficult to calculate just how many lives she saved during the war. By disclosing the location of a German rocket site in northern France, she probably saved thousands of civilian lives in Britain. By deceiving senior Nazis about the true possibilities of building atomic weapons, she may have saved hundreds of thousands. And she did all that while living and working among some of the vilest Nazis that existed.

'On a more intimate level, we all benefitted from Hanna's singular, wonderful ability: her talent at enabling others *to live out their potential.*

'It might have been giving you the confidence to start a business or go on a date. Or tackling an assassin or flying into Berlin ahead of the Red Army to save a man's life.

'Hanna made us all better. I am sure that she is watching over us now'—as he says this, he throws a sly look up at me in the belltower—'urging us to be our best selves. I'm sure you would all agree with me when I say that it was our privilege to have known her.'

The funeral ends and everyone departs.

As she heads off on Raymond's arm, Fanny glances up at me and gives me a quick nod. She, Raymond and Einstein are the only ones who know the truth that I am still alive.

A man steps up beside me in the belltower.

It's Dan. He takes my hand.

'Not a bad turnout,' he says. 'Come on, honey. Time to start that new life. Let's go home.'

I was born on New Year's Day, 1902.

I had turned 46 a few weeks before my 'funeral'.

I was not famous like Einstein although now I worked with him in the physics department at his Institute for Advanced Study at Princeton University under the name Sandra Rose Martin, my mother's name.

I had not won any prizes, Nobel or otherwise, but in a year I would be awarded my doctorate and become, finally, the physicist I had always wanted to be.

Six months after that, I would marry Dan Kessler and take his name, further distancing myself from my old life.

After watching my own funeral, I feel free, liberated.

Born anew.

I have lived one life—a strange, exciting, circuitous and secret life.

Now I have released it, shed it like an old skin.

I have started a new one and it feels right. A clean start. The life I was meant to live. It just began a little later than I planned.

It is a strange thing to watch your own funeral.

To see who comes.

To see how many come.

To see what they say about you.

I made them better.

Einstein's words reminded me of Rule Number 1 at the Graham-Coulson Secretarial School for Ladies.

Your job is to help *your boss to do his job*!

Maybe I was a pretty good secretary after all.

THE END

AFTERWORD

THIS IS A WORK of fiction. Hanna Fischer is fictitious. But many of the events depicted in this novel really happened and many of the characters in it actually existed.

Their real fates were as follows:

ALBERT SPEER survived the war and was tried at Nuremberg. He was found guilty of crimes against humanity and served twenty years in Spandau Prison.

After his incarceration, he wrote several books about his time working under Hitler, portraying himself as a 'good Nazi' who knew little or nothing about the Holocaust. Later authors would conclude that Speer was well aware of the Final Solution (and the use of slave labour). He died of natural causes in 1981.

MARTIN BORMANN's death has long been shrouded in mystery. He participated in a breakout from the Reich Chancellery in 1945 at the height of the Russian attack on the city. For many years, his body remained unfound and it was suspected that he escaped Germany.

But then in 1998, DNA evidence proved that the remains of a body found in Berlin were indeed Bormann's.

FORT BREENDONK was a real concentration camp in Belgium. It was found by Allied troops on September 3, 1944. By then, it was completely empty.

ADOLF HITLER ruled Germany from 1933 until the end of World War II in 1945. When Russian forces arrived at the Reich Chancellery, they found his remains alongside those of his wife, Eva Braun, with bullet wounds to their heads and burned almost beyond recognition.

WERNHER VON BRAUN was captured by American forces in western Germany and spirited to the United States where he would go on to lead the space program.

The technology that he developed for the Nazis' V-2 rockets became the cornerstone of the rockets that sent astronauts to the moon in 1969. That same technology also became the foundation for intercontinental ballistic missiles that would be able to fly nuclear warheads to any target in the world.

WERNER HEISENBERG is known for his uncertainty principle, for which he won the 1932 Nobel Prize for Physics at the age of 31. To this day, he is a controversial figure who ultimately miscalculated the mathematics of the atomic bomb (thinking it required several tons of uranium and not several kilograms). He died in 1976.

THE MÜHLVIERTAL HARE HUNT happened as described in early February of 1945.

THE CENTRAL EAST–WEST AVENUE OF THE TIERGARTEN was used as an emergency airstrip during the final months of the war.

THE KU KLUX KLAN MARCH OF 1925 in Washington, D.C. really happened. On August 8, 1925, an estimated 30,000 Klan members walked through D.C. dressed in their white robes and with their hoods thrown back so that their identities were open for all to see.

THE SOLVAY CONFERENCE OF 1927 is still regarded as the greatest gathering of scientific minds ever.

DOUGLAS 'BABY FACE' MANCINO is a fictional character. (He is named after my good friend Doug Mancino, who is a truly lovely man.) Baby Face is presented as a gangster who sets out to 'organise' crime in New York City with his protégé, Lucky Luciano. Charles 'Lucky' Luciano really did exist and is the guy who is credited with creating organised crime. I just liked the idea that my fictitious Baby Face—a bit like Marty McFly did in *Back to the Future* with Chuck Berry—inspired the real Lucky Luciano.

THE MANHATTAN PROJECT was the name of the American program that produced the atomic bomb during World War II. It is hard to overstate its staggering scale: it employed 120,000 people and cost $2 billion in 1945 (in today's dollars that would be about $24 billion).

ALBERT EINSTEIN is the most famous scientist in history. His presence in certain places on certain dates in this novel—like his tour of America in 1921 and his dinner at the White House—are historically accurate.

He really did write a letter to President Roosevelt in 1939 about the feasibility of an atomic bomb yet he was excluded from the Manhattan Project.

His activities during World War II are, curiously, shrouded in mystery, especially given his worldwide fame then. It is known that he worked with the U.S. Navy during the war but what he actually did with the Navy has never been revealed.

THE GERMAN EQUESTRIAN TEAM really did win all the gold medals in the equestrian events of the 1936 Berlin Olympics, a feat never matched in subsequent Olympic history.

AN INTERVIEW WITH MATTHEW REILLY ABOUT *MR EINSTEIN'S SECRETARY*

WARNING: SPOILERS!

Okay. Where to start? This is a novel about a secretary navigating her way through a world of gangsters, the 1929 stock market crash, Nazi Germany and World War II, with flashbacks and flashforwards, multiple points of view and characters including Albert Einstein, Albert Speer, Werner Heisenberg, and several geniuses of the atomic age. Where does a novel like this even come from?

I think it's safe to say that *Mr Einstein's Secretary* is unlike any of my other novels, including my other historical novel, *The Tournament*.

You know, I had such a good time writing *The Tournament*—with its fictitious characters mingling with real historical figures—that I wanted to do it again.

I loved creating Roger Ascham in that book: the kind and understanding teacher, a genuine seeker (and giver) of knowledge and wisdom. As I contemplated writing another historical novel, I asked myself, *Who would be the ultimate teacher?* The answer, of course, was Einstein.

But he would not be the hero of the story; he would be a mentor figure who assists the hero, Hanna, from time to time.

This book has a very unusual structure with flashbacks and flash-forwards. Tell us about those and why you used them.

In short, I wanted *Mr Einstein's Secretary* to be an epic. To be a story that spanned decades. In doing that, I wanted *time* and *place* to be characters in the story.

Structurally, the story is built on Hanna remembering her life, either during her fake funeral or through the three interrogations she endured.

So if she is recollecting walking through a plaza in Berlin early in her life, then that triggers other memories of being *in that same place at another time*, say, during a book burning years later. Or her drive from Antwerp to Brussels: remembering doing that drive in a limousine in 1927 on the way to the Solvay Conference triggers her memory of doing the same drive with Speer to Breendonk.

But I added a twist. Sometimes it's *not* Hanna doing the remembering.

Sometimes it's Ooma.

Here's how it works:

- Regular text
  If the text is regular, it's Hanna's overall recollections.

- *Italics*
  If a flashforward is *italicised*, it's Hanna remembering incidents from the 20s and 30s from her second interrogation in 1942.

- *Bold and italics*
  If the flashforward text is ***bold and italicised***, then it's Hanna's recollections from 1945 onward (including those from her third interrogation with the Soviets).

- **Bold text**
  If the flashforward text is just **regular bold**, then it's Ooma doing the remembering, not Hanna.

If you check the early flashforwards where our narrator is fleeing Berlin with Bormann, you'll see that they are all in **regular bold**. This is because it is Ooma with Bormann at those times. When the narrator is racing from the Tiergarten to Potsdamerplatz to find Dan, it's Hanna and thus in ***bold italics***.

And, of course—as you now know—Hanna and Ooma collide in the garden at the Chancellery where we get to experience the same scene from both women's points of view, including their different reactions to Dan's speed-of-light question.

As it moves along, our story eventually 'catches up' with all the flashforwards. For example, early in the book, Hanna has a flash-forward of running on the tracks of an el-train. We eventually get to that scene with her and Dan with Baby Face's child fleeing from the gangsters. It's the same with the scenes in Mauthausen and Auschwitz. We eventually reach them as the story progresses.

Why do this?

Well, over the years, as I've written more books—and now

movies—I've always searched for new ways to tell innovative and interesting stories. To that end, a few years ago, I began experimenting with different fonts to add to the tale being told.

I first did this in *The Secret Runners of New York*, with different fonts representing different times. It allowed me to cut back and forth quickly and easily from the present to the future in that time-travel story.

I also did something like this in *Cobalt Blue*. In that book, I used coloured fonts to represent flashbacks for the different characters: green for Cobalt Green, red for Cobalt Red, and so on. (This was a real treat, since getting a book printed with coloured fonts is not easy! I thought Pan Macmillan did a spectacular job on that book; those hardbacks of *Cobalt Blue* with the coloured text are very special first editions.)

You just mentioned Dan Kessler's speed-of-light question. How did you come up with that?

So, here's an admission. I'm no physicist. But I love physics. I wish I knew it better, but it's always just been something my brain struggled to grasp.

Having said that, I love reading about physics and things like time dilation. I'm sure someone will say I'm wrong by a year or something (and the real pedants will whine, 'But you can't ever travel at the speed of light'), but if you were somehow able to travel at the speed of light for a thousand years, you *would* actually travel for a little longer.

Storywise, well, at that moment in the story, I needed Dan to have a question that *only* the real Hanna would know the answer to. This seemed to suit the moment very nicely.

Tell us about starting and ending the novel at Hanna's fake funeral.

I wanted the funeral at the start of the book to read somewhat ambiguously. Readers have read many books where the narrator is, so to speak, watching down from heaven or the afterlife and recalling their life. So I hoped some readers would think that this was happening here: that Hanna is watching her own funeral from the afterlife.

The twist, as we discover, *is that she really is there*, watching over her own funeral from the belltower.

Since it's a story about memories, I thought it was a great way to 'enter' the story and trigger her memories. Also, I just think the same way she does: I kind of want to see who comes to my funeral!

I don't think we've experienced a character like Ooma in any of your novels. Tell us about creating her.

I wrote Ooma as a selfish, petty yet brilliant person who has what's known today as 'borderline personality disorder'.

This story is about Hanna's remarkable journey—and remarkable *growth*—through her life. I wanted Ooma to be a wildcard in that life, a constant danger lurking at the edges of Hanna's world. The way she can change emotions in a heartbeat makes her unpredictable and very dangerous. She was fun to write, especially in the scenes where she coldly tells Hanna about her impersonations of Hanna.

And what about the Soviet assassin–spy Svetlana Sarkovsky?

Svetlana was also really fun to write. Writing a character like her is really just delicious (it's like writing Mother in the Scarecrow books). You can have her say almost anything and it'll be cool. Most of all, I love the way she smells Hanna's distinctive perfume several times.

(Hanna's perfume is something I love in this novel. It's deeply personal to her, a connection to her dead mother, yet it is the thing that reveals her presence to Svetlana.)

And yet Svetlana is the one who saves Hanna at the end in Berlin, because Hanna saved her after the bomb blast at Mueller's Bar. Svetlana can kill anyone without blinking, but she has honour, which I think gives her that little something extra. And that highly developed sense of smell.

This is such a different book for 'Matthew Reilly'. For you, what is Mr Einstein's Secretary *about?*

It is different, yes, although I like to think—like *The Tournament*— it still has that fast and furious 'Matthew Reilly engine' propelling it along.

Hanna's growth in the face of extraordinary change is what drives this story. Her ability to adapt to all the slings and arrows life throws at her and ultimately grow is what carries the narrative. She starts out as a brilliant if somewhat unworldly and timid student who wants to become a physicist—and then ends up in secretary school in the bright, bustling and busy world of New York in the 1920s.

I really love the scene late in the book when Hanna is in Paris at ALSOS headquarters and she's being helped by the young secretaries . . . and they view her with reverence. By this point in the story, Hanna has become someone and she doesn't even know it yet. She is confident. She doesn't care for pleasantries. She is not fazed about going into a room and speaking with someone as senior as Colonel Boris Pash, the (real-life) head of ALSOS.

When I wrote that scene, I was thrilled, because that was the feeling I was after. It took a long time to get there—five years of writing—but that was the goal.

Will you do a book like this again?

Ha! The answer is: I'd like to, but I don't know if I can do it again.

There's always a lot of research involved in writing a novel—like, say, the Jack West Jr books and all the ancient historical research that they required.

But this one required research on another level entirely.

I couldn't have written *Mr Einstein's Secretary* in one year, or even two years. It just took time. I started it back in 2018, and wrote it on and off around the writing of *The Two Lost Mountains*, *The One*

Impossible Labyrinth and *Cobalt Blue* (I even took time off from it to film *Interceptor*). With a large-scale story like this, I needed to step away from it every now and then to regather my energy and then get back into it.

What else is going on? Any more movies on the horizon?

Well, *Interceptor* did amazingly well. It was the number one movie on Netflix in 91 countries and was seen by over 100 million viewers. That was thrilling and I just totally enjoyed the movie-making experience. I'm very eager to do it again, I just have to see which project of mine gets the go-ahead.

And I'm always thinking of new novels to write!

Any final words or comments?

If you're reading this, then you've finished the book, so I just want to say thanks for taking a chance on something a little different!

Because, as always, I just hope you enjoyed it.

Matthew Reilly
Los Angeles
July 2023

Discover more thrilling reads from bestselling
author Matthew Reilly . . .

SCARECROW AND
THE ARMY OF THIEVES

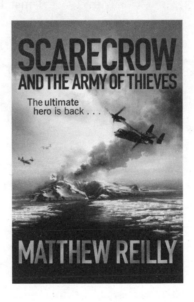

At an abandoned Soviet base in the Arctic, a battle
to save all life on Earth is about to begin . . .

THE FIVE GREATEST
WARRIORS

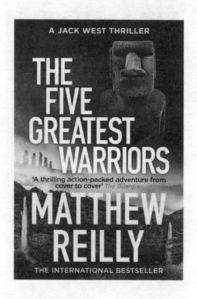

The end is approaching . . . Can Jack West unravel
the ancient secrets of the Five Greatest Warriors
and save the world?

THE FOUR LEGENDARY KINGDOMS

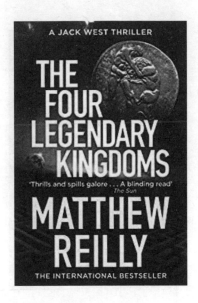

Jack has been selected to take part in the Games,
a series of deadly challenges that will test
him to the limit . . .

THE THREE SECRET CITIES

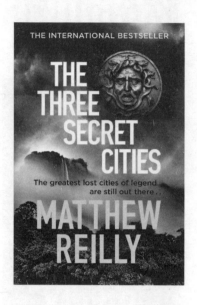

With the end of all things rapidly approaching,
Jack West must find the three lost cities of legend.
It's an impossible task by any reckoning, but
Jack must do it *while he is being hunted . . .*

ONE IMPOSSIBLE LABYRINTH

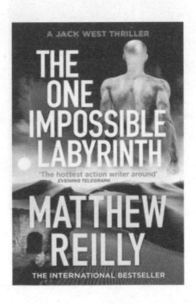

Jack West has made it to the Supreme Labyrinth. It ends here - now - in the most lethal and dangerous place Jack has encountered in all his many adventures. In the face of this indescribable peril there is only one thing he can do . . .